BUDDHISM AND VEDANTA

BUDDHISM AND VEDANTA
Contrast and Similarity

Suraj Singh Sisodiya,
Chandrika Singh

KALPAZ

ISBN: 978-93-5128-057-6

Price: ₹ 890

First Published 2015

Published by

Kalpaz Publications
C-30, Satyawati Nagar,
Delhi - 110052
E-mail: kalpaz@hotmail.com Ph.: 9212142040

Laser Typesetting : Rajender Vashist, Delhi

Printed at : G. Print Process, Delhi

Cataloging in Publication Data--DK
Courtesy: D.K. Agencies (P) Ltd. <docinfo@dkagencies.com>

Sisodiya, Suraj Singh.

Buddhism and Vedanta : contrast and similarity / Suraj Singh Sisodiya, Chandrika Singh.

p. cm.
Includes bibliographical references (p.) and index.
ISBN 9789351280576

1. Buddhism. 2. Buddhist philosophy. 3. Vedanta. 4. Hindu philosophy. 5. Buddhism--Relations--Hinduism. 6. Hinduism--Relations--Buddhism. I. Singh, Chandrika, 1944-, joint author. II. Title.

DDC 294.3 23

Contents

Preface

India has been place of metaphysical philosophy and abode of God's incarnation. Both Buddhism and Vedanta are the products of Indian soil no doubt, but they differ a lot in their philosophical approach, religious belief, social behaviour and ways of living. Buddhism emerged in India as a protest against blind practice of *karmkandas* and ritualism supported by Brahminism. The base of Buddhism is scientific insight, logical investigation, moral attitude and psycho-religious approach. It discards transcendentalism and dogmatism because the Buddha did not believe in speculation. He was a realist and believed in experience. He rejected the subject which could not be substantiated scientifically. His vision merged into the doctrine of *sunayata* (voidness) where scientific vision finds no way to proceed ahead. On the other hand, Vedanta is a philosophy that talks of metaphysics, the world of transcendentalism, soul and God who listens to the human prayer, accepts their worshipping and awards devotees blessing. Surprisingly enough they differ in their angle and approach but both the *dharmas* have similar views regarding doctrines of birth, death, rebirth, transmigration of soul and its salvation. Both accept that the nature of material world is transitory. Both have directly or indirectly been influenced by philosophy of each other.

Deep investigation and critical examination of the tenets of Buddhism makes the point obvious that there is corollary between Buddhism and Vedanta. Though Buddhism differs with Vedanta at several places, but it draws a lot from Vedantic philosophy. In the Vedantic philosophy God, Soul (*atman*) and

World are the base of spiritualism as well as religion. The entire edifice of Vedantic philosophy as well as the spiritualistic views is related to these three words- God, Soul and World. If Soul is removed from the trinities, there is no philosophy of spiritualism. On the other hand, the Buddha denied the concept of Soul and developed the doctrine of *Sarvam Anatman* that means "All is without soul." Upanishads regard *Atman* supreme entity which is identical with freedom, eternality and absolute unity. To the Buddhists, not soul, but consciousness is the carrier of essence of past *karmas* which serves the base of rebirth. They believe in universal principle of impermanence. When the doctrine of impermanence is accepted, in that case, the acceptance of eternality, absolute unity or supreme authority in any case becomes meaningless. As a result, an existence likes soul and God has no place. But the Buddha placed too much emphasis on attainment of *nirvana*. The question is who gets *nirvana*, if there is no soul? Buddhist doctrine of soul is, thus confusing.

Religion, from Vedic angle is *sanatan dharma* which means it is eternal. The ancient *rishis, maharishis, munis* and sheers of Indo-Aryans discovered *sanatan dharma* going deep in meditation. They found religion as a biding divine code in entire universe which keeps all celestial bodies of universe including living beings under binding duties. India has been the land of gods (*deva-bhumi*) where God being kind enough has incarnated from time to time to protect the people from onslaught of devil forces and reestablished religion. Early Buddhism discarding such opinions propagated a religion without *yajana* and worshiping. It is religion of *sadhana* where one has to strive hard to obtain enlightenment and practice prescribed ways to obtain *nirvana*. However, the later Buddhism propounded by the school of Mahayana incorporated a number Vedantic principles and religious ways which brought it very near to Vedantism. As a result, both the *Dharmas* gradually incorporated the principles of each other making it obvious that Buddhism is corollary of Vedantism.

We have applied sincere efforts to investigate into authenticity and utility of Buddhist and Vedantic thoughts in the world of today where scientific angle does not allow unscientific concepts either religious or philosophical to exist. We have taken enough pain to compare the philosophies and tenets of Buddhism, and explain their philosophical boundaries explaining the relevant facts. There may not be two opinions about the fact that Vedas and its appendages are the basic source of Indo-Aryan religion and civilization. Outwardly Buddhism appears a different religion from Hinduism, but inwardly both are similar in many aspects because the primary source of their emergence Vedantic philosophies. While presenting a new religion, the Buddha had been influenced a lot by the existing religious faiths and believes in India based on Vedantism. The truth what the Buddha discovered was not from empty space, but from the Vedantic truth. However, what uniqueness one finds in Buddhism is its scientific angle of thought, psycho-moral aspects of human behaviour and establishment of a mew society devoid of *varna* and caste system. We hope the present work would definitely help readers to understand Buddhism and Vedanta in right perspective. It will also help them to comprehend the fact that though Buddhism and Vedantism are apparently different, they talk of the same universal facts related to physical and metaphysical worlds, but in different manners.

Suraj Singh Sisodiya,
Chandrika Singh

Acknowledgements

Buddhism appeared in India at the time when the practice of *Brahminical Karmkandas* was at its zenith providing fertile ground for the growth and practice of superstitious acts, totally based on blind faith. Religious philosophies falling in the hands of orthodox *Brahmans* in India had lost its scientific values. There was no reason, but purely blind traditional faith that governed philosophy. Both philosophy and religion had become too vague beyond the understanding of the common mass. There were religious people, no doubt, but they lacked religious vision and analysing things from a scientific and philosophical angle. The so-called religious preachers of the time who abundantly prevailed on the religious centres like Banaras, Rajgriha, Gaya, etc., lacked both the sight and purpose of a phenomenon. Buddhism that appeared and prospered on the Indian soil during the 6th century BC lit the flight of wisdom showing the path of reality and reflecting the ways of life. Due to its superiority, it spread over in several countries of West and South East Asia. The number of the followers of Buddhism went on multiplying as the year advanced. The schools of Buddhism such as *Hinayana* and *Mahayana* played dominant role in strengthening Buddhist philosophies by producing various cults in religious philosophies of Buddhism.

The tenets of Buddhism related to human life and humanity are based on scientific approach of metaphysical philosophy. It also relates philosophy with psycho-religious analysis—leading the people a life where there is no chance of sufferings. An analytical study of Buddhism brings the fact to the light that though it differs with ancient Indian metaphysical philosophies and Hindu's religious *karmkandas*, it talks much about Hindu *Vedanta* regarding the world of transcendentalism, birth and death of creatures, existence of soul and its salvation, etc. The comparative study of Buddhist philosophy with Indian *Vedanta* compels one to conclude that Buddhism was very much inclined to ancient Indian *Vedantic* philosophy. It may be said that Buddhism is either a new modified face of the Indian Hindu religious as well philosophical thought or its most of tenets are similar to that of Indian *Vedanta*. However, Indian *Vedantic* philosophy left enough scope for development of ideas and doctrines based on faith as well as belief.

The birth of Buddhism was indeed an expression of revolt against ritualism and formalism prevailed among the Indian masses and practiced by the cult of *Brahminism*. Buddhism, in fact, was a revolt against Hindu's scholarship. The sixth century BC when Buddha was born, was known as the age of great spiritual upsurge. A number of spiritual leaders claiming themselves as the masters of spiritual knowledge had been preaching people spiritualism and teaching the ways to reach salvation. Ascetics and hermits roamed about, from place to place, throughout the Gangetic Valley, advocating mental discipline and asceticism as a means of salvation. Though these so-called preachers and scholars derived their spiritual knowledge from Vedas, they could hardly penetrate into the depth of the Vedic knowledge that was too vague for them to understand. As the ceremonial acts and sacrificial rites prescribed in the Vedic texts could not satisfy the urge of the contemporary philosophers, it became essential to go deeper to fathom the ultimate truth. Here comes the period of the *Upanishads* — (700 B.C–600 BC). The need was felt to do research on ultimate truth which is beyond the limit of Veda's versions related to Supreme God. The questions which perplexed the mind of the philosophers or seers were: What is *Brahman*? Wherefrom do we come? How should we live? Who controls happiness and misery? What is this Universe like? How did it start and who created it? When will it end and so on?

The region of Magadha (South Bihar) situated to east of Kashi on the right bank of the Ganga, was the centre of intellectual and spiritual activities. Among those who fostered the ferment were the Buddha, Mahavira and others. The *Brahminical* scriptures did not regard Bihar as a pious land. Rather it was regarded as a land of sin where the performance of sacrificial rites was prohibited. The inhabitants of this region were considered as 'aliens and infectious fever'. In comparison to the sacred Kashi, Magadha was considered unholy. It is evident from the statement of a Jain pilgrim of 18th century, who referred to a common belief that if a cow died in Kashi, it attained salvation, whereas a man dying in Magadha was considered to reborn as a donkey.

In this circumstances, *Brahminism* covered the mind and practice of people, played dominant role in showing and helping them to obtain heaven (*swarga*). As a result, ritualism and formalism became dominant everywhere in the life of people because it was said that ritualism was the viable base to attain heaven and obtain blessing of various gods to enjoy life in the mundane world. Belief spread that by performing *Yajana* one could achieve the things in this world which one desired. There are a number of gods upholding the creation who ware capable of blessing desired things provided they are pleased, and the way of pleasing was prescribed through performing Y*ajana*. So, people indulged into practice of ritualism assisted by *Brahmans*. *Brahmans* emerged as a spiritual class upholding the responsibility to lead people towards religious life. They commanded supremacy in the realm of *Varna* system of Hindu's social order. Their voices and opinions assumed the status of infallibility which could not be challenged by anyone including kings. People began to treat *Brahmans* next to Supreme *Brahman* on the earth.

Gautam Buddha appeared at this time, and he got frustrated observing various fluctuating views based on faith and ideas regarding aforesaid questions. His mind was so sensitive and scientific that nothing could convince him until he would have personified the truth and established the reality. It led him to find out real as well as convincing answers to the metaphysical questions. So, at the prime of his age Gautam, the prince, leaving all comforts of his life and breaking family relations, became a hermit and continued his efforts to penetrate into the depth of ultimate truth. Gautam Buddha's effort to find the ultimate truth provides the right answer. His goal was to find out the ultimate cause of sufferings and search the ways to get rid of such sufferings and pains. Obtaining enlightenment at Bodh Gaya after a deep penance, Gautam Buddha decided to teach people and his disciples the right path of the life and help them to get rid of worldly miseries. The teaching of the Buddha and the ways prescribed to live the life reasonably attracted number of people from both India and abroad. It was he who challenged frugality of *Brahminism* and attacked severely upon the practice of *karmkandas*. Buddhism propounded by Gautam Buddha and developed by his followers became a cult of religion all over the world. It provided a new vision to approach religion and a new angle to interpret metaphysics. In the findings of the Buddha there is no place for God as the Supreme Being to create, control and govern the universe. He neither approved existence of any such supernatural power nor disapproved it. He maintained silence whenever the question of God's existence came before him. At the same time, he believed neither in the philosophy and nihilism nor discarded natural order that surrounds creatures of the world. The Buddha established the doctrine of *Sunyatvada* which is the ultimate source of origin and dissolution of matters including living beings.

The Buddha's teachings related to humanity; such as kindness, friendship, non-violence; truth, etc., got ascendency not only during ancient India but it is more relevant even today when the standard of human morality has gone too much down overshadowing humanity. It was the growth and spread of Buddhism that caused great changes and modifications in the established *Vedantic* truth. The great Hindu religious philosophers Sankaracharya took the trouble to modify Hinduisms and redefine *Vedantic* philosophy that revitalised the latter.

In our study of Buddhism and *Vedanta*, we have applied the efforts to analyse Buddhism and compare it with *Vedanta*. Various doctrines of Buddhism developed by the Schools of

Hinayana and *Mahayana* have close association with the philosophy of *Vedanta*. It is all because Buddhism that developed in India never remained untouched with *Vedantic* philosophy. That is why, in due course of time, Hindu religion adopted a number of the Buddhist tenets regarding the Buddha as the tenth incarnation of Lord Vishnu. We hope this book would definitely help the readers to understand Buddhism in its right perspective and its relevance with Indian *Vedanta*.

Here we would like to acknowledge thankfulness and obligation to all those who helped us in various ways to complete the work. First of all, we convey our best regards to Professor Arun Kumar Sinha, Professor of Ancient India and Asian Studies, and Professor Ram Sakal Singh, Professor of Political Science, both from Magadh University, Bodh Gaya, who helped us enough by providing the books and materials relevant to the study. They always appreciated our efforts in this regard and encouraged us to write such an authentic book. Secondly, we express our obligation to Shri Gita Prasad Singh, the Senior Advocate of Nalanda District Bar Association, *Biharsharif*. Being an advocate by profession, his interest in religion as well as metaphysical studies is very deep. He took great interest in discussing spiritual philosophies, sitting hours and hours with us. While seating with him and discussing philosophy and religion, we learnt a lot that helped us to write the book. Thirdly, our heartfelt thanks and obligations to Professor Prabhakar Chaudhary, Professor of Mathematics, Magadh University, Bodh Gaya, whose faith in religion is unshakable. We discussed the facts related to Indian ancient *Vedantic* philosophy with him whenever we needed to conclude our religious as well as philosophical concepts. Fourthly, we extend our thankfulness to Professor Deonandan Prasad, Professor of Chemistry and Professor Shashi Bhushan Prasad, Professor of Physics, both from Magadh University Bodh Gaya, who contributed a lot to sharpen our viewpoints by discussing and analysing the relevant facts. How can we forget Dr Manoj Kumar, the IGONU Counsellor to convey our thanks. Dr Manoj took enough pain to collect needed materials even from New Delhi. Besides that, we would like to extend our thanks and obligations to all our friends and well-wishers who helped us in various ways to complete the work. Last but not the least, we thank all those friends and assistants who being kind enough remained co-operative to us till the work was finally completed. We also thank to the librarian of Nava Nalanda Mahavihara who always extended his help in giving the required books from the library for completing this discourse.

Suraj Singh Sisodiya,
Chandrika Singh

1

Introduction

India has been the land of metaphysical prosperity, philosophical insight, religious as well as ritual performances and a place for divine incarnation. It has produced a number of renowned *rishis, maharishis, munis*, sheers, saints, philosophers, thinkers, social reformers and poets of eminent significance who provided new expanding base of Indian *Vedantic* philosophy. No doubt, Hinduism, in course of time, inclined towards *Brahminical* cult of ritualism and formalism paving the way for the growth of blind religious faith and superstitions, but it has been the most prosperous and dominant religion of the country. However, it never remained inimical to other religions. That is why religions like Buddhism, Jainism, Islamism, Sikhism, Christianity, etc., availed the supportive circumstances to grow and prosper in India. India is known as *Dev-Bhumi* (land of gods) because big divine personalities like Lord Shri Krishna, Rama, Mahavira, Gautam Buddha etc., were born here and taught the world the lessons of humanity, new way of life leading towards happiness and eternal bliss.

The highest philosophy of *Vedanta* related to transcendentalism and Absolute Truth emerged in India and it is still the founding base of eternal Hindu *dharma*. Various religious scriptures like *Vedas, Srutis, Smritis, Brahmans, Puranas, Upnishads, Bhagvad Gita,* etc., emanated from the philosophy of *Vedanta* and are the expansion of the *Vedantic* philosophies. The philosophy of *Vedanta*, in the nutshell, talks the Absolute Reality that is eternal, *nirankara, nirvese,* omnipotent, omnipresent, all pervasive, all powerful and final abode of origin and demolition of everything in the creation of mundane world of ours. *Vedanta* basically is related to the concept of God, Soul and World. The creation (world), according to *Vedantic* philosophy, is nothing but reflection of the supreme energy of the all pervasive Absolute *Brahman*. So, the mundane world is not real, but momentary, illusive, being the subject of decay and disappearance. What one talks of *soul* is an integral particle of God that is immortal, illuminative, energetic, stable, and as pure as God and primary cause of creation. It neither gets birth nor does it die because it is eternal.

Buddhism, a word religion propounded by Gautam Buddha, emerged in India nearly 2500 years back. Gautam Buddha popularly known as Siddhartha during the early phase of his life was the son of a Hindu king Suddodhana belonging to Shakya dynasty settled in the surrounding of the Himalayas near Kapilavastu. The curiosity about world's reality, cause of its origin, its nature, fate of humanity, causes of human sufferings etc., haunted the mind of Gautam from his childhood. In pursuit of finding convincing answers to his curiosities and to quench the thirst of his philosophical urge, he became a *sanayasin* leaving aside his royal life and family members at the early age. Rajgriha, that had become the place of various philosophers, preachers, ritual performances attracted him to learn reality, but he soon realised that the thing what he earnestly wanted to know was not available there. So, he left for other places and lastly started his deep penance at Bodh Gaya where he obtained enlightenment. Getting enlightenment, he became Buddha, the knower of truth.

The Buddha, the propounder of Buddhism, being a Hindu confronted with ritualism practiced by orthodox *Brahmans* who overlooking the truth prescribed in the *Vedanta*, had established overwhelming authority over the people and society. At the time when Gautam was deeply contemplating about reality of the world and fate of human beings, there were a number of ascetic preachers, philosophers, saints and religious scholars who were busy with propagating their respective viewpoints related to the metaphysical world and ways of human life. Prevalence of various conflicting philosophical as well as religious doctrines and philosophical viewpoints expressed by these people created more confusion about ultimate reality. The cult of *Brahminism* following rituals was the greatest hurdle for other religious thinking and thoughts. *Brahminism* had developed processes to please various gods and goddesses by performing *yjanas* where sacrifices of animals were abundant. The base of *Brahminism* was blind faith and superstitions while Buddhism talked of logical priority, established wisdom and scientific attitude. Thus, Buddhism and *Brahminism* were bound to clash together so far their philosophical and religious approach and attitudes were concerned.

The vital question before the Buddha was to discover the root cause of world's sufferings and pains and also to find out paths to get rid of *Dukha*. In this course of research Gautam practiced hard meditation and obtained enlightenment ultimately. Gautam, thereafter, became the Buddha which means the enlightened one. He decided to teach people a new *Dharma* called as Buddha *Dharma*, which is still alive not only in India but also in several of the countries of the world especially in the Central and South-East Asia. The wisdom expressed and spread by the Buddha was so enchanting that it attracted many people belonging to different faiths and classes. The Buddha vehemently attacked *Brahminism* and absolutely condemned blind faith and superstitions that had become dominant in the society covering all aspects of human life at this time.

Buddhism propounded by Gautama Buddha and expanded by numerous Buddhist scholars both outside and inside India is based on psycho-scientific approach. Its ideas are various and multifarious. The Buddha's basic concern was not with metaphysics or the world of transcendentalism, but to make the life perfect living in the world by living a disciplined life following moral precepts and principles. He propounded Four Noble truths (*Aryatruth)* and Eight-fold Noble Paths that served as the base of Buddhist thinking and way of living.

A religion once propounded develops into various sects and schools due to internal conflicts and confrontation. After the demise of the Buddha, Buddhism, too, met the fate of internal conflict and confrontation for different interpretations of Buddhism resulting in advent of various Buddhist schools following their respective viewpoints and opinions. These schools presented new light and vision. Though Buddhism remained as central focal point in all these schools, the meaning and philosophy what they presented differed basically from early Buddhism. Thereafter, Buddhism got divided into two prominent schools —*Hinayana* and *Mahayana* having various sects and wings related to either of the two great schools of Buddhism. *Hinayana* school is traditional and stands on actuality and strives to attain Buddha's rank by removing evils. On the other hand, *Mahayana* school which emphasises immaculate human nature holds that, evil is nowhere to be found. Everyone is richly endowed with Buddha's wisdom. Buddha is not an ideal which is to be sought far away. Buddha resides within us. According to this school, the need is to recognise Buddha residing in the inner-heart of the individual and to elevate it to the extent of the highest. As the years rolled down, the school of *Mahayana* achieved more prosperity in inside and outside India.

Buddhism is not a metaphysical speculation, but it is a practice. It emphasises *sadhana* and meditation that is the way to recognise our own Buddha. The Lord Buddha propounded Four Noble Truths. *Dukha* is inherent in the world; it has its roots; it may be uprooted; and one has to learn the path to uproot *Dukhas*. The paths to uproot *Dukhas* taught by the Buddha are divided into Eight-fold Noble Paths that include *Samyak-dristi* (Right seeing), *Samyak-sankalpa* (Right determination), *Samyak-vachan* (Right talk), *and Samyak-karma-(Right behaviour, Samyak-jivan (Right living), Samyak-vyayam (Right exercise), Samyak-smriti (Right memory) and Samyak-samadhi (Right meditation).* Buddhism emphasises on obtainment of *nirvana* and the ways prescribed by the Buddha help one to obtain the goal. So far the case of *Vedantic* philosophy is concerned; it also talks of futility of the mundane world that is the place of attractions towards material prosperity, and that ultimately results in causing sufferings and pains. Hence, emphasis is on *mokhsa* (salvation) that is possible when one totally relies upon saintly life of truth and sincerity.

Buddhism is separate from existentialism and nihilism. Buddhism has relevance to transcendentalism in the sense that *nirvana* is the stage of ecstasy, absolute happiness, free from all sorts of *Dukhas*. *Nirvana* is a state which is 'indescribable', the perfect within one's own self. Buddhism differs from *Vedanta* in the sense that it is silent about the concept related to God and denies existence of soul. Buddhist doctrine of soul, if there is any, is conflicting and confusing. The denial of the soul by the Buddhist philosophy is fully based on the universal principle of impermanence or 'dependent origination' which means nothing is independent due to its constitution of various elements that disperse after decay of the thing or death of the living beings. Lastly nothing remains except *Sunyata* (absolute voidness). Once the doctrine of universal impermanence is accepted, the question to accept the doctrine of eternality, absolute reality or supreme authority does not arise at all. So, logical conclusion of Buddhism is that there is no *atman* (soul).

Buddhism, thus, propounds the doctrine of *anatmavada* (soullessness). However, it accepts the existence of personal ego or provisional soul. Here the question is, if there is no permanent soul, then who avails *nirvana*? In fact, the Buddha adopted the middle path avoiding both contemporary existing doctrines of nihilism and externalism. When he taught that there is no *atman* in the sense of a creator or perceiver or an absolutely free agent, apart from conventional name given to the aggregate of the five *skandhas*, his object was to save man from falling into the opposite heresy of externalism or *samstavada*. Had he accepted complete denial of soul or ego, his doctrine would have fallen into the category of nihilism. So, he developed a different doctrine of soul that is too much vague and conflicting. To the Buddhists, *nirvana* is complete merger into absolute tranquility or complete silence (peace) about which nothing definitely can be said. It appears that the Buddha stopped at the point of agnosticism which means nothing definitely can be said about absolute reality or permanent existence of omnipotent God where enlightened soul merges absolutely. According to A.B. Kaith, "by leaving the matter unexplained the Buddha allowed us to frame our own conceptions of future of the enlightened man after death."

Basic theme of Buddhism is related to *nirvana.* It rejects existing beliefs like theism (*astika*) and atheism (*nastika*) which may be called idealism and materialism. However, it neither rejects Vedic *dharma* nor adopts it. A comparative study of Vedic *dharma* and Buddhism reveals the truth that both the *dharmas* run parallel to the point of salvation, the doctrine of *Karma*, *Samskara* (consciousness), Circle of birth and death, insignificance of the mundane world, etc. To both, the ultimate goal of human life is to strive for liberation of individual from the bondage of the *samsara*. Buddhism condemns the world due to its nature of permanent changes into nothingness. It teaches the beings to rise above the changing state (*anitya*) to an everlasting unchanging state (*nitya*). *Vedantic* philosophy considers the world as false (*mithya*) since it is the reflection or shadow of the Absolute *Brahman*. To a Buddhists only reality is *nirvana* which is negation of everything that is unreal or having impermanent existence. To *Vedanta*, the world is illusion. According to Buddhism *Dukha* is inherent in the world and its root cause is *trisna*, desire, lust, etc., while *Vedanta* treats the world as *maya* which is illusion. Both agree to the point that the ultimate reality is hidden or covered in ignorance. Nothing definitely can be said about absolute reality or permanent existence of omnipotent God where enlightened soul merges absolutely. To the *Vedanta*, Absolute or Ultimate Reality is indefinite and limitless. So, the *Vedanta* declares Absolute Reality as, 'it is not, it is not ...' On the other hand, the Buddha, realising vastness and indescribability of Ultimate Reality preferred to be silent.

The advent of the schools of *Vajrayana*, *Mantrayana* and *Sahajayana* provided new direction to the philosophy and ways of Buddhism. These cults put more emphasis on practice of *upasana* allowing women, intoxication and non-vegetarian food with the result that Buddhism became a cult to obtain *Siddhi* in the shortest scale of time through the use of wine, women, *mantras, mudras* and what not. This created wide and harmful impact upon Buddhism. The advent of Shankcaracharya, (7th century AD) a renowned *Vedantic* philosopher of India, and his successful effort to revive Hinduism provided strong ground for growth of *Brahminism* on the one hand, and presented the

Vedantic philosophy of Absolutism (Monism) on the other. It gave a severe blow to Buddhism. Thereafter, arrival of Muslim rulers in India and their attack upon Hindu's as well as Buddhist's teaching centres, burning of libraries and demolishing temples and monasteries, made Buddhism half-dead. It survived, no doubt, but its earlier fervour and zeal in India began to disappear.

Today, in the light of scientific knowledge has changed human attitude and approach separating traditional ideological values. It is the need to reinvestigate into various doctrines of Buddhism, on the line of empiricism. Secular attitude is challenging religious concepts. Faith in Buddhism should be studied as a doctrine of practical life and relevance of the life to its past and future journey. Buddhism contains solution to the problems of modern life.

The present work, namely *Buddhism and Vedanta: Contrast and similarity* that has been written in about 250 pages and divided into nine chapters is an exercise to investigate deeply into the tenets of Buddhism and its relevance in modern age where a number of problems causing more troubles, sufferings, violence, uncertainty in human behaviours and tense relationship among humanity have emerged. Buddhism that emphasises on a peaceful and honest life and also on a society where there is neither violence, nor hatred, neither social division nor racial discrimination, neither religious conflicts nor ideological fermentation. The Buddha liked the society without violence based on universal brotherhood, truth, sincerity, simplicity, love, friendship and compassion. All these facts have thoroughly been discussed and analysed in the book. Efforts have also been applied to compare Buddhist philosophy to that of Hindu's *Vedantic* wisdom of Absolute monism and their dependence upon each other. An analytical study of Buddhism, its rise and growth, its expansion and decay reveals the truth that Buddhist thoughts are almost a new interpretation of *Vedantic* views where emphasis has been laid down on tractability of human life.

2

A Short Historical Profile of Gautam Buddha's Life and Penance

Buddhism as a religion or a cult of scientific philosophical thinking emerged in India during the 6th century BC its basic philosophies were propounded by Gautam, the son of the king Suddodhana who ruled Lichhavi Ganrajya and its capital was at Vaisali a district of the present day Bihar. His mother, *Mahamaya* who belonged to the clan of the Shakya dynasty died after seven days of giving birth to Gautam. It is said that she gave birth Gautam on the way while she was proceeding towards her parents' house. Regarding the exact year of the birth of Gautam, scholars differ. It is generally believed that Gautam was born in 563 BC in Lumbini that was situated in the forest of Kapilavastu in the surrounding of the Himalayas. However, Smith is of the view that he was born in 563 BC and got *prinirvana* in 543 BC.[1] It is believed that after the birth of Gautam all aims of his father were accomplished. So, he called him Bodhisattva. Before his renunciation, he was known as Prince Siddhartha. The word Buddha or 'enlightened one' was often used for Gautam only after obtaining enlightenment. Prior to that period, he was simply called Bodhisattva (in *Pali Boddhista*) which means a being destined for enlightenment. The Buddha was often addressed by his disciples as *'Bhagavat' or 'Bhagava'*, meaning Lord. He was also called as *Tathagata* which means 'perfect one'. Similarly the term 'Sakayamuni' (the sage of the Sakyas) was common till frequently used in the Sanskrit works. Sometimes, he was referred as 'Gautam' (Pali Gotma) after his clan name, or Mahasramana' or 'the Great Ascetic. However, his personal name was Siddhartha (Pali, Siddhartha) which means one who has achieved all his aim. He renounced his body in BC 477 at Kushinagar in the district of present Gorakhpur. It is believed that the Buddha was born in the full moonlit night (*purnima*) of Vaishakha and he left his body on the same day. That is why *Buddha-purnima* is a central holiday in the Indian gazette and it is celebrated all over the country even today.

Gautam's Childhood

Kapilavastu situated in the surroundings of Nepal was the Capital town of Shakya (*Kshatrya*) dynasty. Today, this place is known as Tilauara Kit. This *gantaantra o*f Shakya, first, was under the rule of Vajjisangh and thereafter it came under the rule of Koshal having some local autonomy. When Buddha got *prvajya*, it was connected to the Kosal Raj. Gautam, though born in a kingly dynasty, remained non-entangled to the material world from his very childhood. His inclination towards worldly luxuries and comforts had been little. He was a different child who preferred loneliness and life of simplicity. His opinion to view the world was different. He had detraction towards the mundane world from his childhood. His thinking and outlook towards the material world was different. He used to remain mostly silent. Various incidents of his early life substantiate the fact that Gautam was—soft, honest, sincere, merciful and kind to all creatures of the world. It is said that when a bird was wounded by his cousin, Devadatta, he did everything to save the life of the wounded bird. He visualised his own self in each and every creature of the world. He was very much sympathetic to all living creatures. His nature was saintly and his behaviour disturbed his father. So, he began to adopt various methods to make his son happy and engage him into the worldly affairs. All sort of comforts available at the time were provided to Gautam with a view to making him happy and involving him towards material world. But nothing could attract Gautam who was deemed to become Buddha. He was born to lead the ascetic life. From his very childhood he looked at the world and its happenings very curiously. Sudodhana, being worried observing the ascetic nature of his son, decided to arrange his marriage with a most beautiful girl. He was allowed to select his life partner from amongst a number of selected beautiful unmarried girls. Yasodhra, the most beautiful young girl, became his wife. But she too could not stop Gautam from becoming a *snayasi* in such an early age. No doubt, a son named Rahul was born to Gautam, but even the birth of son could hardly deter him from giving up his path of renunciation as well as salvation. His destiny was different. Neither the wife nor the son could entangle him in the worldly life. His mission was different.

Gautam's Journey for the Knowledge

It is said that when Gautam was young he used to meet a *sanyasi* named Bharndu Klam, who lived in Kapilavastu.[3] He was disciple of Arad Kalam who was a Brahmin *sanyasi* and well known for his knowledge of *Samkhya Darsan.* Coming in close contact with Bharandu, he heard a lot about spiritual knowledge. Influence of Bharandu was so deep on the mind of Gautam that ultimately it turned him towards the life of spiritualism. Thus, during his early life when he was living with his family, he had learnt a lot about the significance of the life of *sanyasi* and *Samadhi.*[4] Thereafter, nothing could entangle Gautam in this world, neither his wife nor his son, neither luxuries nor comforts, neither family nor kingdom. Rather he remained confined to his thought and thinking that was quite different from the thought and thinking of others. He had begun to realise the truth-related to transitory nature of the world and things. It appeared to him that the world is full of miseries and pains. Here the pleasure that is available is a little and that also is perishable. No one could be happy in such a world. The incident that took place during his journey brought turning point in the life of Gautam. One day, while on journey along with his chariot Chhandak, he saw a suffering old man, a sick man and a corpse of a man. It made him unhappy. He was told that oldness, sickness and death are the fate of the creatures. Everyone has to pass through such stages of life sooner or later. He was also told that destiny of the man is such that he has to bear all odds of this world. It made him sadder and proved as a turning point in his early life.

His apprehension that the world is the place of pains and pangs got confirmed. The question that perplexed his mind more was, if the life of creatures living in this world is to suffer, then what is the need to live in such a painful world. His curiosity was to know the root cause of suffering. He wanted to know the remedy to get rid of such painful stages of human life. If pain, uncertainty and diseases are so common in this mundane world, the life is meant for what? Is it the destiny of the life? Is a man born here is to suffer and die? All these questions that hounded his mind could not get satisfactory answer. So, in search of the proper answer to the questions and find out remedy to get rid of worldly pains and miseries, he decided to quiet the kingdom stealthily, living behind his whole family.

At the age of 31, in one midnight he along with his chariot Chhandak and the horse Kanthak, left his whole family and kingdom behind, reached to the bank of the river Achirabati. Since he was determined to renounce the world and follow the ascetic life, he gave up his princely dresses. He also gave up his princely style after having cleaned shave of the head and the beard. He put on yellow coloured clothe and turned into a *sanaysi.* This incident in the religion of Buddhism is called *Mahabhiniskraman*. His aim was to know the reality of the life and the world both. Young Gautam had fully realised that it was difficult or rather impossible to obtain full knowledge leading the life of *Garhastha* where one had to face a number of worldly problems. His chariot Chhandak had nothing to do, except shedding tears. After his departure, his horse Kanthak could not bear the mental agony caused by the pang of separation of his master, and died there. Later on, at this place the *Kanthak Vihara* was founded.

Journey towards Rajgriha and Vaisali

Gautam, after renouncing the family and kingdom in the dress of a *sanyasi,* moved towards Rajgriha. At that time,

Rajgriha was the capital of Magadh Empire ruled by the famous king Bindusara. Since *Rajgriha* was the capital of a famous empire, it was a famous place having richness and prosperity. The inhabitants were Hindu and *Brahminism* as a cult of Hindu religion was at the climax. *Rajgriha* was also known for the place of religious activities. A number of philosophers, *sanaysi* and scholars used to gather there. The fame of their knowledge and penance had spread all over the region. Besides that, the 24th Tirthankar of Jain *Dharma* had also established his reputation in the field of knowledge at *Rajgriha*. Hearing all about the significance of *Rajgriha*, Gautam after becoming a *sanyasi* reached Rajgriha and met several religious people. Lastly, he began his penance and meditation. The theory and practice of Brahmin *Karmakanda* based on religious scriptures and propagated and practiced by *Brahmans* had established supremacy everywhere in Bihar as well as in northern India. Rajgriha had become the centre of Vedic scholars. A number of *sanyasis* had gathered there for penance. They lived nearby the capital in surroundings of various mountains. Rajgriha was, in fact, the centre of spiritual knowledge. That is why Gautam with the determination to obtain truth moved towards Rajgriha renouncing his home and family. While reaching here, he availed the opportunity to meet various scholars and sages. At Urubela he lived six years and practiced penance, but he was not satisfied because his curiosity and questions were not answered properly. No one could guide him. The scholars whom he met could hardly convince young Gautam. The answer what he sought was not available with them.

Thereafter, Gautam moved towards Vaisali where he came in close contact with Arad Kalam or Uddak Ramput who was the famous scholar of *Sankhya Darshan. Sankhya Darshan* is based on Vedic philosophy which believed in the philosophy of non-dualism. According to *Sankhya*, God who is alone and formless *(nirnkara)*, is the supreme cause of all causes, omnipotent, omnipresent and inapprehensible etc. What exist except Him is nothing, but is the power of His re-election and shadow. Except Him nothing is permanent. He has neither beginning nor end because He is eternal. Eternity, consciousness and light are his power that has been prevalent everywhere.

Things emerge from him and merge into Him. Nothing definitely could be said about the God of *nirnkara*. Whatsoever is said about Him is not the final. Something more is there and the process of that something never ends.

It appeared to Gautam that Arad Kalam, perhaps, could have the answer to his queries. Hence, he decided to adopt him as his Guru. However, Gautam's close association with Arad Kalam and his philosophy of *Sankhya* could not convince him. His thirst for knowledge remained unquenched. Gautam was in search of the absolute knowledge that could have given him satisfactory answer to the question that had been perplexing his mind from his childhood. According to *Mahaparinirvana,* Kalam was well-known for his ascetic meditational life. He had obtained to different stages of *Samadhi*. The last stage of *Samadhi* where he had reached was the stage of *Sunya* (nothingness). Gautam had learnt it all from Kalam's disciple Bharandu. However, being the disciple of Kalam Arad, he practiced meditation and reached to the stage of *Sunya,* no doubt, but he was not yet satisfied because it was not the answer which he sought. He wanted to realise absolute truth.

Thereafter, getting permission from his *guru*, he returned back to Rajgriha where he met king Bindusara. The king was very much attracted by his body language. He wanted to employ him in royal service, but he rejected his offer to join the service of the kingdom. Thereafter, he came in close contact with Rudrak Ramputra whom he accepted as his second spiritual *guru*. In association with Ramputra, he learnt the relevance of action (*karma*) and soul that is *Naivsangyana Sangayaytan.* According to this spiritual theory, the essence of human actions as well as activities never disappear because they made an indelible impression on the consciousness of human mind. Consciousness is the quality of soul that reflects from the inner soul. Consciousness, in fact, is the base where essence of human activities is deposited. Since the essence of action is not destroyable, it remains intact even after the death and being the seed it serves as the cause of next birth. Such essence is called *sanskara* according to Hindu's philosophy. Thus, the *Samskara*, which carries the essence of action even after one's death causes rebirth, and one has to harvest what he sows in the present life. Each action (*karma*) has its fruit and the person who acts has to eat the fruit.

The philosophy of Ramputra, too, could hardly satisfy Gautam. He wanted to know the nature of the absolute truth and its permanent abode. He also wanted to know how this absolute truth is related to the world and the life of the creatures. What is the root cause of human sufferings? How does the destiny of man is governed? What are the methods and means to get rid of such destiny? The life is meant for what? Though the philosophy of Ramputra could not convince the thirsty mind of Gautam, but he learnt the theory of *karma* and rebirth from his second *guru*, Ramputra. The theory of soul that was preached to him by his *guru* remained vague. To him it was still perplexing that how soul is the base of everything and how it is the cause and carrier of human bondage. If soul that is the particle of Supreme God is formless and beyond the reach of human understanding, how can superiority and authenticity of soul could be justified? In fact, he was not ready to accept the existence of soul. He accepted the theory of *karma*, no doubt, but so far as the case of permanent existence of soul and its universality was concerned, he was not convinced. So, he left his second *guru*, too. The theory of *karma* and soul would be discussed in the succeeding chapter. Here it is notable that Gautam was not a blind follower. Rather he believed in application of mind and wisdom to accept the things, finally.

Movement towards Gaya

At Rajgriha nothing could satisfy Gautam, neither the companion of great Brahmin scholars, nor meeting of famous *sanyasis.* While living at Rajgriha, he had heard a lot about religious as well as spiritual significance of Gaya. Gaya at the time had become the centre of religious activities. People from different places visited there for religious performances. There were number of sacred places nearby Gaya which have mentioning in the Indian religious scriptures of the Hindus.[5] Gaya had become the place for religious as well as spiritual activities. Several noted scholars, philosophers and preachers were available there. Even the forefathers of Gautam had visited Gaya to perform religious activities. It has been popular for redemption of dead souls. So, after hearing all about the sanctity and sagacity of Gaya, Gautam moved towards Gaya with a curiosity to obtain real knowledge about God and the world.

Gautam moving from Kurkihar reached Uruvela (Gaya). Near Uruvela there was a village known Senanigram. He preferred the place very much due to its natural surroundings. At Gaya, there was a small mountain called Mundeshwari at the meeting point of the rivers Mohna and Nirnjana. At this mountain Gautam started doing his penance for several years. In the Indian *Purana* this mountain is known as Mundprisat.[6] The mountain was very much famous due to its transcendental stories. He began his hard penance at this mountain.

The Life of Penance

Gautam being fully convinced that he could not get the satisfactory answer to quench his spiritual thirst from so-called spiritual *gurus*, he made up his mind with strong determination to enter into the life of hard penance by controlling his wordly thought, concentrating his mind and punishing his body. He had learnt that deep penance meant sitting in full concentration renouncing food and other requirements. Then he started into hard penance living with five Brahmin followers. He controlled his diet and respiratory system. What he began was the practice of *pranayama.* In the name of food he took small quantity of some rough food grains including even cow dung and dung of goats. He sat long in meditation. As a result, he lost his weight, physically he became too weak to sit even. His physical condition became very feeble. Despite all his efforts in doing meditation he failed to realise his goal. Gautam while narrating about the experience of his hard penance, said to his best disciple Sariputra:

O, Sariputra! then I got deeply involved into hard penance throwing out off my entire clothe. I became totally naked. I could not accept invitation of anyone. I gave up all social thinking and behaviours. I began to live on small quantity of food that collected from one to seven nearby households. Afterward I gave up that also and started to depend on grass, paddy etc. Thereafter, I left that, too, and cow dung and goat dung became the source of my food. I used deer's skin and used the blanket made of human hairs. I used to take off the hairs of my beard and moustache by hand. In sitting position, I performed penance. These were the methods of my penance. O, Sariputra! My condition was such that I could neither stand nor sit properly. When I tried to get up I fell down again and again. I do not feel natural call. Despite all that I got nothing out of this hard penance.[7]

Gautam, who had faith in getting knowledge through hard penance, realised that it was meaningless and futile to punish the body. He also felt that those who were punishing the body in the name of penance were, in fact, wasting their time to get nothing. So, he changed the method and decided to go through the middle way. He began to take food to sustain his body and for survival of life.

Though he continued in his penance, no doubt, his weak and feeble body did not allow him to sit long. At that moment, a miracle happened to the life of Gautam. A lady called Sujata, the daughter of a rich farmer family came there to offer *khir* to the tree-god where Gautam was engaged in penance. It is believed that the lady Sujata had no issue, and she had promised to the tree-god to offer *khir* provided she was blessed with a son.[8] Thereafter, a son was born to her. Being too happy, she prepared good quality of *Khir* to fulfill her promise. Along with the *khir* she reached near the tree-god where she found Gautam sitting in penance. Seeing Gautam there in the mood of penance, she took him as tree-god and happily offered him the *khir*. Gautam, too, accepted it and ate it. His hunger was vanished. Having eaten the *khir* offered by the lady Sujata, Gautam experienced unique change in his mind and body. He felt quite fresh and found that his mind was full of unique awareness. At that moment, realisation came to Gautam that to punish the body in the name of penance was not the satisfactory way to attain the knowledge. He knew that the reliable way to obtain absolute truth is meditation. After having *khir* from Sujata and accepting some grass offered to him by a grass cutter namely Srotriya, he moved from Senanigram to the Bodhi Tree. He decided to meditate for realising truth sitting under it. He said to himself that the place that had been deserted by all Buddhas was the place where root causes of

Dukha could be abandoned. So, he took the vow with great determination to do continue meditation there at any cost until he obtained enlightenment. He had the determination to face any difficulty even at the cost of his life.[9] It was this place where Gautam got enlightenment and the place was called *Vajrasan*. He used the grass offered to him by a grass cutter namely Srotriya for sitting. His five followers, who had been waiting him to share the fruit of knowledge with him, became upset. They thought that Gautam had failed to achieve knowledge and his penance was not pure due to having food. Hence, they all left him alone.

Attainment of Knowledge through Samadhi

The second stage of Gautam's penance began under the Bodhi Tree at Bodh Gaya near the Falgu river. He reached there crossing the Niranjana River and he sat under a Bodhi Tree. It is said that the reflection of the light that began to appear from his face and body disturbed God Mars. Hence to break his penance up, he applied natural forces such as flood, earthquake, wind, etc., to disturb Gautam, God Mars sent all these forces to disturb him and test his determination. However, he remained so firm in his penance that nothing could stop him in his mission. He had decided either to obtain truth or give up his life. Even some forces in the guise and appearance of beautiful ladies appeared before him to disturb him and test his patience, These forces were sent by him to break up his penance, but Gautam was so firm and determined to obtain knowledge that nothing could disturb him. Eventually, God Mars appeared before him and blessed him. God told him that he was happy with his penance and he was found fit for having absolute knowledge.

The story of God Mars and his activities to disturb Gautam has no historic relevance. It appears that it all happened in his mind. Perhaps these were his mental states during the course of his penance. It is under the Bodhi Tree where Gauatma's thirst for knowledge was fully quenched. Gautam continued his penance despite various obstacles and disturbances. He went deep into various stages of *Samadhi* and obtained knowledge (enlightenment) in different phases which are mentioned below:

1. **First Stage:** This is the stage, where the person sitting on meditation gets knowledge based on pure logic and thought. It gives pleasure. Gautam crossed this stage.
2. **Second Stage:** In this stage, the *sadhak* rises above the logic and enters into the stage where the logic and thought both disappear. What remains there is the fact above logic and intelligence. Gautam crossed this stage also.
3. **Third Stage:** In this stage, one gets pure pleasure due to absence of entanglement into the worldly affairs. Reaching at the stage Gautam detached himself from world's thinking.
4. **Fourth Stage:** In this stage, there is no feeling of pain and pleasure. Here neither pains nor pleasure exists. While reaching this stage Gautam's thought remained detached from any sort of feeling and thinking.
5. **Fifth Stage:** This stage of *Samadhi* one rises above all worldly thinking and there appears pure and selfless wisdom related to inner consciousness. At this stage, one visualises truth as it stands. He crossed this stage also.
6. **Sixth Stage:** This is the stage where one obtains the knowledge of his past lower and upper births and deaths according to his past *karma*s and *sanskara.* While reaching this stage, Gautam obtained the knowledge of his past births and deaths.
7. **Seventh Stage:** When one reaches to the seventh stage, he visualised there the inner consciousness that is quite pure and free from any kind of imprints of the life. In this stage, Gautam realised what is pain and pleasure and how to get rid of pain.
8. **Eighth Stage:** This stage of *Samadhi* where absolute truth is attained. In this stage, Gautam fully realised inner conciseness and knew that all the causes of his rebirth disappeared. He found that the main cause of birth and death are deposition of *sanskara*. Once the inner consciousness is clean, there is no cause of birth and death. He also realised that nothing definitely can be said about 'Absolute Truth' because there is complete

tranquility and which can not be expressed in any form. It is beyond the reach of mind and language.

Attainment of Enlightenment at Uruvela

Thus, Gautam obtained full enlightenment within 49 days of *Samadhi* at the age of 35 years. The enlightenment would be described separately in this book. It made him Buddha which means knowledge of Absolute Truth. He achieved the goal and came to know the causes of endless circle of birth and death, worldly miseries, *avidya, maya*, etc. He also discovered the remedies of how to get rid of such bondage. He obtained knowledge in three phases. First, he regained the knowledge of his past births and deaths, in the second phase, he got divine vision through which he could see the entire spiritual world and in third stage he found truth, in two parts. First part is relative truth that exists related to the thing and disappears with the disappearance of the thing. This truth reflects through the boundary of the time and speed. The truth in this stage which he visualised was concealed in ignorance. The second truth is permanent un-related to anything. It is imperishable and non-transitory. This absolute truth exists beyond time and speed. He visualised truth in three phases. According to *Majjhim Nikya,* during the first phase of the last night of *Samadhi,* he obtained the first *vidhya* where he remembered his past life. At the midnight, he obtained divine eyes and through it he got the visualised *pratityasmutpad knowledge.* Through his divine light he found absolute truth in two parts. First truth what he realised was concealed, temporary and dependent while the second was independent and permanent. The first truth is relative truth that reflects through the entity which conceals it. It is not permanent. The second one is eternal, pure and free. It has no concern with anything or anybody. According to *Vinya Pitaka,* the Buddha after getting enlightenment remained confined to his thinking, enjoying it. This stage is called *Vimuttisukh* in the language of Pali. He also knew four *aryastya* which are mentioned below:

1. *Dukha* is related to *trisna.* So, it has the cause.
2. So, long there is cause of *Dukha,* it would continue.
3. With the abandonment of *trisna, Dukha* would also disappear, and

4. The way and method to abandon *trisna* is eight-fold *yoga* and by practicing and following it would definitely end *Dukha*.

What Buddha obtained at Uruvela in a nutshell became the focal point for the growth and development of Buddhism. The knowledge what he got was related to *Dukha* (pain). He fully visualised what pain is, what is the root cause of pain, how pain could be uprooted and what are the ways to uproot pain. After six years of hard penance these truths appeared before the Buddha. That is called four *Arya-satya*. The Buddha knew that the world is full of *Dukha*; it has its root; it can be opposed and it may be uprooted. Buddha called them four *Arya-satyas* which are mentioned below in *detail*.

1. *Dukha* is inherent in the world,
2. Root cause of *Dukha*,
3. Control of *Dukha*, and
4. Ways to Uproot *Dukha*.

Dukha-: Lord Buddha had fully visualised that the nature of the mundane world is such that, it is full of pains. There are various kinds of pains. He realised that human life was full of pains and pangs. Pains exist in different forms. According to *Digh Nikaya* pain comes out of birth, old-age, death, sorrow, weeping, parivedan, enmity or ill-will, companionship of ill-motive persons or things, severance of pleasant one, deprivation of desired things etc.[10] Lord Buddha took these five elements present in the world as *Rupa, Vedna, Sangya, Sanskara,* and *cit* .

1. Rupa: Excluding sky, he treated earth, air, water and fire as visible part of the universe.

2. Vedna: Vedana comes out of having in touch with the worldly things or to thinking about them.

3. Sangya: It is the imprint of *sanskara* in the wisdom and through it one recognises the thing by name.

4. Samskara: *Sanskara* is based on consciousness. The essence of actions in the life remains present on the consciousness that results in *sanskara*. It is *sanskara* (essence of good or bad activates) according to which one is to act and perform.

5. Cit – Cit is the base of creation. According to *Samkhya Darsan* cit is *Mahttatva* from which or from where, everything originates. *Mahattava* is the most subtle, invisible, pure and having all seeds of origin. To the Buddha *cit* is the super most layer spreading above the sky that causes creation. Since he denies the concept of soul, it is *cit* that is the ultimate source of consciousness.

Causes of Pain: The root cause of worldly pains is *trisna* (dissatisfaction and desire to have more). It is related to pleasure of organs, desire for wealth, prosperity, name and fame, and enjoy sex etc. It is *trisna* of the man that involves him into action causing rebirth where all agents of pains become active and dominant. Man is constantly desirous of material utility. This is called insatiable desire which never dies. Man through his sensual organs such as eyes, ears, nose, tongue and sensation, establishing contact with scene, colour, smell, noise, test, runs after them to obtain and enjoy and thus falling the prey to lusts and desires, in this process, he gets completely entangled into the worldly matters and worldly affairs for his entire life.

Control of *Dukh*: *(Dukha Nirodh):* To Lord Buddha, renunciation of all kinds of *trisna* can control *Dukha*. The castle of Buddhism has been built on the foundation of *Dukha Nirodh*. The root cause of *Dukha* is *trisna* which means insatiable lust for worldly pleasures. *Trisna* is dark devoid of any reason. It is a thirst that has no end. Hence to renounce *trisna* is the most effective way to control pains. Man getting attracted towards material things, gets involved into them, and that involvement causes a number of actions (*karmas*) which ultimately result in rebirth. Until *trisna* is renounced one cannot get rid of *Dukha* of the world.

Means and Ways to Renounce *Trisna:* Behind every activity of man there is *sanskara* which is deposition of essence of the actions of the past life. What everyone does, he does according to his *sanskara.* It is *sanskara* that reflects through human actions. The mind along with various organs known as *karmendriya* (legs, hands, mouth, genital organ and organ for passing tool) and *janendriya* (two ears, two eyes and one nose) at the instigation of *sanskara* is constantly active. Its activities are related to *sanskara*. The way to change and remove *Samskara* is meditation (*yoga*). Buddha developed eight-fold *yoga* to correct *Samskara* and finish it forever. These are:

1. *Samyak-drishti-* (Right Vision or Outlook),
2. *Samyak-Sankalp-* (Right Determination),
3. *Samyak-vachan-* (Right Talk),
4. *Samyak-karma* (Right Behaviour),
5. *Samyak-jivan* (Right Living),
6. *Samyak*-vyayam- (Right Exercise),
7. *Sayak-smriti-* (Right Memory),
8. *Samyak-samadhi-* (Right Meditation).[11]

It is right vision or right seeing that distinguishes between right and wrong. The determination that is aloof from violence and attraction towards worldly lusts is called right determination. Right Talk is that where there is no place for unpleasant, harmful, meaningless, causing quarrelling, and inciting talks. Right talk is always related to truth and love. The right *Karma* or action is the action which is devoid of theft, violence and misbehaviours etc. Right living means prohibition to kill other creatures with weapons for food. Right exercise is to control *karmendriyas* and *janendriyas*, renouncing bad thinking, and adopting good sentiments and feelings for others. In right memory it is noted that the world along with its all properties and creatures is always momentary. There is an end to everything. Even the body, mind, consciousness etc., are perishable. Right *samadhi* is that where mind is completely free from all sorts of thinking. Here, *cit* becomes stable. There is no wave of *sanskara* on it. It means in *samadhi* one is fully detached from the mundane world.

In eight-fold *yoga* of Lord Buddha except *Samadhi*, other seven *yoga* are known as *Saptang* (seven-fold). Buddha called Right balanced vision and Right determination as the wisdom that keeps the *sadhaka* stable. He contributed *Panchseel* (five behaviours) for Right talk, Right action and Right living. For Right exercise, Right *smiriti* and Right *samadhi*, the Buddha prescribed different processes.

The Buddha after Getting Enlightenment

According to *Vinaya Pittaka*, Lord Buddha after gaining enlightenment under the Bodhi Tree rejoiced it for a week. The next week, he moved a little northwards and sitting at *vajrasan* continued to look at the Tree for a week with great rejoicement. The place where Buddha stood for a week to gaze at the tree for another week is known as *Animech Chait*. From the third week, he walked between the Bodhi Tree and the place *Animech*. While walking he was still enjoying the truth which he had obtained. The place where he walked for a week is called *Ratnchakaram Chait*. It is said that God Mars once more appeared and requested him to leave the earth and get *Mahaprenirvana*, but he denied because his mission was incomplete. In the beginning, he was hesitant about spreading of Buddhism, but in the interest of the people, he decided to let the light of knowledge everywhere. In the Pali literature, it is mentioned that gods provided a house for Buddha a little far from the *Ratnachakram Chait* where he lived for another week rejoicing enlightenment. This house where he lived is known as *Ratnaghar Chait.*

Thus, after rejoicing his enlightenment, the Buddha once more reached to the tree where he had eaten *khir* offered by the lady Sujata. Thereafter, he visited many places nearby Bodh Gaya making people all pious. All these places including the Bodhi Tree became the places of pilgrimage for the world. This shows the divinity and greatness of Lord Buddha. The Bodhi Tree at Bodh Gaya where the Buddha got enlightenment and after getting it continued looking at it for a week became the tree of great faith and honour. The tree is yet available. Thousands of visitors come to this place to have a look of the tree and they bow down before it with great honour and faith.

Thus, the Buddha obtained enlightenment under the Bodhi Tree in Bodh Gaya that has become the central place for Buddhist pilgrimage. Gautam who became the Buddha was born not in Bihar, but the Buddha a highly developed personality of Gautam was definitely born on the pious land of Bodh Gaya that is in Bihar. Rahul Sanskritiyan is of the view that, it is a matter of great pleasure and pride for the people of Bihar that a godly personality like Buddha was born here.[12]

Bodh Gaya along with Bihar became popular all over the world due to the advent of Lord Buddha here. The light of knowledge that the Buddha lit from Bodh Gaya is still illuminating the world. After obtaining enlightenment, he remained there for several days to enjoy the status that he reached through hard penance. First, he thought to enjoy it himself and remain silent. Later on, the idea came to him, to help the people who are suffering a lot due to ignorance or *avidya*. So, he decided to preach people the ways and means to get rid of worldly miseries and endless cycle of birth and death. Now, he fully visualised *nirvana* and obtained the way to get rid of *Dukha* that is inherent in the world. He had also searched the way to get rid of the worldly miseries. So, he liked to share the knowledge with his followers and spread it among millions of the ignorant people. Gautam who had become the Buddha decided to spread the knowledge through travelling.

Tapassu and Mallik who belonged to Orissa, met the Buddha when he was rejoicing enlightenment at the Rajayatan tree where he had eaten the *khir*. At their request, the Buddha accepted them as his first disciples. Both of them were counted as the first and most reliable disciples of Lord Buddha.[13] Thus, it is evident that he decided to impart his teaching to Alarm Kalam and Ruderk Ramputra whom he had accepted his first and second spiritual *guru*, but both of them had died. Now, he decided to impart knowledge to those five *Brahmans* who had deserted him during the time of his penance and meditation thinking that he had lost the way. All these *Brahmans* had gone to the forest of Saranath for penance. He reached there and included them in the list of his disciples. These *Brahmans* were *Kaundinya*, *Vapya, Bhadrik, Mahanam* and *Ashvjit*. This incident in the Pali literary history is called *Dhammacakarapravertan.*

The Buddha's Travelling to Impart Knowledge

Thereafter, he travelled different places and preached his followers by spreading the divine light. As the years rolled down, the number of followers went on increasing. Not only the common mass even big scholars as well as famous rulers like Bindusara of Magadh Empire got influenced and helped the Buddha with great honour to spread Buddhism. Though he did not contribute any written scriptures, his sermons and words what he delivered here and there became the ultimate source of Buddhism. So, long as he remained alive, Buddhism was consolidated one without any variation or change in its meaning, but after his *Mahaprinirvana* in BC 547 at Kushinara in the district of Gorakhpur, Buddhism was divided into several branches. It was interpreted and reinterpreted with new angles and outlooks. Different schools of Buddhism appeared with the rise of its popularity and also due to advent of new Buddhist scholars. Among them the two schools *Hinayana* and *Mahayana* remained very much dominant even today. Both the schools have been discussed in detail in the succeeding chapter.

Buddhism has a long history. Its ideas are various and multi-coloured, but all the Buddhist attitudes fall into either of the two notions. The first one holds the view that man is utterly ignorant and has no wisdom. He cannot lead a right life. He is ugly and sinful. The other view holds that man is neither ugly nor sinful in his true colour. He is good and beautiful. He is pure and has wisdom. The depth of the Buddhistic doctrine and the attitude of thought depend on which attitude a particular school assumes. Generally speaking *Hinayana* school stands on actuality and strives to attain Buddha's rank by removing evils while *Mahayana* school which emphasises immaculate human nature holds that evil is nowhere. Buddhism arose in India and was propagated in China and Japan. Doctrinally speaking, Indian and Chinese Buddhism may be characterised as intellectualistic. The intellectualism reached the peak in Ancient China. Later it became practical with the rise of Sen who interpreted Buddhism from new practical angle. In Japan Buddhism bloomed as the religion of faith. Dogen, Shinren and Nichiren contributed much to its rapid development. Buddhism based on the idea of 'original enlightenment' seems to have reached its highest peak here.

Buddhism is not a metaphysical speculation. Rather it is a practice. Truly speaking, it is a *sadhana* which encompasses various methods. The Buddha was a *Bibhajyavadi* which means this world is not real. It is a conglomeration. The world where we live, according to Buddhism, is *panca skandhatmaka-Rupa, Vedna, Sanjya, Sanskara, Vijyana*. All these elements are not real entities. Like the philosophy of *Vedanta*, Buddhism believes in transitory phase of the material world that is on constant change. Though the Buddha does not talk about speed and time, he knew that things in the universe either living or non-living are on constant change or the series of changes are not governed by any external force, but it is automatic. This is the nature of the world. Nothing is static in the world. Things are changing moment to moment. Things perish and the process of perishing of things is so continuous that outwardly it appears that thing stands as they are. The momentary nature of things has been described in the *Vedantic* philosophy, too.

Conclusion

Gautam also known as Siddhartha, or the Buddha spent his childhood at Kapilavastu. He was brought up by his aunt Mahaprajapati. As a young boy he learnt warriorship including the technical and athletic skills of man-to-man fight. He also learnt the art of archery. At the yearly age of sixteen he married his beautiful cousin princess Yasodhara who was of equal age. He spent thirteen years with his wife in the royal court of his father. He was provided with all comfortable facilities. He enjoyed lavish court life while his father was trying to screen him from all troubles and worries. A son, namely, Rahul was born to him at the age of twenty. Despite having all material pleasures, at the age of 29 he was dissatisfied and became a monk leaving aside his family, wife, son and kingdom. After long and exhausting years of searching he finally became disillusioned with the Indian caste-system, Hindu asceticism, and the religious doctrines of his time. He obtained truth through the way of meditation. While meditating under the Bodhi tree at Bodh Gaya, Siddhartha experienced great wisdom (enlightenment) which made to realise him the way of salvation. He spent seven weeks meditating in the vicinity of the site of the Bodhi tree and attained the status of a fully realised Buddha at the age of 35. Thereafter, he travelled different places to spread the knowledge what he obtained and met different people whom he made disciples. His travelling is mostly related to northern India. Thousands of people followed him. There were not only his admires but he had to face those who were envious and jealous to him. He was criticised, but ultimately his fame and popularity went on spreading far and wide.

Having achieved the goal of spreading the teaching to the greatest number of people, Buddha obtained *Mahaprinirvana* at the age of 80 (483 BC) years as a result of food-poisoning. He took his last breath in a forest near Kusinagar (Nepal) in the company of his followers. Before his death his last talk was:

"All compounded things are ephemeral; work delightedly on your salvation."

The Buddhist scriptures of Pali Canon consist of three sections:

1. The *Suttas*–Discourses,
2. The *Vinaya*–Rules of the monks and nuns, and
3. The *Abhidhamma*–The higher doctrine of the philosophy and psychology of the teaching written only in 'Ultimate Truth'.

The complete Pali canon is roughly about 20,000 pages long, setting aside the stories and the bibliographical/historical information in the scriptures. The Buddha wrote nothing. The scholars related to Buddhist philosophy produced various accounts of Buddhism in course of time.

The philosophical contribution of the Buddha has uniqueness not in its originality, but in the manner and way that he represented. What he talked about the universe, world, birth, rebirth, death, mind, consciousnesses, are not knew. A lot has been said about in Indian great ancient epics like *Vedas*, *Vedantas*, *Upnishads*, *Bhagvad Gita*, the *Ramayana* and the *Mahabharata* etc. All these epics present in detail about momentary nature of the world and involvement of the *jivas* into *jagata,* the world due to *trisna*, lust, desire etc. For instance, when Arjuna asked Lord Krishna what force compels man to involve into worldly affairs, the Lord replies:

It is lust only which is born of contact with the material mode of passion and later transformed into wrath, and which is the all-devouring sinful enemy of this world.[14]

It is further said,

The senses, the mind and the intelligence are the sitting places of lust. Through them lust covers the real knowledge of the living entity and bewilders him.[15]

To control lust, the way to control minds establishing the hold of knowledge upon them. The *Bhagvad Gita* talks much about the significance of meditation and prescribes how to conduct it. Thus, it is evident that what the Buddha said has the relevance in ancient Indian religious scriptures. As stated above, the Buddha's concerned was not metaphysics or the philosophy of pure abstraction or to develop the theorem of transcendentalism etc., but to provide people the way of living and open the mind to realise the practical truth. He avoided the path of nihilism, externalism, absolutism, etc., and propounded the middle path accepting the truth from nihilism and absolutism both. Thus, Buddhism as a religion is like 'old wine in a new bottle'. Those who have the knowledge of Indian *Vedanta* finds nothing new in Buddhism except that it discards existence of souls and God in first hand, and ultimately reach to the same truth prescribed in the *Vedas* and *Upnishads* related to God, Soul and world. This is another matter that Buddhist's explanation of such spiritual philosophy is not direct, but indirect. What the Buddha and his followers talk of the doctrine of *Sunyata* or dependent origination is the doctrine of Zero in the Indian philosophy. Perhaps these are the similarities between Buddhism and Hinduism that ultimately merged together and the Buddha was considered as the Tenth Incarnation of Lord Vishnu in India.

References

1. B.A. Smith, *Early History of India,* Oxford, 1924, pp. 49-50.
2. *Sutnipat, (pravajyasuta)*, 18-19.
3. *Angutar Nikya, (Atkatha)*, 2, 4, 5.
4. Dharmanand Kosambi, *Bhagwan Buddha*, p. 93.
5. The *Mahabharata, perva, one,* Chapter 84, 82–103.
6. Jagnnath Das, *Bodh Gaya Itkatha, Bodh Gaya,* 1956.
7. *Majhimnikay, Singhnad Sutanta.*
8. *Jatakath Katha*, 54, p. 51.

9. *Mahima Jatak*, 479.
10. *Dighnikaya,* 2, 9, 5, 16.
11. *Majjhim Nikay, Chulvedalsut*, 44, Also see – *Lalit-Vister*, Part-26.
12. Rahul Sanskritiyan, *Attkatha, Vinya Pitaka*. p. 77
13. *Mahavaggi,* 1, 1, 4, 5.
14. *Bhagvad Gita*, Chapter 3, Verse-37.
15. *Ibid.,* Chapter 3, Verse-40.

3

The Buddhist Way of Life and His Four Noble Truths and Eight-fold Noble Paths

Buddhism was not started as a new and independent religion. It was an offshoot of the more ancient faith of the Hindus. Perhaps schism or a heresy that occurred in Buddhism after the death of the Buddha and where the school of *Mahayana* (*Theravada*) appeared inclined much more to the ancient Indian philosophy. While on the fundamentals of physics and ethics the Buddha agreed with the faith he inherited, he protested against certain practices which were in vogue at the time. He refused to acquiesce in Vedic ceremonialism. His main object was to bring about a reformation in religious practices and a return to the basic principles. His humanism crossed the racial and national barrier. The Buddha revolted against the ignorance and superstition, the dread and the horror, which accompanied popular religion. Besides, theistic views generally fills men's minds with dogmatism and their hearts with intolerance. It is said that doctrinal orthodoxy has filled the world with unhappiness, injustice, strife, crime and hatred. What the Buddha established was a way of new life and it has no room for social injustice, strife and crime. The eight-fold noble paths prescribed by him is useful to all. This is the way that may bring out universal brotherhood avoiding violence and advancing ethical as well as moral conducts of mankind. To attain such things one has to follow the way prescribed by the Buddha-based on his principles of Four Noble Truths and Eight-fold Noble Ways. These two noble things prescribed by the Buddha not only became the base of Buddhism but also provided further growth of the Buddhist philosophies and tenets. Buddhism is not a metaphysical speculation. Rather it is a practice. Truly speaking, it is a *sadhana* which encompasses various methods. The Buddha was a *Bibhajyavadi* which means this world is not real. It is a conglomeration. The world where we live, according to Buddhism, is *panca skandhatmaka, Rupa, Vedna, Sanjya, Sanskara, Vijyana*. All these elements are not real entities. Like the philosophy of *Vedanta*, Buddhism believes in transitory phase of the material world that is on constant change. What we see and observe through our sense organs is not true, but illusion. Truth is ultimate, different and it can be grasped through *sadhana* (meditation) that leads one to the goal of ultimate reality. This chapter, by explaining the Buddha's Four *Arya-staya* and Eight-fold Noble Path, examines the relevance of these principles in the life of modern man.

The Buddha Wanted to Replace Brahminism

The birth of Buddhism was indeed an expression of revolt against ritualism and formalism practiced by the cult of *Brahminism* and an aversion to scholarship. The sixth century BC when Buddha was born, was known as the age of great spiritual upsurge. Ascetics and hermits roamed from place to place throughout the Gangatic Valley, advocating mental discipline and asceticism as means of salvation. As the ceremonial acts and sacrificial rites prescribed in the Vedic texts could not satisfy the urge of the contemporary philosophers, it became essential to go deeper to fathom the ultimate truth. Here comes the period of the *Upanishads* (700 BC-600 BC). The need was felt to do research for ultimate truth that is going beyond the limit of Veda's versions related to Supreme God. The questions which perplexed the mind of the philosophers or seers were: What is *Brahman*? Wherefrom do we come? How should we live? Who controls happiness and misery? What is this Universe like? How did it start and who created it? When will it end and so on? Gautam Buddha's effort to find the ultimate truth provides the right answer. His goal was to find out the ultimate cause of sufferings and search the ways to get rid of such sufferings and pains.

The region of Magadha (south Bihar) situated east of Kashi on the right bank of the Ganga, was the centre of intellectual and spiritual activities. Among those who fostered the ferment were the Buddha, Mahavira and others. The *Brahminical* scriptures did not regard Bihar as a pious land. Rather it was regarded as a land of sin where the sacrificial rites was practiced. The inhabitants of this region were considered as 'aliens and infectious fever'. In comparison with the sacred Kashi, Magadha was considered unholy. It was evident from the statement of a Jain pilgrim of 18th century who referred to a common belief that if a cow died in Kashi, it attained salvation, whereas a man died in Magadha was reborn just as a donkey.[1]

In this circumstance, *Brahminism* that covered the mind and practice of people, played dominant role in showing and obtaining people heaven (*swarga*). As a result, ritualism and formalism became dominant everywhere in the life of people because it was said that ritualism was the viable base to attain heaven. Belief spread that by performing *Yajana* one could achieve the things in this world which one desired. There are a number of gods upholding the creation who ware capable of blessing desired things provided they are pleased, and the way of pleasing was prescribed through performing *Yajana*. So, people indulged into practice of ritualism assisted by *Brahmans*.

Charvaka's Attack on *Vedantic* Knowledge

During those period, different philosophers began to interpret absolute reality in different ways creating more confusion. There were also philosophers who denied the existence of God and believed in the theory of non-existence of any Absolute power. Among them the school of Charvaka appeared more dominant. Charvaka denied the authority of Vedas as having supreme origin and rejected the usefulness of sacrificial rites, enunciated by the priestly class. They denied the existence of an intelligent first cause of this universe. They did not believe in efficacy of caste and enunciated the thesis that it is not through birth but through one's own deeds, a person either an untouchable or a *Brahman*, should be recognised. A philosopher like Charvaka who believed in the philosophy of materialism attacked *Vedantic* knowledge. He did not believe in the existence of soul apart from the body. The school of Charvaka held that consciousness was not the quality of any unperceived non-material or spiritual entity, but a by-product of material elements such as the fire, earth, water air and ether. To substantiate his fact, the school of Charvaka quoted a passage from *Chandogya Upanishad* which stated that "If there is no separate existence of soul, it is useless to believe in the next world, rebirth, good or bad deeds and merits and demerits"[2]. Therefore, in the opinion of Charvaka, as long as we live we should live happily because there is no life after death. He totally denied the theory or philosophy related to existence of God and soul. They have quoted Brihaspati, the propounder of their philosophy, saying : "Oblation to fire, the three Vedas, the three staves and besmearing ashes to the body – all are nothing but the means of livelihood for those who are devoid of intelligence. They are more sarcastic about the priestly class." They further pointed out: "If killing of animals for sacrificial purposes, leads to heaven, why does not the sacrificer kill his own parents. And, if the *sradha* ceremony observed in honour and benefit of dead relatives causes them satisfaction, then this provision for those who undertake a journey is not necessary?" Furthermore, "if the same colour of blood flows in the vein of a *Brahman* and a *Chandala* (sudra), and both look alike, where lies the question of their being either high or low?"[3]

Buddha's Emphasis on Scientific Empirical Approach

It is the matter of great pride and honour for Bihar that the truthful tree of Buddhism, originated on the most pious, religious and spiritual land of Bodh Gaya, situated in Bihar. The noble path branches of the tree of Buddhism spread not only inside the country but also in a number of foreign countries. The light of divinity and spiritualism that Buddhism reflected, spread far and wide leading millions of people to the right path of knowledge. Buddhism, in fact, appeared at the time when wisdom in India had been enveloped by blind faith and superstitions falling in the hands of orthodox *Brahmans* who were badly engaged in *Brahminical* cult of religious ceremonies performing *karmkandas.* They hardly paid any heed to evil consequences of the religious performances practiced by them. At that time, the ancient Indian Hindu philosophy that had reached to the climax of philosophical knowledge had become out of the reach of common mass. Kurwkauds has become a slave to so-called orthodox *Brahmans* who were actively and whole-heartedly busy with practice of *karmkandas.* It was the practice of *karmkandas* widely prevailed in India that taught people *Yjanas* and sacrifices. Rituals and formalities had superseded the truth. Sacrifices of animals during *Yjanas* had made people merciless towards all sorts of animal and birds. So, their survival was in constant danger.

It is Buddhism that explained the truth from the veil of ignorance and taught common man that, philosophy and religion both needed scientific understanding. People need to believe in faith, but not in blind faith. Superstitions or superstitious beliefs must be verified with the logical eyes of reason. While accepting religion and philosophy and performing religious norms one must consider its evil consequences in the society. Buddhism also emphasised that philosophy and religion are not meant for a particular high as well as developed classes, but it must be applicable to all without the barrier of caste and *varna*-system. Religion must be approachable to all and salvation, if there is anything like that, must be open to all. Lord Buddha taught that each amoeba has inner quality as well capacity to evolve into the level of Buddha (supreme consciousness). Universality of religion depends upon its applicability to each one at every door. Buddhism achieved the status of universalism due to its scientific and liberal approach.

Buddha's Thought is Scientific

It is scientific? It is an approach where a hypothesis is verified, analysed, tested and examined. Before coming to the conclusion various methods are applied to confirm the truth. Science is practical, not dogmatic. It needs reason and logic. So, scientific truth once established becomes universal because there is no variation. The Buddha was a thinker, a monk, a saint and a scientist. He did not believe in blind faith and superstition. Rather he preferred reason. He had the reason to distinguish between right and wrong, good and bad, acceptable and non-acceptable etc. So, his thought and actions all had been reasonable. He believed in the knowledge that is gained through logical experience. He observed reality and ultimate truth applying reason from the deepest levels of insight and enlightenment of his mind-body. What he discovered, he discovered it with great pain and experience. Though his followers observing his qualities and achievements regarded him God, he never claimed himself as God or incarnation of God. Regarding existence of God he preferred to be silent because the concept of God is so vast and vague that human mind cannot even rightly comprehend about it. He neither approved God's existence nor denied it. It is all because he was not able to say scientifically whether there is God or not. So, he preferred to remain silent on this issue. The subject of his observation and verification was the physical world, not the metaphysical world. His objective was to teach the people reality related to the present life, not to attempt for attaining heaven.

His outlook was broader, balanced, analytical and observational. His vision was based on his inner-insight. He did not accept any truth until it was reasonably verified. It is true that what he said or taught was not new. It was said and taught before his advent. But the way and the method of his teaching the truth was very much different because of its reliability on scientific attitude. The philosophical truth that he established related to existence or denial of God, salvation, the way of attainment of truth, etc., are all scientific. His various doctrines like *sunyata, anatmavada,* theory of *karma,* death and rebirth etc., are scientific. His way of thinking and angle is scientific. The truth which he talked about is not new, but the method and style to establish truth are new. The philosophies which he carried were based on scientific understanding. His teaching became popular because it was simple and understandable even to common mass. Moreover, his teaching helped number of people to come out from the captivity of *karmkandas* and ritualism. That is why the orthodox *Brahmans* became bitter critics of the Buddha and Buddhism both. However, it did not dampen the courage and block the way of the Buddha. He remained firm in his postulates and hard in his behaviours.

Buddha's Teachings

Buddha, who was a progressive thinker in the guise of a super monk, taught people about their ignorance. He laid emphasis on advancement of society by laying down new social, religious and philosophical values. He discarded dogmatism and authoritarianism in thinking. He did not favour miracles and superstitions. Rather he applied the power of reasoning-based on scientific spiritualism. He preferred moral and social values to metaphysical and dogmatic discussions. He postulated that there is no absolute truth, it is only relatives. If there is any absolute theory of ultimate truth, that stands above human sense and reasoning. Nothing scientifically and definitely can be said about that and no scientific theory regarding the existence and nature of ultimate supreme power can be established. Therefore, we should try to understand the point of view of others. In this regard he confirmed the Vedic version about God that *"Na Iti, Na Iti"*, which means whatsoever is presented about existence and meaning of God is not final. There is something more to be said about endless reality.

Buddhism preached non-violence brotherhood and love. It taught people that hatred cannot remove hatred. Rather it is love and compassion that may govern and correct others. It put emphasis on self-controlled and disciplined life. The Buddha and his followers condemned superiority and inferiority of caste, and held that everyone can attain the highest status through perseverance. The Buddha believed that each amoeba has the quality to become Buddha. His emphasis was on *Meta* (friendship) and *Karuna* (compassion). He asked people to be kind enough to all creatures of the world and let them live. All beings are the same in their inner-quality. Weaker beings need sympathy from the higher one. Since man is the highest being, he must be friendly and sympathetic not only to other people but to all living beings including animals, birds and even insects. This is the right path of living. Ill-will and hatred bring about more problems and harm to the society.

The Buddha did not teach a sectarian religion. He used the word *Dhamma* in Pali which means truth and law. *Dhamma*, according to him is the way to liberation and to the end of suffering. His teachings are universal and applicable to all religions and people from all backgrounds. He put emphasis on *vipassana* which means insight. It is *vipassana* that leads to the inner calm of relaxation and also to the insight or wisdom of reality. He emphasised that the truth would be realised through the practice and not by the sermon or preaching of some individuals. The answer to life and the end to suffering are found by oneself as one own teacher and discoverer. Truth is achieved through the practice of insight meditation, not by hearing sermons and performing *Yjanas.* The base of a religion must be universal humanity. Without humanity a religion is useless.

Buddhism, thus, is a religion of kindness, humanity and equality. The Buddha aimed at a new spiritual existence attained through *jnana or Bodhi* or absolute illumination. Buddha deemed "the highest goal of a man to the stage in which there is neither old age nor fear, nor disease, nor birth nor death, nor anxieties, and in which there is no continuous renewal of activity."[4]

The Triple Gem: *Buddha, Sangha* and *Dhamma*

All Buddhists take refuse in the Triple Gem *Buddha, Damma* and *Sangha*. It is called Gem because of their immense value. Refuge simply means taking comfort in the Triple Gem to assist one on the noble path. It is something that 'keeps us going' by giving one support and encouragement. The first part of triple Gem is '*Buddha*'. This refers to the historical *Buddha* who lived 2,500 years ago. It also refers to *Buddha* (wisdom) inside us. According to Lord *Buddha*, everyone has consciousness that is the base of wisdom. If properly guided, and rightly followed everyone may reach to the stage of perfect *Buddha*. *Buddha* that symbolises absolute wisdom is the shelter of everyone. Those who come to Buddha or accept the way shown by Lord Buddha may definitely reach to the destination of the life and may avail *nirvana*. *Buddha* in Buddhism means the final abode of life where there is no darkness. It is the stage of illumination of wisdom. A *Buddha* is he who knows reality and who is fully convinced what is real truth. To a Buddha there is no suspicion about the life and a *Buddha* knows well what is right and what is wrong. He is capable of following the life that ultimately merges into the great ocean of *nirvana*. So, *Buddha* symbolises wisdom, knowledge, light, goodness, etc.

Taking refuse in *Buddha* does not mean to worship Buddha or his statue. Worshipping cult in Buddhism developed later on where emphasis has been laid down to worship and pray before Buddha's statue or other deities enunciated by the school of Theravada. The Buddha was enlightened one, who is the worthy of the highest respect. The Buddha never taught people to worship God or apply certain prescribed measure as well as processes to appease Him as it is done in Hindu religion where different gods are worshiped in different manners. Early Buddhism, in fact, was basically related to wisdom, understanding and knowledge. Here there is no place for faith and trust. It is the subject of self-realisation. It is the way which is to be covered. It is the doctrine that has to be understood. Becoming a Buddhist means to follow the path of wisdom prescribed by Lord Buddha with full determination.

The *Dhamma* refers to all of the teachings of the *Buddha*. This gives one comforts and solace. As stated above, *Buddha Dhamma* is not sectarian or dogmatic, but it is related to universal or natural law. The Buddha realised that creation is based on reason where everything is resting on established law. There is cause and effect. Products, evolution and decay all are the results of cause-effect relationship. Every effect has a cause and every cause gives birth to something. In other words, a cause results into effect and each effect brings forth some happenings. Nothing happens automatically. The need is to understand or know the cause of happenings so that it may be controlled. According to Hindu philosophy, *dharma* that is the base of creation is duty. All the elements and creatures that are in the creation have their own *dharma*. Wheel of creation is moving on the movement of *dharma*. *Dharma* is universal. It is spread everywhere. The wheel of *dharma* is constantly moving. In Buddhism *Dhammacakra* has great significance. The wheel of *Damma* is in every heart. If it is propelled rightly, it produces good fruits, but if it is taken to wrong direction, it yields poisonous fruits. *Dhammacakra in* Buddhism carries great meaning. It is the endless cycle of nature. It is moving from upwards to downwards and the vice-versa. It moves in right and wrong both the ways. It is up to the understanding of the man whether he moves *Dhammacakra* right or wrong, upward or downward. At the temple of Bodh Gaya, there is *Dhammacakra* and the visitors propel it towards right direction. It symbolises the universal *dharma* that must be followed in right direction. Thus, in Buddhism, *Dhamma* stands for purity, sanctity, sagacity, right thinking and right behaviour. It is not a religious cult or a sectarian religious understanding that confine *dharma* to a particular community expressing its supremacy over other religions. So, *Buddha Damma* is universal, equally applicable to everyone. *Buddha Dhamma* is not a mere belief in some unseen supreme power, but a method of perfect understanding and a way of reasonable behaviour.

To handle *Dhammacakra* properly, one must have the wisdom and determination both. It comes when one joins *Buddha Dharma*. That teaches how to live, what to do and what not to do. In fact, every religion teaches people the sanctity of life and leads them towards light to get rid of troubles and pains. Like that *Buddha Dhamma* is the light that calls upon its followers to move towards right direction and perform the duties for improving his personality and the well-being of others.

Sangha generally refers to the community of monks and nuns, but generally became known as the entire Buddhist community of monastic and lay people. *Sangha* has prescribed rules and the followers have to strictly practice and follow them. *Sangha,* in fact, is a type of organisation of Buddhists. *Sangha*, in theoretical aspect, is pious where there is no place for any kind of evils. It emphasises on purity of life and shows the way of salvation. *Sangha* has certain prescribed rules which must be followed strictly by the members of a *Sangha*. Thus, the *Sangha* in Buddhism carries great meaning and contains big purpose. While living in the *Sangha* one learns a lot about Buddhism and avails the opportunity to became Buddha. It is an organisation based on moral principles and religious ways. It has the authority to punish those who either dishonour *Sangha* or break up its sanctity. Those who are in *Sangha* have to abide by its rules and regulation. It teaches monks discipline first and then knowledge.

Basic Rules of Buddhism

Thus, in Buddhism three Gems in *Buddha*, *Sangha* and *Dhamma* are very popular and also provide the base of the religion. In the beginning, the *Bhikhus* had to travel from one place to another one and they had to live the life according to certain rules and order prescribed by Lord Buddha. The rules what the Buddha framed for the *Bhikhus* have been collected in *Patimokha.* From time to time, some changes have occurred in that, no doubt, but they are still sacred to Buddhism. These rules may be divided into seven categories mentioned below:

1. Ordination *(Diksha),*
2. Monastic system *(Vihara),*
3. Stay at Rainy Season *(Varsavasa),*
4. Dress,
5. Food and Medicine,
6. Regulations for nuns, (lady *Bhikhu*), and
7. Religious constitutions.

Ordination *(Diksha)*

While awarding *Diksha* directly performed by the Buddha the initial words uttered by him were, 'Come, O Monk'. Later on, when the number of followers increased, he allowed some of his trustworthy disciples to give *Diksha* to interested one. In that course, three noted and pious words, *Buddha, Damma* and *Sangha* came to be used while awarding *Dikhsa.* The following slogans were to be uttered twice by one who wanted to obtain *Diksha:*

1. *Budham Sarṇam Gachhami,* (let us go to the shelter of Buddha);
2. *Dhammam Sarnam Gachhami, and* (let us go shelter to the *Dhamma);*

3. *Sangham Sarnam Gachhami.* (let us go to the shelter of *Sangha).*

The process of *Diksha* was called *pravajya.* There are two phases of *pravajya*—the phase of probation and the phase of permanent. The period of probation was for five years. If the character of the *Bhikhu* after getting proper *Diksha* was found satisfactory, he was allowed to enter into permanent phase of *pravajya.* Some of the important rules for *pravajya* are mentioned below:

1. One must not be below fifteen years,
2. One must not take *Diksha* without the permission of parents. One must not be a slave.
3. One must go for clean shaving of head and beard before obtaining *Diksha.*
4. After obtaining *Diksha,* one must wear the yellow clothe.
5. The person indoctrinated must lead ascetic life.
6. He/she must follow the life of *Brahmcharya* till lifelong,
7. One must not speak lie.
8. One must not take things causing intoxication.
9. One must take food at the time prescribed.
10. One must not sleep on comfortable bed.
11. One must not decorate body, and
12. One must not accept wealth in forms of gold and silver.

Vershava and *Vihara*

The *Bhikhus* had to move from one place to another. The main source of their livelihood was begging. During the rainy season, the *Bhikhus* were allowed to stay at a particular place till the rainy season was over. Normally, it began from the month of July and after end of the season they had to move again. The Buddha along with his disciples passed his first *Varsavasa* at Saranath, second, third and fourth at *Rajgriha,* fifth at Vaishali, sixth at Mankulgiri, seventh at Tarvartilok, eighth at Sumsumarigiri, ninth at Kaishambi, tenth at Prilegyak, eleventh at Balgram, twelfth at Mathura, thirteenth at Chaliyagiri, fourteenth at Shravasti, fifteenth at Kapilavastu, sixteenth at Alki and seventeenth at Rajgriha. Buddha preferred Shravasti most appropriate place for *Varsavas*. It is evident from the fact that he stayed at Shravasti at least 21 times during the rainy season. His stay at Shravasti made the place so pious and popular that it came to be known as Saranath where a number of visitors travel every day. The place where the *Bhikhus* used to stay during the *Varsavas* was provided by the people living nearby. In *Rajgriha* the king had given Benuvan to *Bhikhus* for *varsavas*. The supporting necessary requisites were available. Each *Bhikhu* had to live in a hut that was prepared. Generally such *Vershavas* that was called *aram* was built near a river. No luxurious facilities were made available.

The base of the *Buddha Sangha* was democratic. During *Vershavas* provision was to have assemblies chaired by the *Bhikhus* having at least ten years of experience. Quorum was fixed for meeting of the Assembly. If the number of the members was less than the prescribed quorum, the meeting was not held. Minimum number for an assembly in the border areas was fixed not less than four. The Buddha started fortnight assembly and made it compulsory for the *Bhikhus* living nearby to attend it. Decision on a proposal was taken by majority after proper discussions. In the assembly only those persons were allowed to be present who had the right to vote. The proposal was placed before the assembly by giving three readings. The members in the *Sangha* discussed truth and established norms.

Dresses and Food

The dresses which were used by the *Bhikhus* resembled to that of a *sanyasi*. It was called *chiver* that was made with rough clothes. In the begging, the colour of the dress was yellow, but later on *Bhikhus* began to adopt *geruya* colour like Hindu *sanyasis*. They were both vegetarian and non-vegetarian. Eating meat was not prohibited. However, they were not allowed to demand something special in the name of food from supporters. In case some *Bhikhus* suffered from any kind of disease, they could take medicine to get cure. But in the name of medicine nothing was allowed that could have created intoxicative effect. Gradually, *Bhikha* remained formal. Most of the *Sanghas* had sufficient collection to support them.

The dress gave them a status to be recognised in the society.

Rule Related to Bhikhuni in Sangha

In the beginning, there was no provision for ladies to become *Bhikhuni*. The Buddha had established *Bhikuni Sangha* after five years of the foundation of Buddhism. In the beginning, the Buddha was not in favour of including ladies in the *Sangha*. He changed his mind when he reached Kapilavastu where Gautami requested him to grant *Diksha*. At the denial, she requested his most trustworthy follower Ananda to plead her case. Ananda accepting the request of Gautami persuaded the Buddha to include ladies in the *Sangha*. He agreed after several requests to allow ladies to join the *Sangha* with certain conditions. There were some *Bhikhus* who disliked the inclusion of ladies into the *Buddha Sangha*. The Buddha knew well that inclusion of ladies in the *Sangha* would definitely affect its sanctity, but there was no way out because of requests and pressures. It was this point that was raised in the First Council after the death of Buddha and the point became one of the factors for division in the *Buddha Sangha*.

The conditions which were laid down for the *Bhikhuni* were:

1. To honour *Bhikhu* even though he was junior to her.
2. No criticism of a *Bhikhu* by a *Bhikhuni*.
3. Where there is no *Bhikhu, Bhikhunis* cannot live together during *Vershavas*.
4. The conditions framed for the *Bhikhunis* must be strictly applied.

No doubt, *Bhikhuni Sangha* was set up by permitting ladies to come and join the system, but the Buddha always remained doubtful. His apprehension was that inclusion of ladies would affect the sagacity and durability of the *Sangha*. Prajapati Gautami was the first lady to obtain *Diksha*. Thereafter, the daughter of Gautami, Nanda, was the next to have *Diksha*. Yasodhara, the wife of Gautam, also obtained it. When Lord Buddha reached Kapilavastu, several persons obtained ordination along with close relatives and friends of Gautam. Even his son Rahul obtained *Diksha* from Lord Buddha.

The Four Noble Truths of the Buddha

Lord Buddha had fully experienced that to live means to suffer, because the human nature is not perfect and neither the world is fit for living. However, man is bound to live. So, the Buddha set up certain good principles to be followed in the life to avoid *Dukhas* that came to be known as the Four Noble Truths. During our life time, we inevitably have to endure physical suffering such as pain, sickness, injury, tiredness, old age and diseases related to old age, and lastly death. One has to endure psychological suffering like sadness, fear, frustration, disappointment and depression etc. The pleasure that one receives in the world is temporary. Nothing is permanent in the world. Everything is momentary. So, he discovered that life is suffering. His Four Noble Truths that he discovered during the time of getting enlightenment are mentioned below in detail.

1. Life is suffering.
2. The origin of suffering is attachment.
3. The cessation of suffering is attainable, and
4. The path to the cessation of suffering.

1. Life is Suffering

Buddha's entire philosophy originates from the popular term *'Dukha'* which means suffering. According to the Utilitarian theory of Bentham man prefers pleasure and avoids pain. According to the Buddha, pleasure attracts mankind but in pursuit of pleasure man gathers pains because he lacks proper knowledge to distinguish between sources of pain and pleasure. To the Buddha pain or suffering is such that it has deep root in the world and everyone is in the ambit of *Dukha.* The Buddha visualised that suffering is the universal fact and everyone is in its hard catch. There are various kinds of sufferings. One suffers because he knows neither the root cause of suffering nor the ways how to get rid of suffering. Man creates suffering from his own mind, body, action, feeling, and thought. Too much attachment to the worldly affairs and too much desire for material things mean to invite more sufferings. Man in search of pleasure gathers more pain due to ignorance and greed. He lacks the right knowledge. Ignorance leads him towards pain that goes on multiplying. Selfish desire, greed, dissatisfaction, lust for material gain and prosperity etc., are the agents which tempting man take the path of sufferings. Believing the theory of cause and effect, he was fully convinced that every action has its effect and it is one who performs the action has to harvest the fruits of actions. Since man lacks proper understanding while performing action (*karma*), he indulges into prohibited acts which are the root of *Dukhas*. Falling in the lap of lust and *trisna* man overlooks painful results of actions and he has to suffer. The process of suffering continued till man dies and even after his death, the effect of his *karmas*, bad or good, remains alive and active that causes his next birth. Thus, the process of suffering becomes endless.

2. The Origin of Suffering is Attachment

Lord Buddha established the truth that the origin of suffering is attachment to transient things and the ignorance thereof. Transient things do not include only objects that surround us, but also ideas, and, in a greater sense, all objects of our perceptions. Ignorance is the lack of understanding of how our mind is attached to impermanent things. The reason for suffering is insatiable desire, passion, lust, un-ending thrust for worldly things, ardor for wealth and prestige, striving for fame and popularity. In short, craving and clinging are basic cause of suffering. The Buddha called it *trisna*. Because, the objects of our attachment are transient, their loss is inevitable. Man wants to possess or gather as much as he can. His wish is to establish his ownership over enormous wealth forever. While doing that he forgets that nothing is certain and durable. What will happen even at what moment to him is not known. Though he knows that he shall have to depart from this world one day leaving all what he collected, but he overlooks the fact and falling in temptation, goes on gathering wealth even by applying wrong means. Once the things that he has gathered are ruined or destroyed by any reason, he falls in great disappointment. This all cause suffering which makes man upset and sad. Objects of attachment also include idea of 'self' (ego) that is delusion. What one says self is imagined entity. It is the pride of self that keeps man constantly busy to collect the means of comfort and luxuries. It is self that makes one proud and selfish. It is self that is the cause of quarreling because it makes one proud and mad. Conflict between two egos is the root cause of violence and ill-will against each other. It is the nature of every creature that when his ego is damaged, he becomes blind and he does not hesitate to harm the interest of enemies. He overlooks the reality that every creature and everything of the world is a part of the ceaseless becoming of the universe. The process of coming and going and appearing and disappearing is constant. Everyone has to meet the process. So, creatures of the world falling prey to the lust and desires, are entangled with pain and suffering.

Buddhism, sometimes, is called as pessimistic religion because it terrifies people in the name of suffering. According to Buddhism the world is full of miseries and sufferings. It creates sadness to man and makes him disappointed. Such thing makes man non-active and keeps him away from engagement in life's activities. But reality is different. Buddhism talks reality. Life is suffering this is universal truth. It has been accepted by other religions also. However, it does not have to be this way. Suffering in the life is to those who are un-enlightened. The enlightened person has no need to fear. Life is pleasant to those who obtain enlightenment. Enlightenment itself is pleasure. It brings out real and permanent pleasure. It is happiness, which never perishes. It is said:

"I do not say that the breakthrough in the Four Noble Truths is accompanied by suffering or displeasure. Rather, the breakthrough to the Four Noble Truths is accompanied by the happiness and joy."[5]

3. The Cessation of Suffering is Attainable

One suffers because one does not know the cause of suffering. In the Hindu philosophy it is called *Maya (delusion)* that is veil of ignorance. Man has reason, no doubt, but it is covered with ignorance. What he thinks real is, in fact, not real, but illusory. Reality is under the cover. Due to universal prevalence of lust, greed, desire, hatred, jealousy, etc., man's wisdom does not reflect. Until vision appears from the inner-heart, reality of thing is not known. In the absence of right wisdom he falls prey to *Maya*. Temptation attracts him towards worldly things and to get them, man is ready to go to any extent. Reason is enveloped. Man hardly looks into the innerself. So, these are the causes of sufferings. The creation of the universe is such that it is outwardly attractive but inwardly painful. Here everything is momentary including the life. Death is certain and things are to change. Changes take place in bodies also. *Trisna* (insatiable desire) is so strong that man overlooks the bad consequences of *trisna*. It takes man to the trap of *Maya* where there is nothing but sufferings only. The pleasure or happiness that comes is temporary. Lord Buddha was confident that if there are suffering and causes of suffering, there are ways to cease suffering. Suffering may be opposed. The cessation of suffering can be attained through *nirodha*. *Nirodha* means the unmaking of sensual craving and conceptual attachment.

To cease the cause of suffering man shall have to awake his wisdom that is inside. *Nirodha* to lust and desire is possible. One has to distinguish between right and wrong, and that can be done with the help of reason only. However, it needs determination, a strong will to get rid of suffering. It is right wisdom that enables one to avoid lust and *trisna*. Until man fully visualises the cause of suffering, he may never come out of the net of sufferings. Even the death cannot release from suffering because man will have to take another birth. Even after death it is the unfulfilled desire that serves as the cause of rebirth and sufferings again and again. To finish suffering forever it needs complete abandonment of worldly desires and lusts. It is not possible until one learns the means to abandon the causes of suffering. Buddhism teaches these ways and means.

The third noble truth of Buddha expresses the idea that suffering can be ended by attaining dispassion. *Nirodha* distinguishes all forms of clinging and attachment. This means that suffering can be overcome through human activity, simply by removing the cause of suffering. Suffering is there, but not forever. It may be uprooted. Though the root of suffering is very deep and strong, but it can be cut off forever by the axe of wisdom and strong determination as well as complete detachment. While applying the prescribed methods one may reach to the final stage of *nirvana* where there is no suffering. *Nirvana* is such that all sorts of *dukhas* end there. There is permanent peace and pleasure. According to Hindu religious scriptures *nirvana* (salvation) is the stage of imperishable *ananda* (bliss) which is permanent. It is *sat-cit-anand.* It is the place of eternity where there is no *Dukha.* In the universe there is *Ananda* (bliss) that is permanent because it is attached to *sat* (truth) that never dies or disappears. *Cit* is consciousness or *chetna*. So, the need is to remain always conscious about the nature of thing and also remain attaché permanently to the truth that is known through consciousness. It is true that everything is changing moment after moment, but the truth or essence of the thing remains always as it is. It is that which never changes or disappears. So, in the Hindu philosophy, the term *sat-cit-anand* has been used and God is called as *Schidanand* which means one who is symbol of permanent truth and bliss.

4. The Path of Cessation to Suffering

What the Buddha discovered or realised is not only suffering of the world, but he also found the ways how to get rid of it. There is a path to be free from suffering. It is the middle way between the philosophy of agnosticism and nihilism that has been elaborated in this book somewhere else. The way the Buddha prescribed is *Samadhi* or meditation. Through *Samadhi* or meditation one would definitely know the truth and would get the will to get rid of sufferings. In normal condition of life man is totally engaged in outward world. He lacks the idea of inner-world or inner-self. The Buddha knew well that the base of human activities or even the life of all creatures is inner-consciousness where essence of each activity is noted. This essence is called *sanskara* which guides one to act. Everyone is acting according to his own *sanskara* that he had gathered in his past life. He has prescribed Noble Eight-fold ways which are mentioned below. In the present life, one has to harvest what he sowed in the past life. There is no escape from it. Until the imprint of *sanskara* is removed from inner-consciousness, it is not possible to get rid of suffering. To remove the essence or imprint of *sanskara* is to know it, and one can know it through *samadhi* that is deep thinking or go back to his own inner-consciousness as Lord Buddha reached there during his deep *Samadhi*. After obtaining enlightenment, he established Eight-fold path to obtain *Samadhi* and lastly to get rid of suffering.

The Noble Eight-fold Paths

The Noble Eight-fold Paths describe the way to the end of suffering, as it was laid out by the Buddha. It is a practical guideline to ethical and mental development with the goal of freeing the individual from attachment and delusions. It finally leads to understanding the truth about all things. The Noble Eight-fold Paths of the Buddha constitutes the base of Buddhism. In Buddhism great emphasis has been laid down on the practical aspects. With practice one can achieve a higher level of existence and finally reach *nirvana.* The eight aspects of path are not to be understood as a sequence of single steps, instead they are highly interdependent principles that have to be seen in relationship with each other. It also leads to understand the truth about all things. Together with the four Noble Truths, it constitutes the gist of Buddhism.

The Noble Eight Path of Buddhism, which the Buddha himself described as the Middle Way, may be called the quintessence of the Buddhist ethical system. It was called the Middle Way because of the context in which the Buddha preached. During the time there were people who believed that man's spiritual elevation depended on self-mortification, and there were those who completely disregarded spiritual values and preoccupied themselves with sensuous indulgence. The Middle Way of the Buddha is sometimes described as a scheme of the three-fold moral training consisting of virtuous practice-*sila* (mental composure), *samadhi* and wisdom.

1. Right View or Understanding *(samma ditthi)*

The things which we see or view in our daily life stand not as they are, but they are different from reality. They are concealed under ignorance. To know their real nature one has to go deep into understanding and find out reality. So, they need right vision. In Buddhism right understanding means to understand aforesaid Four Noble Truths. So, it includes right understanding of four noble truths. One begins with an understanding based on the logic of the teachings, then knowledge, then experience through meditation and finally an understanding through the wisdom of enlightenment experiences. Such understanding is real and non-flexible or non-variant. The Buddha while expressing the significance of Noble Eight-fold Path said to the *Bhikhus:*

Bhikhus, this is the forerunner and precursor of the rising of the sun.... So, too, *Bhikhus,* for a *Bhikhu* this is the forerunner and precursor of the breaking through to the Four Noble Truths as they really are, that is, Right Understanding.[6]

Right view is the beginning and the end of the path. It simply means to see and understand things as they really are and to realise the Four Noble Truths. Right view is the cognitive aspect of knowledge. It also means to grasp the nature of things that are on constant destruction. Worldly objects have the nature that is impermanent and imperfect. Right view is not necessarily an intellectual capacity. Right view is attained, sustained and enhanced through all capacity of mind. It begins with the initiative insight that all beings are subject to suffering and it ends with complete understanding of the true nature of all things. Right view yields right thoughts and right action. It is a reasoning capacity which catches reality through penetrating into the nature and depth of the thing or being. Right view is related to love and non-violence extending to all beings. It is not simply to see the thing but to understand its nature, quality and utility. Man suffers in the life because he does not view things properly. It is obtained through deep thinking. So, in meditation one observes the real nature of a thing and forms the good idea. Man is the product of his own thought. The same reality has been described by Lord Buddha in the following words:

All we are is the result of what we have thought. It is founded on our thoughts. It is made up of thoughts. If a man acts or speaks of a pure thought, happiness follows him like a shadow that never leaves him.[7]

Another Quote from *Ddhammapada* States

Your worst enemy cannot harm you as much as your own thoughts, unguarded. But once mastered, no one can help you as much, not even your father or your mother.[8]

Thus, it is quite obvious that the Buddha put emphasis on the right view or right understanding of a thing. When one comes in contact with a thing, he must deeply think about its goodness and harmfulness. Man does what he thinks. If thinking is improved or highlighted, there is no fear of suffering because the root cause of suffering is ignorance.

2. Right Speech or Talk

Speech is expression of one's mind. What one thinks and feels is expressed through a language. Words can break or save lives, make enemies or friends, start war or create peace. To stand from slanderous speech and not to use words maliciously against others make man perfect and wise. Violence is not only in action, but in words also. To speak harsh words to anyone is also a kind of violence because it may hurt his ego or mind. Like that if one talks idle things or utters nonsense words, his image is tarnished and he loses his value among people. The Buddha is very much particular to speak right thing, avoid telling lie, use friendly as well as polite words and to talk only when it is necessary. Hatred speech is harmful. The Buddha was of the view that when one person attacks another through filthy speech, two people gets hurt. He said that when one is harmed even through speech, he becomes angry he uses the same harmful language which ultimately may result into quarreling and fighting. Moreover, a filthy or dirty language or hatred talk may cause agitation to both sides (speaker and listener) ultimately resulting in diseases like hyper tension, blood pressure which may again result in heart-attack. So, one must be attentive and careful while delivering speech. To spread rumour is harmful to everyone. The language is the best that resolves problems not complicate them. That is why a language is an art and its beauty relies upon one's wisdom who uses the art. The Buddha knew well that words can break or save lives, make enemies and friends, start war or create peace. Speech is the way to convince people or to make them aggressive. The Buddha explained right speech as follow:

1. To abstain from false speech, specially not to tell deliberately and not to speak deceitful;
2. To abstain from slanderous speech and not use words

maliciously against others;

3. To abstain from harsh words that offend or hurt others;
4. To abstain from idle chatters that lacks purpose or depth, and
5. Abstain from Alcoholic drinks, drugs, or intoxication that clouds the mind.

It means one must speak truth and must use friendly words. One must talk when it is necessary. It is said that speech is silver and silence is golden. Offending words harm both the person who uses it and to those against whom it is used.

4. Right Livelihood

Right livelihood means to earn one's livelihood by applying honest means. Wealth should be gained applying proper skill and labour. To store things more than need by applying insincere methods is a kind of theft and also crime against the society. Moreover, one should not earn wealth indulging oneself in wrong profession such as killing animals, dealing in human trades and illegal arms, prostitutions, narcotics, intoxication, poisons etc. If it is done, it will definitely harm the principles of Right Speech and Right Action. The Buddha had compassion for everyone. So, he prohibited people from doing anything in the name of livelihood that becomes harmful to others. Bread and butter are must for everyone. The step that devoid others to get the required share are always wrong, and it may result in anger, hatred and bloodshed. Dealing in wrong professions may cause troubles to others and it may also be dangerous to the life of many.

6. Right Effort

Right effort can be seen a prerequisite for the other principles of the path. Without effort, which is in itself an act of will, nothing can be achieved, where as misguided effort distracts the mind from its task and confusion takes place. So, determination is needed to do something that has been selected, applying wisdom. Mental energy is the force behind the right action. It can occur either in wholesome or unwholesome states. The same type of energy that fuels desire, envy, aggression, and violence can on the other side fuel self-discipline, honesty, benevolence and kindness. Right effort is detailed in four types of endeavours that rank in ascending order or perfection. These are:

1. To prevent the arising of not yet arisen unwholesome states;
2. To abandon unwholesome states that have already arisen;
3. To arouse wholesome states that have not yet arisen; and
4. To maintain perfect wholesome states already arisen.

Persistence and determination are omnipotent to achieve success. Nothing can be done successfully with half-mind or less determination. Regarding persistence and determination the American President Calvin Coolidge said:

"Nothing in the world can take the place of persistence. Talent will not; nothing is more common than the unsuccessful man with talent. Genius will not, unrewarded, genius is almost a proverb. Education will not; the world is full of educated derelicts. Persistence and determinations are omnipotent."

In this regard The Buddha said:

Therein, *Bhikhus*, the mediator who is both a thorough worker and a persistent worker regarding concentration is the chief... the most excellent of the mediators.[9]

Determination is the firm decision to do something. One has to set the goal and apply the effort to achieve it. The Buddha sat under the Buddha tree with full determination to obtain enlightenment. He remained firm despite various troubles. He did not care even for his life. He did it persistently without any break. Lastly, he achieved the goal that he had set for. So, everyone desired who wants to achieve goal in the life must be wise in selecting the goal and makes a strong determination to achieve it.

7. Right Mindfulness

Right mindfulness is the control and perfected faculty of cognition. It is the mental ability to see things as they are, with clear consciousness. Usually, the cognitive process begins with an impression induced by perception or by a thought, but then it does not stay with the mere impression. Instead, one almost always conceptualises sense impressions and thoughts immediately. One interprets them and set them in relation to other thoughts and experiences, which naturally go beyond the facility of the original impression. The mind then posits concepts into constructs, and weaves those constructs into complex interpretive schemes. All this happen only half consciously, and as a result one often sees things obscured. Right mindfulness is anchored in clear perception, and it penetrated impression without getting carried away. Right mindfulness enables us to be aware of the process of conceptualisation in a way that one actively observes and controls the way one's thoughts process. The Buddha accounted for this as the four foundations of mindfulness. They are:

1. Contemplation of the body;
2. Contemplation of feeling (repulsive, attractive or neutral);
3. Contemplation of the state of mind, and
4. Contemplation of the phenomena.

8. Right concentration.

The eighth principle of the Eight-fold Path is right concentration which refers to the development of mental force that occurs in natural consciousness, although at a rate of relatively low-level of intensity, namely concentration. Concentration in this context is described as one-pointedness of mind, meaning a state where all mental faculties are unified and directed onto one particular object. Right concentration for the purpose of the Eighth-fold Path means wholesome concentration, i.e., concentration on wholesome thoughts and actions. The Buddhist methods of choice to develop right concentration are through the practice of deep meditation. The meditating mind focuses on a selected object. It first directs onto it, then sustains concentration, and finally intensifies concentration step by step. Through this practice, it becomes natural to apply elevated levels of concentration in day to day situation.

There are actually two types of meditation as taught by the Buddha. They are *samatha*, which is the calm, tranquil technique and then there is *vipassana,* which is the type leading to insight. Most meditation techniques in the Buddha's and before and even still today are primarily the *samatha* type. That is, they lead to a relaxed peaceful state and sometimes to great experience of joy, bliss, even trance, but no ultimate insight of enlightenment. Right concentration primarily deals the *samatha* type of meditation which is aimed at these highly concentrative states. On the other hand, *vipassana* meditation, when done correctly, can prove the inner calm of *samatha* and also can lead to the insight wisdom of *vipassana*. It can be direct one-pointedness concentration on a devotional figure such as a statue of Buddha, Jesus or Mary. The common subject for beginners is awareness of *pranayam*. The mediators remain in the present moment focussing on the inhale and outhale of the body. The mind and the body become calm and free of negative thoughts.

Meditation in the Hindu Religious Scriptures

The great religious scripture of Hindus, the *Bhagvad Gita* talks much about meditation. According to it, meditation is the process of concentration of mind sitting on a right posture outly prescribed. One has to be cool and calm keeping the mind in full control so that it may not vary. The attention is concentrated on the nose or in the mid of the two eye-brows. While concentrating, entire attention is confined to the object which is concentrated. No other thinking should take place in the mind except the object. In this way, the mind is disciplined. Once the thought is stable, the mediator penetrates deep into the consciousness; the attention becomes firm and invariable. This needs constant practice. Here all logics and arguments applied by reason disappear. This is the state of *samadhi*. The person meditating remembers nothing, neither his body nor his wisdom. He enters into a state of complete calmness. His attention is fully concentrated on the figure which he meditates. In this state what one sees is vision not scene. Prescribing the ways of *Samadhi* Lord Krishna says to Arjuna:

Shutting out all external sense objects, keeping eyes and vision concentrated between the two eyebrows, suspending the inward and outward breaths within the nostrils, and thus controlling the mind, senses and intelligence, the transcendentalist aiming at liberation becomes free from desire, fear and anger. One who is always in this stage is certainly liberated.[10]

Regarding the posture of *Samadhi* or *Dhyan Yoga,* Lord Krishna further states:

To practice *yoga*, one should go to a secluded place and should lay *kusa* grass on the ground and then cover it with a deer skin and a soft cloth. The seat should be neither too high nor too low and should be situated in a sacred place. The *yogi* should then sit on it very firmly and practice *yoga* to purify the heart by controlling his mind, senses and activities and fixing the mind on one focus point.[11]

It is further said:

One should hold one's body, neck and head erect in a straight line and stare steadily at the tip of the nose. Thus, with unanimated, subdued mind, devoid of fear completely free from sex life, one should meditate upon Me within the heart and make Me the ultimate goal of life.[12]

A lot has been said in the book *Yoga-Pantanjali,* written by great Indian scholar Patanjali Muni, who was expertise in the method of *Yoga* or *Samadhi*. According to him *yoga* means to control the desires that have constantly been coming out from the consciousness. He has presented details about the various stages of *yogas* and achievements out of *yoga*. When the Buddha talks of meditation where he suggests controlling senses and emphasises on concentration, it appears that he had the knowledge of *Yoga* prevailed in the ancient Indian Hindu society. The right way to obtain real knowledge and have closeness to God is *Samadhi* that is method or practice to be done under the guidance of a perfect *guru*.

It appears that Gautam knew the method of meditation. He might have learnt it from his earlier *gurus* or from someone who knew it. So, Gautam while performing *Samadhi* (Meditation) under the Bodhi tree at Bodh Gaya applied these methods and obtained enlightenment. It has already been stated that while entering into *Samadhi* he had taken some grass from the grass-cutter. He used to sit on the grass. It was *kusa* grass. He sat under the tree for as many as 39 days and nights continuously concentrating his mind to the fixed point controlling his all senses. Thus, it is evident that the impact of

Hindu religious scripture on Gautam's mind was present. He applied the ways prescribed in the *Bhagvad Gita* or mentioned in some other religious scriptures.

The Buddha's Eight-fold Middle Path has been summarised to the three main categories:

1. Wisdom,
2. Morality, and
3. Concentration.

Right Understanding and Right Thought come under the wisdom category. Right speech, right action and right livelihood come under the category of morality. Right effort, right mindfulness and right concentration come under the concentration category.

The Precepts

The precepts are the condensed essences of Buddhist ethical practice. They are often compared with the Ten Commandments of the Christianity. However, in Buddhism these commandments are not compulsory to follow. They are to be taken as recommendations, not commandments. This means the follower is encouraged to use his/her own intelligence to apply these rules in the best possible way. Secondly, it is the spirit of the precepts, not the text. The first five precepts which are mentioned below are mandatory for every Buddhist, though the fifth precept is often not observed, because it bans the consumption of alcohol. Precepts number six to ten are laid out for those in preparation for monastic life and for devoted lay people unattached to families. The eighth precept put together number eight and nine and omits the tenth. Lay people may observe the eight precepts on Buddhist festival days. Ordained Theravada monks undertake no less than 227 precepts. The following are the precepts to abstain from:

1. Harming living beings;
2. Taking things nor freely giving;
3. Sexual misconduct;
4. False speech;
5. Intoxicating drinks and drugs causing insanity;

6. Taking untimely meals;
7. Dancing, singing, music and watching grotesque mime;
8. Use of garlands, perfumes and personal adornment;
9. Use of high seats, and
10. Accepting gold or silver.

References

1. *Pracina Thirthamala Samngraha*, I, p. 4.
2. *A History of Indian Philosophy,* III, p. 537 also see p. 528 ff.
3. Jagdish Chandra Jain, "Two Great Religion of Magadha", in P.N. Ojha, (ed.) *Homage to Bhikhu Jagdish Kashyap*, (1986), Shri Nava Nalanda Mahavihara, Patna. pp. 153-160.
4. *Asvaghosa, Buddhacrita,* XI, 59.
5. *Samyutta Nikaya*, 56.35.
6. *Dhammapada*, Chapter 3.
7. *Dhammapada*, 1st verse of the 1st chapter.
8. *Dhammapada*,Chapter 3.
9. *Samyutta Nikaya,* 34.53.
10. *Bhagvad Gita*, Chapter 5, Verse 27-28.
11. *Ibid.,* Chapter 6, Verse 11-12.
12. *Ibid.,* Chapter 6, Verse 13-14.

4

Buddhist Philosophy and its Similarity and Contrast to the Philosophy of Hinduism

Each religion contains certain tenets, precepts and doctrines. It establishes moral and ethical values and attempts to interpret metaphysics and speculate about transcendental world. Buddhism, too, has precepts, doctrines and golden path to get rid of worldly suffering and obtain *nirvana*. Though the Buddha's intention was not to set up any particular religion, with growing strength of his followers both inside and outside the country, and also coming of new interpretation of Buddhism, gradually it assumed a state of a religion. It became *Buddha Dhamma.* The basic purpose of Lord Buddha was to oppose excessiveness in the practice of Hindu *Dharma* by orthodox *Brahmans*, who had developed the cult of *karmkanda*-based on ritualism and formalism. The Buddha wanted to set a new philosophy devoid of blind faith and superstition. However, Buddhism became a religion. Whether it is a religion in true sense or not one has to know the meaning of religion. This chapter investigates into the religious concepts of Buddhism and analyses its philosophical as well as social values. It also examines various tenets of Buddhism that came into being even after the death of the Buddha.

Meaning of Religion

What is a religion? The greatest factor that is responsible for building-up a vast superstructure in the core of a religion is its institutionalisation. As long as a religion is a matter of personal faith, piety (devotion to God) or inner experience, it does not come into conflict with secular laws and institutions. But once a religion is institutionalised, it becomes interested in maintaining its hold on the populous and social institutions, and develops a rigid form of creed, sect of rituals and laws which are declared as binding upon its followers.[1] So far the case of Buddha *Dhamma* is concerned, during the life time of the Buddha it became an institution in the form of *Sangha*. However, its nature remained universal and secular also. Again, religion is the main instrument for the expression of values. It is the carrier of ethics and the moulder of personal and social behaviour. It supplies the ethos, the prevalent tone or sentiment of a given culture. According to Encyclopaedia Dictionary of Society, religion is a "system of belief, practice and philosophical values concerned with definition of the sacred, the comprehension of life, and salvation from the problem of human existence." Again, "Religious traditions are the results of man's attempt to capture and enshrine his philosophical and spiritual insights so that they are available to the individual as he faces life and its stresses, confusion and complexities."[2] "Religion is a social phenomenon because it necessarily stresses fellowship in the development, teaching and perpetuation of religious insights and knowledge. It also deals with concepts of supernatural part of salvation."[3]

Keeping in mind the definitions of religion mentioned above it appears that Buddhism, in fact is a religion. It established norms, related to moral values, social behaviour. It developed spiritual and philosophical insight, directing followers to attempt for achieving salvation with a purpose to get rid of the worldly life that is full of miseries and sufferings.

God, Religion and Devotion

Before we have a detailed discussion about Buddhist's religious philosophies, it would be better to have a cursory glance over religion, God and devotion. Each religion is related to the concept of God Who is supreme, transcendental, invisible, omnipotent, omnipresent, all powerful, capable of doing anything, creator, sustainer and destroyer of entire creation etc. He is permanent, imperishable, ultimate truth, source of power and qualities. These all are the faith which cannot be proved scientifically. A devotee has to believe in existence and supremacy of God-based on his own intuitional feeling and understanding. A number of views, opinions and doctrines have been developed to understand God by various metaphysical schools, thinkers, philosophers, seers, poets etc. Their views and opinions are different and conflicting. There is also a school that has no faith at all in existence of God or any particular religion. The School of *Carvaka* denied the existence of God. To this School the creation is not the result of God's power, but it is eternal and there is automation in the creation. Even the Indian Vedas though believe in God's supreme power, say nothing definitely about God's existence. While presenting the perception about Supreme God the Vedas simply concludes: '*Na Iti, Na Iti* (that is not, that is not). The school of agnosticism is doubtful about existence of God. It maintains to keep silence in this regard because the concept of God is beyond the catch of human senses and understanding. To the Nihilists there is no God at all. They have no faith in a concept related to God. To them the ultimate reality is material world. Various religions, like Hinduism, Islamism, Jainism, Judaism Jewish, and Christianity etc., talk much about God, soul and world, but they come to different conclusions and prescribe different ways as well as methods to apprehend God and visualise God. However, they are unanimous about God's supremacy and transcendency. Once the existence of God is accepted or belief in God's supremacy is developed, it requires devotion to obtain His blessing and kindness. So, devotion to God in a religion is a must. Devotion is complete faith and absolute surrender to God. Here there is no scope for any logic or argument. It comes out of heart, not mind. The base of devotion is complete faith and total dependence on God's mercy and kindness. Once the devotee devotes to God, it is God who takes care of him. The devotee totally relies upon God's mercy and remains in peace and pleasure forever. It is believed that with devotional force anything at any moment can be achieved. He may even personify God.

According to Sankaracharya parmarthika standpoint, *Brahman* alone is real. There is no creation, no creator like God or *Isvara*, no created effect like *Jiva-Jagta.* Creation is illusion (*Maya*). So, there cannot be any question of religion at all. No question of sweet relation between God and soul because the soul or *Jiva* itself is *Brahman.* So, there cannot be a worshiper of *Isvara.* The proposition of *Sanskara* is related to the Vedas. It is *Sankhya Darshan* which emphasises on pure knowledge. This doctrine believes in Monistic Theory of God. Except God there is nothing. What we see or feel is reflection of that Absolute Power which alone exists. The reflection is like shadow and it is not permanent. Its nature is temporary and illusory. There is rope only, no serpent. If one sees a serpent, it is his illusion only. According to *Sanskara,* religion is possible and has value only from the *vyavaharika* (empirical) standpoint. *Isvara* and Saguna *Brahman* is creator, the object of the worshipped, while the *Jiva* is the created effect and the worshipper. The relation between *Isvara* and devotee is not real, but adopted. Since there is nothing except Absolute *Brahman*, the question of existence of *Jiva's* soul does not arise. However, this doctrine of *Sanskara* has been criticised by many others.

Vedanta's Doctrines of Monism and Monotheism

In Indian Vedic philosophy two distinct trends developed—Monism and Monotheism. The former is a doctrine of one reality and only one God or Absolute *Brahman. Brahman* and *Brahman* alone or Absolute and Absolute only is the sole reality. *Jiva-jagata* or this universe of souls and matter is *mithya* or false. So, there is only one *Brahman* and one Reality. Monotheism is a doctrine of one God only and not of one Reality. There is only *Brahman*, no doubt, but there are three realities—God or Absolute *Brahman*, *Jiva* and *Jagata.* (God, Soul and Matter). According to Sanskara, *Brahman* or Absolute is *Ekemevadvityam* (*Chandogya Upanishad,* 3, 14.1). It means there exists permanently only one *Brahman* and everything that comes out, follows from Him. The *Brahman* is *nirvisesa* or without quality or *visesa or bheda or* difference of any kind whatsoever. So, *Brahman* is *nirvikara* (absolutely pure) and all pervasive. He is absolutely changeless. He is totally free from any kind of qualities that are the major cause of change. He is *nirguna* (without quality), *Gunas* (qualities) are three in number- *Sattva*, *Raja* and *Tamsa*. Since *Brahman* stands above three *Gunas*, it is *Nirguna*. The attributes of *Brahman* are *nirvikar, nirguna, nirnkara* (shapeless) *nistriya, sudham* (absolutely pure) free, and without sin.

Sanskara's doctrine of *Ekemevadvityam* was modified by Ramanuja, the great Indian philosopher who appeared after Sanskara. Though he accepts oneness of Absolute *Brahman*; he denies that He is *nirguna.* Rather He is *saguna.* He is not *niskriya*, (without action) but *sakriya* (having activities). He possesses heavenly qualities and powers. He is the creator. Being unchangeable, He changes in the form of universe of souls and matter. He is *niranjana*, (non-visible), absolutely pure, sinless and perfect. *Jiva* is the part of *Isvara* or *Brahman*. The difference between *Brahman* and *Jiva* is like the sky and the sky surrounded in a jar. Once the jar is broken, the surrounded sky merges into the greater sky. It is *Maya*, *avidya* (ignorance) that has been covering the soul. Once it is removed, the soul is free and pure. According to Ramanuja, *Brahman* and *Jiva* and *Jagata* also are different in attributes otherwise they are identical in nature (*swarupa*), and so they are inseparably connected and form beautiful synthetic harmonious organic whole or unity like a tree and its different branches, leaves etc.

Ramanuja founded the *Bhakti-marga,* the way of devotion. Since soul is encircled by *Maya* that is all pervasive and powerful, the only easiest way to be emancipated from the clutch of *Maya* is devotion *(Bhakti)*. Since God is kind enough and merciful, He listens to devotee's prayer and grants him blessing. God is the soul of souls, rescuer, protector and supporter and controller of all beings.

Religion talks about God and teaches devotion to Him. Explaining the meaning of religion the *Mahabharta* says that in this infinite universe and great world the universal element which integrates different elements of the world is nothing, but religion. It is religion which combines both the external and internal worlds (physical and spiritual). Religion, in fact, is a quality which is inherent in every animate and inanimate object. Religion is duty entrusted upon each and every component of the universe living or non-living, visible or invisible. Everyone is bound to perform duty because duty is the base of the universe. These duties have been prescribed in each religious scripture. To act against the prescribed duties in religious scriptures is irreligion. *(Shrimad Bhagvada Gita* 6/1/40). The sun, earth, water, air, fire, and all gods/goddesses as well as semi gods etc., are bound to perform duty because duty upholds the universe. The duties prescribed in the religious scriptures like *Vedas*, *Upanishads*, *Smritis*, *Sutras* etc., are pious and meaningful. To go against such duties means to commit sin and follow those sincerely means to earn *punya*. Sin takes one to hell (place of sufferings), while *punya* preserves place for one in the heaven (place of enjoyment and pleasure).

Buddha's Views about God, Universe and Religion

Traditionally and popularly Buddhism is generally accepted as atheistic. But this does not state the whole picture on the issue for many reasons. The Buddha was not so much atheistic as he was opposed to discussing metaphysical questions in general. He described his teachings using the analogy of a physician, who treats the patient without keeping in mind who he is or what caste and community does he belong to? The doctor's only mission is to cure the ailment of the patient. The Buddha without going into depth of the metaphysics simply adopted that it is the human mind that creates the world. So, there is no creator, except for what mentally wish to create. The Buddha adopted the middle way whereby his emphasis was on the reality, not the abstract idealism. He had no faith in abstraction. Some Buddhists tend to be atheistic because of the measurable silence of the Buddha on such issue. The Buddha was, in fact, opposed to a concept of an all powerful God who exists somewhere. He rejected the idea of a first beginning or creation or that there is a creator sitting somewhere. It is his adoption that some people take him as atheist. In other religions, existence of God, His mercifulness and benevolence are described in such a manner that He listens to the prayers of mankind and grants blessing being pleased.

The Buddha discarded such faith. God has been taken as a personal entity in other religions, but in the Buddha's mind or opinion there is no place for personal God.

The term *nirvana* that is very much popular in Buddhism means to enter into Divine Ocean or the ocean of complete tranquility or in the unlimited *Sunyata* where there is no noise, no movement, no activity, no pain, no birth or death. There is eternity. According to the Buddha one may enter into the ocean of *nirvana* through enlightenment that is to be achieved by oneself. Since the Buddha believed in the cycle of birth and death-based on *karma* and *sanskara,* and also in *nirvana,* it appears that there is something beyond our universe. It is this something which seems that the Buddha was not atheistic. Rather he was theist or pantheist. Even the Buddha, after getting enlightenment, became something as a symbol of worshipping in heavenly realms. The Western thinkers while analysing the Buddha's concept of theism and atheism advance the logic that how can there be a religion without a belief in a personal God figure. The Buddha's God is not like the God of other traditional religions. His God is different about whom nothing definitely may be said anything. So, it is better to remain silent. He neither approved the issue of God nor rejected it and adopted a middle path.

When Gautam Siddhartha was born, Hinduism in India was passing through turbulent period. It was the class of *Brahmans* that was highly devoted to Hindu religion prescribed in various religious scriptures. Along with the cult of devotion, emphasis was on *karmakanda,* which base was ritualism. Number of rituals regarding God's worshipping had been developed and these were performed by *Brahmans*. The *Vedantic* philosophies prescribed in the religious scriptures including Vedas were out of touch to common mass because of their complicacy to understand them. So, the common mass became simply believers and followers of religion, religious philosophy and religious performances. It resulted in supremacy of superstitions and blind faith suppressing reason. Real knowledge related to religion and metaphysics was wrongly interpreted for material gain and prosperity. Wisdom had been replaced by blind faith, and pious duties were covered by traditions and conventions. There was too much talk about God, soul, reality, devotion, salvation and emancipation, but in action there was neither right direction nor committed followers. The Buddha, observing all these, liked to spread the light of wisdom and lead people towards light and reality. In that course of thinking, he decided to found Buddhism. Since the concept of God had been very much vague from the beginning, he preferred to keep silence about God's reality and existence. He did not like to fall into the controversies regarding existence of a supreme Power that is the ultimate source of creation and destruction. His emphasis remained confined to release mankind from the captivity of worldly sufferings and troubles, and leading them towards the light of wisdom.

Guru Nanak, the founder of Sikhism, once told that a religion is without its moorings till it joins the life current of humanity and socially and spiritually insulates itself into them.[4] According to the Buddha, development of morality, truth, concentration and purification of the mind are the important aspects of a religious life for salvation.[5] The Buddha, in fact, was a realist, an empiricist. His entire concern was related to the present life that is shrouded in miseries and pains. The Buddha talked much about the mundane world, the world of ours and the people living in this world. His purpose was to release mankind from sufferings and pains of the world. He found that despite various sects of religion man had been suffering from different kinds of pains both mental and physical. He had realised the root cause of pain and sufferings. So, what he contributed religiously or philosophically is mostly related to this world where we live. While setting his doctrines, he explained birth, death, oldness, disease, *nirvana,* etc., prescribing certain right ways to get rid of these worldly miseries. Buddhism from analytical point of view is, in fact, not a religion like Hinduism, Islamism or Christianity, but a way of the life of sanctity, sagacity, purity, simplicity and what not. His faith in existence of soul does not stand. His explanation is mostly psychological where status of mind and consciousness is largely discussed and explained. The Buddha did not write any scripture. It was his followers divided into various schools who developed written scriptures that present details of Buddhism.

So, Buddhism is a religious way having its own texts, meanings, costumes and the method to perform worshipping. While doing so a lot has been borrowed by the Buddhists from the Indian religion (Hinduism). While observing Buddhism the imprint of Hinduism may easily be discerned. However, it stands differently and differs much from the metaphysical Hindu's philosophy.

The Buddha was a Traveller and Preacher

After getting enlightenment at Bodh Gaya, he wished to preach the knowledge he gained. So, he said:

I shall go to Banaras where I will light the lamp that will bring light unto the world. I shall go to Banaras and beat the drums that will awaken mankind. I shall go to Banaras and there I shall teach the Law... I will preach the *Dhamma*.[6]

He travelled from place to place, touched the life of thousands high and low, princes and peasants. They all came under the spell of his great personality. He taught for forty five years the beauty of charity and the joy of renunciation. There are two sides of the Buddha— individual and social. Individual Buddha is a sage, *yogi*, absorbed and withdrawn lot in the joy of his inner-meditation. Another Buddha is concerned with sorrow of men, eager to enter their lives, heal their troubles and spread his message for the good of the many.[7] To the *theravadians,* the Buddha is a man not God, a teacher and not a saviour. However, all of Buddhism agree that the Buddha was the founder, that he strove and attained transcendental wisdom as he sat under the Bodhi tree, that he pointed a way from the world of suffering to a beyond, the undying, and those who follow the path for liberation may also cross to the wisdom beyond.[8] In the words of Radhakrishanan, "The Buddha did not feel that he was preaching a new religion. He was born, grew up and died as a Hindu. He was restating with a new emphasis the ancient ideals of the Indo-Aryan civilisation".[9] He aimed at a new spiritual existence attained through *jnana* or Bodhi absolute illumination. He said:

Pade tu yasminn na jara na bhir na run na janma
Naivoparano na cadhayh

Tan eva manye purusartham uttmam na vidyate.

Yatra punch punch kriya. (Asvaghosa Buddhacarita, XI, 59).

It means, "But I deem the highest goal of man to be the stage in which there is neither the old age nor fear, nor disease, nor birth, nor death, nor anxieties, and in which there is no continuous renewal of activity."

The Buddha was dead against the ignorance and superstition, the dread and the horror that are found in other religions. He disliked dogmatism. He knew that doctrinal orthodoxy bans the door of intelligence. It filled the world with unhappiness, injustice, strife, crime and hatred. To quote Radhakrishanan once more, "The Buddha did not concede the reality of an unchangeable 'self', for the 'self is something that can be built up by good thoughts and deeds, but yet he has to assume it. While *Karma* relates to the world of objects, of existence in time, *nirvana* assumes freedom of the subject of inwardness."[10]

Thus, it is evident that the Buddha did not found a new religion. He took the personal troubles and pains to spread the message among the people about goodness of life and he prescribed the new ways for mankind to follow and get relief from worldly pains that exist in the life of the man due to his ignorance. Rather he collected some evidential elements of other religions especially from Hinduism and branded them in the form of Buddhism. He accepted metaphysics of Hinduism, no doubt, but did not go into depth because his basic concern was to the world where humanity lives and suffers. Due to his inclination towards Vedic philosophy and acceptance of the theory of birth and death, theory of *karma* and salvation, he was, later on, regarded as incarnation of the Hindu god Lord Vishnu. He utilised the Hindu inheritance to correct some of its expressions. He came to "fulfill Hinduism, not to destroy it." He left his footprints on the soil of India and his mark on the soul of the country with the habits and convictions. Slowly Buddhism became an integral part of Indian culture. Radhakrishanan is right when he says that "In a sense the Buddha is a maker of modern Hinduism."

Buddha's Concept of Soul

Buddhist philosophy related to acceptance and existence of soul is apparently very much different from India's *Vedantic* philosophy, but when this concept of Buddhism is deeply analysed and investigated, it explicitly becomes obvious that Lord Buddha believed in permanent and imperishable existence of the substance that is the basic cause of creation of the universe. Since he adopted the middle way of his thinking, he dropped the faith in Nihilism or *Uccedavadas* expressed by the thinkers who denied existence of any supreme power or God on the one hand, and he rejected the transcendental doctrine propagated by philosophy of *Vedantism* on the other. His concern was different. He talked of the universe that we feel and think about. The basic question before the Buddha was how to reduce the sufferings of the mankind in this world and how to get rid of worldly miseries, troubles, sufferings, fear, uncertainties etc., forever. So, the way he preferred and adopted and also taught the people is the middle path. To elaborate and interpret the path he thought it wise to drop the idea of self-ego or soul as the base of every individual. Buddhist philosophy is universal in character because it is fully based on the undernoted essential principles:

All is impermanence

There is no soul,

Nirvana is the only calm,

All is suffering, and

All is without soul *(Sarvam Anatman).*

Soul According to Indian *Vedanta*

Soul, according to the philosophy of Indian *Vedanta*, is permanent universal element that has consciousness, light, energy and that is the base of everything in material world and light of the spiritual world. It is the basic cause of causes being fundamental cause of creation and sustenance. According to the *Bhagvad Gita,* soul is immortal and eternal like God because it is the integral particle of God. *Bhagvad Gita* says:

> For the soul there is neither birth nor death at any time. He has not come into being, does not come into being,

> and will not come into being. He is unborn, eternal, ever-existing and primeval. He is not slain when the body is slain. (*Bhagvad Gita* 2.20).

Talking about immorality of soul, Text 22 of the Chapter 2 of the *Bhagvad Gita* says:

> As a person puts on new garments, giving up old ones, the soul similarly accepts new material bodies, giving up the old and useless one.

It is further said:

> The soul can never be cut to pieces by any weapon, nor burned by fire, nor moistened by water, nor withered by the wind. This individual soul is unbreakable and insoluble, and can be neither burned nor dried. He is everlasting present everywhere, unchangeable, immovable and eternally the same. It is invisible, inconceivable and immutable. Knowing this you (Arjuna) should not grieve for the body.
>
> (*Bhagvad Gita* 2/23, 24, 25).

Thus, it is evident that soul is as pure as God; it is as bright as God; it is as immortal as God. Being the integral part of God, soul is deathless and eternal. God is the primary cause of creation. So, in the human life it is soul that upholds everything. Soul is wisdom, light, illumination and what not. The relationship between God and soul is not only integral but indivisible also. The individual soul in a body is the captive of material world. Since the material world is subject to decay, body meets to the fate of destruction, but not the soul due to its immortality. It changes body in the form of rebirth where soul remains as it is. The human body has two aspects mental and physical. Mental aspect is made of mind. Mind is related to the *cit* (consciousness) that upholds consciousness (awareness), ego (I) wisdom and activity through sense as well as physical organs. Except soul, all these elements are impermanent. The *cit* that is very near to soul is the upholder of the essence of all *karmas* that results in rebirth of a *jiva*. According to *Upnishads*, soul and *jiva* are two different aspects. *Jiva* is the living being having effects of *karma* and enjoys the fruits of *karma* while soul is upholder, witness of every activity of *jiva* and illumination of the heart.

Buddha's Conflicting Theory of Soul

The denial of the Buddhist philosophy of soul is fully-based on the universal principle of impermanence. When the doctrine of universal permanence is accepted, then, in that case, the acceptance of eternality, absolute unity or supreme authority in any case becomes meaningless. As a result of it, an existence like the above cannot have *atman*. However, the Buddha accepted the provisional existence of personal ego. This is evidence from the statement mentioned below:

> The Tathagata, sometimes, taught that the *atman* exists and at other times he taught that the *atman* does not exist. When he preached the *atman* exists and said to be the receiver of misery of happiness in the successive life as the reward of its *karma*, his object was to save man from falling into the heresy of nihilism. When he taught that there is no *atman* in a sense of creator or perceiver or an absolute free agent, apart from conventional name given to the aggregate of the five *skandhas*, his object was to save man from falling into the opposite heresy of externalism or *sasvatvada.*[11]

The question is which of these two views are correct? It creates more conflict and the conflict is very much difficult to be resolved. Nagarjuna further says:

> This doctrine is so difficult to understand. It was not intended by the Buddha for the ears of those whose intellect is dull and in whom the root of goodness has not thriven. And why? Because such man by hearing the doctrine of *anatman* would have been sure to fall into the heresy of nihilism. The two doctrines were preached by the Buddha for two different objects. He taught the doctrine of *atman* when he wanted to impart to his listeners the conventional doctrine. He taught the doctrine of *anatman* when he wanted to impart to them the transcendental doctrine.[12]

The existence of *atman* and the *dharma* of the ego and the phenomenal world are affirmed in the sacred canon provisionally and hypothetically and never in the sense of possessing real and permanent nature.[13] The similar view is also recorded in the *Samyutta Nikaya* of the Pali canon and Vasubandhu's own commentary on his *Abhidharmakosa.*

Thus, it is very much evident that the Buddha followed the middle path where he neither rejected the theory of absolutism nor he accepted the theory of nihilism. He did not approve the existence of an independent supra-soul as it has been presented in the *Bhagvad Gita* or other religious books of Hinduism. However, he does not deny about the existence of intellect, though that is not immortal. Immorality is *nirvana* which can be achieved through individual personal effort. His basic purpose was to teach people how to get liberation from pains and sufferings of this world. The fact is that he accepted an identity that does not die even after death of the individual and it carries the imprint of past *karmas* and causes rebirth accordingly. He talks of *Hinatma* and *Mahatma.* The former is cause of suffering having resemblance with the egoism of *Samkhya* philosophy, while *anatman* can be attained by the practice of the highest motive. This motive is Buddhahood. *Mahatman* means *Tathagatagarabha* which means the womb of *Tathagata.* To be more explicit, it is the treasurer or store in which the essence of Buddhahood remains concealed under the veil of *avidya.* It is also the womb of the universe. In the terms of psychology, *Tathagatagarabha* means "the transcendental court of man coming under the bondage of *karmic* causation." Some scholars are of the view that *Tathagatagarabha* has correspondence to the *Pramatma* or the universal soul of the Vedantians. Despite that there is a great difference between the meaning of the *Pramatman* of the Buddhists and the meaning of *Pramatman* of the Vedantians. In the case of the former the *Pramatman* is complete tranquility, without any form and shape. It is ocean of complete peace that has no concern to the universe at all. In the case of the latter, the *Pramatman* is creator, sustainer and destroyer of the universe. It is *Narayana*, the Primal ultimate source of all powers, who sleeps in the ocean of tranquility and being the ultimate source of origin of things, governs the universe through His various elements and agencies. It is Lord Vishnu who is called as *Hirnayagrabha* and it is He who upholds the entire universe at his will.

Hirnayagrabha means the ocean of infinite from which Lord Vishnu is the first to appear automatically. So, He is called *swambhu* (self-born). *Upanishads* talk that Vishnu sleeps in *Chhirsagar* (ocean of milk) which symbolises the sign of absolute purity. The ocean in which the Lord Vishnu sleeps is absolutely peaceful, pure, without any noise, disturbance and movement. The ocean is His expanded or manifested form which is fathomless and unfinished treasury of intelligence, consciousness and all sorts of divine energies in subtle form. He is known as *Hirnayagrabha* because of His emergence from Infinite Ocean of power and energy. The entire creation has emerged from this Ocean and after its dissolution, it merges into it. Thus, Vishnu who is self-born is the Lord of the universe and base of the divine manifestation. Lord Vishnu is first manifestation of eternal unmanifestation.

The Buddha who had learnt the theory of soul prescribed in the Indian religious scripture denied the existence of soul as it has been stated in the scriptures. However, he accepts consciousness instead of soul that follows one even after death. It means it is not mortal. It exists and causes the rebirth. Denial of soul of the Buddhist philosophy is fully-based on the universal principle of impermanence. Once this doctrine is adopted, there is no case of the acceptance of eternality, absolute unity or supreme authority. So, there is nothing like 'Ego' or *Atman* that exists and governs. Like Sancaracharya, the Buddha believes in one Absolutism about which nothing definitely or determinately can be said. However, it is the only reality and there is nothing except it. The Buddha believed in universality of universal nature, but he denied that there is any supreme power that governs the nature. It means there is no God or supreme commander. The world is as it is. There is automation and everything is moving by losing its original shape in this continuous or endless automation of time and space. Man is the captive of his own nature that is full of *trisna*, lust, desire etc., and he suffers because he is ignorant. He is wrapped in the thick cover of *Avidya*.

Regarding *Avidya* (ignorance) the *Hindu Dharmashastra* says that it is *Maya* of Lord Vishunu (*Naryana*) that has covered the divine light. The ordinary people cannot view God or soul unless his wisdom, the light of the soul, is uncovered. Under the spell of *Maya* man is ignorant about divine wisdom, and he remains involved in this world of impermanence facing births, rebirths, suffering and troubles. Once the darkness of the human soul is removed, he obtains salvation, and to remove darkness he needs divine blessing that comes under the influence of devotion to God.

The question is whether the Buddha discovered that there is no soul. Most of his philosophical thoughts and principles are very much related to the *Vedantic* philosophy such as theory of *karma*, theory of death and theory of rebirth, theory of salvation etc. An investigation made into the thoughts of Buddha, it reveals the truth that he was not much confirmed about non-existence of soul. He, sometimes, thought that the *atman* exists and at other time he taught that *atman* does not exist. Prabhkar Mishra has rightly observed that the Buddha was of the view that *atman* exists and as "to be the receiver of misery or happiness in the successive life as the reward of his *karma*."[13] The Buddha mentioned about the existence of soul with the marked object to save man from falling into nihilism. When he taught that there is no *atman,* in the sense of a creator or perceiver or absolutely free agent, apart from conventional name given to the aggregate of the five *skandhas*, his object was to save man from falling into the opposite heresy of externalism or *sasvatyavada*".[14] The Buddha knew well that common man whose intellect and understanding about God, universe and soul is vague, not sharp, would definitely fall into the category of nihilism if the doctrine of *atman* is not propagated. Perhaps under this understanding he supported the view of *atman*, but in different form. Once it is accepted that one has to go through the process of rebirth due to one's past *karmas*, then there must be something immortal like the soul being the upholder of the essence of *karmas*. Otherwise who dies and who gets birth? Who carries the essence of *karma* and who eats the fruits of *karma*? Consciousness about which the Buddha talks is a psychological term and it may dismantle with the dismantling of the body.

The existence of *atman* and *dharma* of the Ego and the phenomenal world is affirmed in the sacred canon provisionally and hypothetically and never in the sense of possessing a real and permanent nature.[15] The similar views are also recorded in the *Samyutta Nikaya* of the Pali canon and Vasubandhu's own commentary on his *Abhidharmakosa—Sastra*. Thus, it is evident that Buddha, with a view to maintaining the middle way, preached sometimes the principles of *atman* and sometimes *anataman*. If there is concept of salvation, question arises that, who gets salvation? Who is in the body that suffers? Salvation is freedom from the material world and it is related to one who is in the captivity of the material world. It is soul that is the captive of the material world which is governed by *Maya* or *Kalcakra*. So, long as soul is not liberated, it shall have to suffer.

The Buddha has no faith in individual soul. He followed the theory of *Sarvam Anatmam* which means 'All is Egoless' and there is no such element that is subtle and upholds individual's will, desire, his account of action and other things. There are no such things that inspire the individual to act and obtain. It is lust and desire, entanglement with the worldly affairs for pleasure that activate him and binds him to remain confined to the circle of birth and death. Buddhist philosophy has always spoken of the denial of existence of an everlasting individual soul which is reflected in numerous earlier Buddhist writings. In other religious theories soul is regarded as the most subtle non-visible element and it is difficult to differentiate it from nominal and phenomenal concept. But reality is that if existence of soul is denied, entire mansion of Buddha *Dhamma* would collapse then and there. It is true that lust inspiries one to act for material guru, but common experience shows that man as acts for good causes also. Who does inspire man to act for good causes? It is soul of the man which is always good and pure.

Transmigration of Soul

In the Indian philosophy the theory of *karma* and transmigration of soul is very common. The individual gets another body in the next birth according to his *karma* and *sanskara*. The supreme reality is the law of change and that is causality. The universe is governed by causality. There is no chaotic anarchy or capricious interference. According to the

Buddha, carving or lust felt in the previous life causes the birth of new individual who was to inherit the *karma* of the former one. Immortality of soul is one of the cardinal principles of all theistic religions. However, the teaching of the Buddha in this regard is unique. The Buddha denied the existence of soul in the narrow sense of the word. According to him, the narrow self-related to the individual is not the real self. The narrow self-needs to be subdued and spiritualised. Transmigration posits continuity from one life-span to another. The Buddha believed in rebirth. The question is, if there is no soul who takes rebirth or how rebirth is possible. The Buddha resolves this problem by the analogy of fire which maintains itself unchanged appearance yet is different at every moment. The Buddhists admit the continuity of an ever-changing identity. The seeming identity from moment to moment consists in a continuity of an ever-changing identity. The individual is only a bundle of changing *skandhas,* changing from moment to moment, and from life to life, and it was only *nirvana* which could bring about their final dissolution.

Observing the transient nature of things, Buddhists reduced things and soul to forces and functions and movements and processes and he adopted kinetic conception of reality. Life to them is nothing but a series of manifestations of becoming and extinctions. The Buddha repudiated the popular delusion of the individual ego. The objects with which one identifies oneself are not true self. Even body, mind are not true self. The Buddhists adopted the 'theory of non-self' which means anything perceived is not the self. Accordingly, body, feeling, perception, dispositions and consciousness, all these are not-self because nothing of them is substantial. They are appearances, empty of substance or reality. Buddhism is not a metaphysical conception, but it is a practical aspect of religion. So, it does not believe in spirituality of soul.

Buddha's View of Self-enlightenment

The Buddha was a *Vibhajyavadi* which means this world is not real. Like *Sanskara*, he believed that the world is *mithya* (false) having no permanent existence. Everything in the world is on constant change due to constant motion of the universe. It is a conglomeration. It is made of *punch skandhatmaka* (*rupa, vedna, sanjya, sanskara, vijyana*). They are not real entities because they are ceaselessly changing. Change is there, no doubt, but continuity remains intact. Things come and go, appear and disappear, but the process of coming and going or appearing and disappearing in different forms remain static. *Cit* (inner-consciousness) of common man governs human activities and behaviours either good or bad. Theravada tradition believes that *cit* is full of *cetasikas* as quality of *cit* due to which it is considered *kusala or akusala*. To observe *cit's* qualities and human activities one should stand above it being pure neutral. Question is who stands above it? The Hindu philosophy states that it is soul that stands above all in human body. Soul living in the body, remains aloof from any kind of activities. Soul is the base or rather upholder of consciousness, mind and other organs of the body. Consciousness is the quality of soul. It is soul that supplies energy to all and give light to wisdom. Until one reaches to soul or realises it closely, he cannot understand reality nor may he obtain salvation. In Buddhism it is consciousness that is upholding essence of human *Karma* and until it is destroyed because it is not permanent, liberation is not possible. It contains the seed of rebirth because the *sanskara* is there having the essence of past *karmas*. Action ends, not the imprint of action which is printed on consciousness in the form of *sanskaras*. Thus, *sanskara* is the nature of a being. It is formed out of actions or behaviours. Good *karma* means good *sanskara* and bad *karma* means bad *sanskara*. The individual falling prey to the lust and *trisna* indulges in prohibited *karmas* with the result that he gathers bad *sanskara* which not only causes rebirth but also brings about miseries and troubles in the present birth. What the Buddha said about consciousness, is infact, soil consciousness is a quality of soul. It follows soul even after death of a being.

As it has been stated above, according to Hindu philosophy the Self is immortal and it is integrally related to the Absolute. So, it is self-consciousness of the Self that is related to the Absolute. Self and Absolute is one. They are united, but it does not mean that heterogeneous factors are brought or bonded together. It means the need is to know the two which are originally one. Separation is due to ignorance. Once the *avidya* that has covered self, is removed, its union with the Absolute that is already there, will soon be visualised. There is also the need to know that these two elements that are basically one, is not different or separate. It seems separate due to effect of continuous *sanskara* gathered in different births. The individual self, constantly living in body, thinks that it is body, not spirit. It seems to the individual self that it dies with the death of body. This is *avidya* (ignorance). So, once it is firmly realised that soul is without death and eternal, the ignorance disappears. It is right realisation that there is no Absolute outside. It exists within the soul. That is called self-realisation. The concept of 'I' is an illusion. All animate and inanimate things between heaven and earth are nothing, but shadow of self. This is the fact that the Buddha what found was found within the Self. When emphasis is laid down on the self the whole universe is self and when emphasis is shifted to the universe, the self will be submerged into the universe and there will be no such thing as the self. This is the merger of self into the Absolute. That is called salvation or *nirvana*. To attain this enlightenment is the vital concern of the seeker of the Self-conscious or seeker of the truth. This stage can be achieved through meditation. What the Buddha achieved through meditation is self-enlightenment. The difference between the religion of prayer and the religion of self-enlightenment lies in the fact that the former finds it outside the Self while the latter finds it within the self. The Buddha found it within the Self without prayer and ritual of *karmkanda.* He applied the method of meditation and went deep into the ocean of knowledge. So, he became Buddha, which means the embodiment of absolute reality. The first man that ever found the absolute within himself was Sakyamuni, the Buddha. Therefore, Sakyamuni was at once a man and the Buddha.[16]

Buddha's Two Aspects of Absolute Truth: The Buddha saw two aspects of Absolute Truth—the first universal, unmanifested, all pervasive, free, independent and untouched by anything, and the second manifested through creation, dependent, and concealed. It is dependent on material world not for its energy, but for its reflection. It is concealed in the cover of ignorance due to lack of real wisdom. Describing about the nature of the Absolute Truth *Bhagvad Gita* states that it is *nirankara* (shapeless) that lies beyond the perception of the senses, all pervading, inconceivable unchanging, fixed and unmoveable.[17] Every living being from amoeba to *Brahma* is endowed with such light of absolute truth in the centre of the heart. This is another matter that un-enlightened one is ignorant about it. Once ignorance is removed, the reflection of the light is clearly visible. To remove ignorance means to apply the prescribed methods. The cover of ignorance is too hard to penetrate into and too difficult to overcome. In the *Bhagvad Gita* the way prescribed is either to pray God with full devotion or to know the Absolute Truth through meditation. The truth that is manifested or unmanifested is one and indivisible. It appears different due to ignorance. Once ignorance is away, both aspects of truth unites together as the sky surrounded in a jar merges into the sky after destruction of the jar and becomes one. After getting full realisation, the self-residing in the body merges into Absolute Truth forever since there is neither ego nor individuality. The individual becomes universal and universal becomes individual. Individual's thoughts, actions and behaviours all become universal. He is now for everyone because he sees himself in everyone. The Buddha obtaining self-enlightenment became Buddha and the only purpose of his life was to release ignorant people from the darkness and worldly miseries, and lead them towards the light of absolute wisdom. Visualising the absolute Truth the individual Gautam became the universal Buddha.

Shrikanta is also of the view that in the religion of prayer, man seeks to be emancipated from the suffering of the world and enjoy a beautiful life through reliance on the Absolute Being termed as God. But in the religion of self-enlightenment man strives to realise the Absolute within his individual self. Both in the religion of prayer and the religion of self-enlightenment, the central idea is the Absolute (God in Christianity, Islamism and Hinduism and Buddha in Buddhism). Describing the difficulty to be faced in the self-realisation, Shrikanta says, "But in the world of ours, we cannot expect this aspiration to be gratified. Consequently, man tries to seek a solution by conjuring the Absolute (Buddha or God). That which cannot be realised in the world of ours must then be realised in the realms of God or Buddha. Thus, we prostrate ourselves before the absolute."[18]

The method that Buddha prescribed to achieve *nirvana* through meditation, not prayer, is not easy for everyone. It is a difficult path. It is the path of *sanaysis* or *yogis* who devote the whole life in penance and meditation living aside the family and renouncing the materialistic world. For common man, who lacks understanding, the path that is the easiest is either the path of *karma-yoga* or the path of *Bhakti-yoga* (devotion). One can reach to Absolute Truth or God by performing right duties in the name of Almighty or one may also attain salvation by devoting his life in the service of God. But the Buddha who did not believe in any concept of super-being that governs the universe, taught that man has to attain the stage through his own self- effort. He has to learn the way and be determined to achieve salvation. The way suggested by the Buddha is Four Noble Truths and Eight-fold Nobel Ways that has already been described in the preceding chapter.

According to Shrikanta:

> The statement that the universe is the Buddha sounds pantheistic to use a term of religious philosophy. But Buddhism is no pantheism. The unity of the absolute and the self means the knowledge of the absoluteness of the self. He reached the insight into the true nature of things, right wisdom to see things as they are, therefore his enlightenment is called supreme enlightenment or supreme universal wisdom. He clearly perceived the law pervading all things in the universe. He achieved the 'Path'.[19]

Thus, the Buddha's enlightenment is the acquisition of right universal wisdom capable of seeing things as they are. He reached to the spiritual stage which was open and free world where everything was embraced and the distinction of self and non-self had been done away with. "The shell of egoistic self had been smashed. His eyes (divine) saw things as they are. The opposition which hitherto had stood between the self and non-self disappeared. He was the only being in the whole universe who became one with the whole universe. He attained such a conscious and became Buddha."[20]

The Three Bodies Doctrine of Mahayana

The Buddha is regarded by the *Mahayana* Schools as the universal saviour and bestower of deliverance. He is master over space and time. The Mahayanists believe that there are so many Buddhas. There are as many Buddha as grains of sand on the bank of the Ganges. Buddha appears in all regions of the world taking many forms. Like the Hindus they believe that Buddha is omnipotent and omnipresent. However, they developed the *Triptitaka* doctrine which means three bodies of Buddha as mentioned below:

1. The *Dharmakarya*—(Dharma-Body)

It is the inner nature of the Buddha. In all the innumerable earthly Buddhas and the countless transcendental Buddhas, there is only one *Dharmakarya*. It is the Absolute Reality, besides which there is no other reality. *Dhamma* is the partial manifestation of natural law, namely, 'facts'. *Dhamma* is the technical form for 'factors of existence'. The *Dharmakarya* is, thus, base-consciousness of existence. The Buddha had direct connection with the Absolute.

2. *Sambhogakaya*—Body of Bliss

It is the transcendental Buddha that cannot be interpreted or perceived by the senses. It may be experienced spiritually. In *Sambhogakaya* Buddhas are seen as mental creations, the idea of the Bodhisattva. It is the manifestation of the absolute. Transcendental *Sambhogakaya* Buddhas are regarded as objectively existing supramandane and subtle beings. The most transcendental Buddha is the *Amida* Buddha. He is said to possess paradise in which believers are reborn there. They are the teachers of the Bodhisattvas and spiritual fathers of the earthly Buddhas. They project their compassion for all beings into the world by their meditation.

3. *Nirmanakaya*—Physical Body

Nirmanakaya belongs to those Buddhas like historical Gautam Buddha, appearing in the world in physical shape. They are called *Nirvana* or 'manifesting beings'. They are subject to misery and aging, illness and death, because they are persons of flesh and blood. They are distinguished by thirty two bodily characteristics and some supernatural abilities. The function of the earthly Buddha or *Nirmanakaya* Buddha is to teach and spread *dharma* to formulate into the world.

It is notable that in the Hindu *dharma* there is mentioning of incarnated God, who incarnates with the purpose to re-establish deteriorating *dharma* on the earth by teaching people right path and suppressing anti-*dharma* forces. Since, He incarnates in human form for well-being of human beings, He appears like a man having flesh, bone, blood, desire and so on. Time comes when His body perishes and He leaves the world. The Buddha in that sense is incarnation of God. He incarnated with the marked purpose and fulfilling the purpose he departed giving up his body.

Arahatahood in Buddhism

An *Arahata* in Buddhism is he who is an emancipated being, free from all internal and external pollutions. His further evolution is over. He is no more in the stream of the life-force. He is an ideal man, a saint, completely free. He is a man of pure consciousness. He rises from a common man whose consciousness is impure due to *karma-sanskara*. But due to his gradual inclination towards Buddhism, his consciousness develops and becomes pure. Due to the favourable turning of the wheel of *karmic* forces he gets an opportunity to hear the discourses of the Buddha or his disciples and gets acquaints with the *Dhamma*. Thereafter, he concentrates on *Dhamma* which gradually makes him pure and helps him to attain *Arahatahood*. A man who sets on the Noble Path is called a *Yogavacara*. To reach to the stage of *Arahatahood*, one has to cross seven stages. The first effort of the *Yogavacara* is to destroy the first fetters—*Sakkaya-ditthi, Vicikiccha* and *Silabbata-paramasa*. They are the embodiments of ignorance. The *Sakkaya-ditthi* generates the notion of the existence of a permanent soul. Unless free of this bondage, one cannot throw off one's sickles. *Viccikiccha* is hindrance to right knowledge. The *Silabbata-paramasa* imprisons the mind, creates confusion between means and ends and bewilders one in the thickest of misunderstanding.

The *Yogavacara* with his sincere efforts becomes able to destroy evils and thereby becomes *Sottapana* or a stream-winner. Thus a *Sottapana* is one who sets on the path leading to *Nibbana*. He cuts the three aforesaid fetters. If he does not realise *Nibbana* in this life, he has to come seven times on the earth. The first stage to get *Arahatahood* is the state of *Sottapana*. The second stage is *Sakadagami*. It literary means one who returns only once. Here the *Yogacara* establishes control over his *Kama-raga* and *Patigha,* the desire to harm others. The third stage of Arahatahood is *Anagami.* Reaching this stage the *Yogacara* fully understands the evil potentialities of the fetters and tries his right efforts for their destruction and succeeds in eliminating them. The *Yogacara* reaching to this stage does not come to this world again. However, if he fails to achieve the purity, he may come again here. The same truth has been described in the *Bhagvad Gita*. it is said that a *Sadhak* achieves salvation taking re-birth.

Forth stage is *Arahata* which is the last stage to obtain Arahatahood. The devotee attains it after total destruction of five fetters—*Rupa-raga, Arupa-raga, Mana, Uddhacca* and *avijja.* The functional forces of these fetters are curtailed to the maximum in course of the practice of *Sila* and *Samadhi*, yet their potential energy remains crystallised within them. It means the seed of evil fetters are suppressed but not totally destroyed. The charm of *Rupa-raga* may attract the *Yogacara. Mana* may generate a strong ego feeling. The ignoble acts of *Uddhacca* may be marked by the way it takes the mind away from essential things. *Avijja* has still the power of creating mischief. The *Yogacara* understands all these fetters, no doubt, but he has to apply hard and sincere effort to win them over for becoming perfect *Arahata.*

The *Arahata* is an ideal personality in Buddhist tradition. Attainment of *Arahatahood* in Buddhism is 'summum-bonum of life.' To achieve it one has to become *Bhikhu* giving up his house-hold. Once it is achieved, the achiever is known as *jivana-mukta.* He lives here on this earth for as long as the *karmic*-forces continue to maintain his body. Neither has he had a carving for its continuity nor a desire for its destruction. He is as detached as the lotus which lives in the pond. He moves in society to gather whatever he requires, but develops no attachment for anything because he is free from all attachments.

The Bodhisattva

The Bodhisattva is the name ascribed to those beings that strive to systematically for enlightenment or who have already obtained but postpone their own Static post-mortal *nirvana* until all beings are liberated. Bodhisattvas live exclusively for others. They are full of mercy and compassion, wishing love for all without self-interest, only for the happiness of others. They encompass wisdom to give, compassion to help others in any way to bring others closer to enlightenment. He sacrifices things for others. The Bodhisattvas have wisdom to see others and lead others. There are two types of Bodhisattvas— the earthly one and the transcendental one. The former follows the way of life striving for enlightenment while the later are those who through realising perfection and wisdom, sainthood and liberation have refused to enter static *nirvana* to stay in active *nirvana* in a state of deliverance in which they can work for the benefits of the world. They can assume any form, playing the illusory reality to help those caught in to seek the truth and absolute. Their status is like gods and demi-gods mentioned in the Hindu *dharma*.

Concept of *Nibbana* in Buddhism

The primary postulate on which the entire ethical system of Buddhism rests is the fundamental premise that there is a supreme end in human life that all rational and intelligent persons ought to aim at achieving *Nibbana.* This goal, the *summum bonum* of Buddhism, is referred to the Pali sutras as *Nibbana* (*nirvana*). It is the goal which is aimed at, either remotely or immediately, by both lay man and recluse (*bhikhu*). The religious or holy life is said to be lived to achieve this goal. The goal of *Nibbana* is the guiding principle for moral action in Buddhism. *Nibbana* itself is conceived as a state of moral perfection and purification. It is defined in the *suttas* as the elimination of lust and greed, the elimination of hatred and the elimination of delusion. It is characterised as the highest *kusala* which means goodness. Since goodness is the base of *Nibbana,* in Buddhism, emphasis has been laid to be good in the life, forever. Later on, the term *Nibbana* was interpreted in metaphysical term. It has been interpreted as a transcendental reality, beyond any form of conceptualisation or logical thinking. This has been largely the result of the influence of the absolutistic and transcendental views stemming from the Vedic tradition. Dr Radhakrishanan, observing the fact in this regard said:

> *Nirvana* is an eternal condition of being, for it is not *sanskara*, or what is made or put together, which is impermanent. It continues, while its expressions change. This is what lies behind the *sakandhas*, which are subject to birth and decay. The illusion of becoming is founded on the reality of *nirvana*. Buddha does not attempt to define it, since it is the root principle of all and so it is indefinable.[21]

The Buddha never spoke of *Nibbana* on the metaphysical ground that explains the empirical universe. Metaphysical concepts such as God, *Brahma*, *Alman*, *Purusa*, presenting ultimate metaphysical grounds as explanations, are discouraged in Buddhism. Radhakrishanan furthers states:

> *Nirvana* is timeless existence, and so Buddha must admit the reality of timelessness. There is a being at the back of all life which is unconditioned, above all empirical categories, something which does not give rise to any effect and is not the effect of anything else.[22]

Thus, such concepts at describing the nature of Buddhist *Nibbana* have transformed its character from being a concept having ethical and psychological significance to being a concept having metaphysical and ontological significance, and this seems to be contrary to what was intended by the Buddha. This view has resulted in the interpretation of Buddha. *Nibbana* is an escapist and life denying ideal which involves the most radical form of salvation doctrine. Some have gone to the extent of saying that the highest spiritual attainment in Buddhism transcends morality together. For instance, Tachibana says that one who attains *Nibbana* is free from such distinctions such as good or evil, pleasantness or unpleasantness, purity or impurity on so on. When one reaches this stage of culture, distinctive ideas will be absolutely abolished. In his own words:

> He (the Buddha) has reached the mental condition where there is not consciousness of moral, aesthetical, or logical

> distinction; the relative ideas therefore of good and evil, pleasure and pain, agreeableness and disagreeableness, right and wrong are all annihilated for him.[23]

However, there are Buddhist scholars who deny that in Buddhist culture of *nirvana* transcendency has preceded or finished morality. Morality is still the base of Buddhism. The scheme of moral evaluation in Buddhism can be clearly seen to be relative to the goal of *Nibbana*. In the moral evaluation of persons, one who has attained *Nibbana* is judged to be the most praiseworthy person. A disciple who has confidence in the Buddha and who has his ultimate aim in attainment of *Nibbana* is described as a noble disciple. The *Dhammapada* describes the *arahantas* the highest being extend, as far as the end of the realm of becoming, the *arahantas* are the highest, the supreme being in the universe.

Concept of *Moksha* in Hinduism

The concept of *nirvana* originated in Hinduism and is similar to the Buddhist concept, meaning to blow out, extinguishing the flame. Conflict in understanding this term has lead to divergent views of the Buddha and Buddhism. Some Buddhists worship the Buddha as a divine being: other Buddhists view him as an ordinary man. Tibetan Buddhists, see the Dalai Lama as the reincarnated Buddha, who was not annihilated into *nirvana* but chose to come back and help those still here. Encyclopaedia Britannic states:

> The living process is linked to a fine burning. Its remedy is the extinction of the fire of illusion, passion and cravings. The Buddha, the enlightened one, is one who is no longer kindled or enflamed. Many poetic terms are used to describe the state of the enlightened human beings – the harbour of refuge, the cool cave, the place of bliss, the further shore. The term that has become famous in the West is *nirvana*, translated as dying out—that is, dying out in the hit of the fierce fire of lust, anger, and delusion. But *nirvana* is not extinction, and indeed the craving for annihilation or known existence was expressly repudiated by the Buddha. Buddhists search not for mere cessation but for salvation. Though *nirvana* is often presented negatively as 'release from suffering. 'It is more

accurate to describe it in a more positive fashion: as an ultimate goal to be sought and cherished.[24]

The view of *nirvana* contrasts with the *Brahman* Hindu views those teach that *nirvana* means to be united with the universal soul. The Buddha believed, according to some that the soul elements along with individual identity are extinguished at *nirvana.*

The philosophies of Hinduism related to *nirvana* or *Moksha* is different. It is soul, the integral particle of Almighty God and surrounded in mysteries as well as ignorance, is released. *Moksha* that is complete merger of individual soul into the absolute *Brahman* is a process that is achieved through various ways, such as having complete faith in God and absolute surrender to God's mercy, realising God fully, controlling actions and performing pious duties in the interest of the society as a whole etc. Individuals living in the world are in constant ignorance. They are far away from reality with the result that their activities are impure that cause circle of birth and death. The *Bhagvad Gita* stating the fact says: "all living entities are born into delusion, bewildered by dualities arisen from desire and hate."[25] Regarding liberation of the soul it further says:

> "Persons who have acted piously in previous lives and in this life and whose sinful actions are completely eradicated, are freed from the dualities and delusion, and they engage themselves in My service with determination."[26]

Performing pious duties and knowing God fully, the person never comes back to this world. It is evident from the statement of the *Bhagvad Gita*. It says:

> After attaining Me, the great souls, who are *yogis* in devotion, never return to this temporary world, which is full of miseries, because they have attained the highest form of salvation.[27]

It further says:

> From the highest planet in the material world down to the lowest, all are places of misery wherein repeated birth and death take place. But one, who attains to My abode, never takes birth again.[28]

Regarding the God's supreme abode the *Bhagvad Gita* says:

> That which the *Vedantists* describe as unmanifested and infallible, that which is known as the supreme destination, that place from which, having attained it, one never returns – that is My supreme abode.[29]

Thus, it is quite obvious that in the Hindu religious philosophy *Moksha* means rising above the worldly desires, lusts, affections and having everlasting association with noble principles set by Almighty. Those who have complete faith in God and have totally devoted to God's principles, later or sooner avail *Moksha.* A divine consciousness is needed that leads one to *nirvana*. It is said:

> By virtue of the divine consciousness of the previous life, he automatically becomes attracted to the *yogic* principles— even without seeking them. Such an inquisitive transcendentalist stands always above the ritualistic principles of the scripture.[30]

To attain *Moksha* is a continuous process that continues even after death of the individual. The efforts applied in this direction never ends. In the next birth, consciousness having religious performances or devotional acts remains intact. *Moksha* needs purity of life. It is an understanding. It is the final goal of mankind. It releases one from the shackles of death and birth forever. It releases man from all types of worldly sufferings forever. *Moksha* means to avail the status where is complete peace, no quos, no repentance, no birth, no death, no fear, no worry, no scarcity etc. It is a status of reaching to the point where there is no variation in thought and action. In the *Bhagvad Gita* such status is known as *sthita-prajnah.* (Transcendentally situated). According to *Bhagvad Gita sthita-Prajnah is he*:

> Whose happiness is within, who is active and rejoices within, and whose aim is inward is actually the perfect mystic. He is liberated in the Supreme, and ultimately he attains the Supreme.[31]

Again:

> Those who are beyond the dualities that arise from doubts, whose minds are engaged within, who are always busy

> for the welfare of living beings, and who are free from all sins achieve liberation in the Supreme.[32]

The goal of *Moksha* is a Supreme goal. It is difficult to achieve because it needs renunciation. One who has fully controlled his sensual organs, and who is living in the world as if he has no concerned with it at all as he is very near to the goal. After death such man will never be born again. The *Bhagvad Gita* declares:

> A person who has given up all desires for sense gratification, who lives free from desires, who has given up all sense of proprietorship and is devoid of false ego—he alone can attain real peace.[33]

A Comparative View about *Nirvana* as per Buddha and Hindu *Dharma*

Thus, it is evident that the concept of *Nibbana* of Buddhism has too much similarity with that of Hinduism. In Hinduism the concept has largely been explained. Both the concepts related to *nirvana* are similar in the sense that both talk of freedom from life or to get rid of the circle of birth and death, forever. Both emphasise on the renunciation and the life of purification where there is no lust, no desire, no worldly willingness, no attachment, no greed and no falsification. Both believe that there is continuity of life even after death and one has to harvest the fruits of actions what one does. To attain *nirvana* wisdom is required that comes out of meditation. *Nirvana* is a status of complete peace where there is neither any upheaval, nor any noise, neither beginning nor end. To both the *Dharmas* the mundane world is illusion having no permanent essence. So far the case of dissimilarity is concerned they are mentioned below.

According to Buddha *Dharma* there is no Supreme God whose mercy or kindness is needed to avail *Nibbaana*. Rather it is attained with the self-help of the individual through the path of meditation. While the Hindu *dharma* believes that *nirvana* cannot be achieved without God's mercy. Hence not only faith in God is needed but blessing of God is also essential.

According to Hinduism, *Moksha* means to reach to the abode of supreme God that is beyond any type of destruction or annihilation while the Buddhism maintains that there is no any such place called God's abode. If there is anything, it is *Sunyata* (voidness). *Nirvana* means to merge into voidness. Hinduism believes that after availing *Moksha* one lives in the abode of Supreme God and enjoys all heavenly amenities. On the other hand, the Buddhists believe that since *nirvana* means merger into *Sunyata,* question of enjoyment or rejoicement does not arise.

The Buddhism denies the concept of soul and to it there is mind and mental consciousness, i.e., while achieving enlightenment one realises reality that there is nothing except *Sunyata* that is complete emptiness. But Hinduism maintains that soul is permanent and it is soul that is liberated completely while getting *Moksha*. Buddhist concept of *Nibbana* is psychological while the concept of *Moksha* in Hinduism is spiritual. It is transcendental.

Notes and References

1. Sart Jhingru, "Religion and Communalism", P. Bidawai, H. Nukhia and A. Vainik, (eds.), *Religion, Religiosity and Communalism*, New Delhi, 1996, p. 76.
2. Quoted in D. Smith, *India as a Secular State*, Princeton University Press, 1963, p. 373.
3. *Encyclopaedia Dictionary of Society*, Vol. 4, B.B. Sharma (ed.), New Delhi, 1992, p. 766.
4. Maheep Singh, "Guru Nanak: Bridge Across all Paths", The *Times of India,* 14th November, 2000.
5. Mahatherra Narda, *Nutshell of Buddhism*, pp. 35-57.
6. Quoted in Sarvapalli Radhakrishanan's Forewords *in 25000 Years of Buddhism,* Bapt P.V. (ed.), Publications Division, Ministry of Information and Broadcasting, Govt. of India, New Delhi, (sixth reprint), 1919, p. vi.
7. *Ibid.*, p. vii.
8. *Ibid.*, p., viii.
9. *Ibid.*, p. ix.
10. *Ibid.*, p. xi.
11. Nagarjuna in the Commentary on the *Prajnaparamita Sutra*
12. *Ibid.*

13. Dharmapalacarya in his commentary on *Prajanaparmita Sastra*.
14. Prabhakar Mishra, "The Doctrine of Self-lessness (*Sarvam Anataman*)" in Rabindra Pant, ed., *Buddhism in Universal Perspective*, 2001, Nav Nalanda Mahavihar, Nalanda, p. 61.
15. *Ibid.*
16. Dharmapalacarya, in his commentary on *Vijnanamattra Sastra*,
17. *Bhagvad Gita*.
18. Shrikant Singh, "Zen Buddhism", in Pant, R.B. (ed.), *Buddhism in Universal Perspective,* Nava Nalanda Mahavihara, 2001. pp. 203-04.
19. *Bhagvad Gita*, 12/3-4.
20. Shrikant Singh, "Zen Buddhism", in Part I, R.B. (ed.), *Buddhism in Universal Perspective*, *op. cit.* p. 202.
21. S. Radhakrishanan, *Indian Philosophy*, London, George Allen and Unwin, 1929, Vol. I, p. 449.
22. *Ibid.*, p. 452.
23. Shundo Tachibana , *Ethics of Buddhism*, Colombo: The Buddha Sahitya Sab, 1943, pp. 37-38.
24. *Encyclopaedia Britannica*, 2004, *Nirvana*.
25. *Bhagvad Gita*, Chapter 7, Verse 27.
26. *Ibid.*, Verse 28.
27. *Ibid.*, Chapter VIII, Verse- 15.
28. *Ibid.*, Verse 16.
29. *Ibid.*, Verse 21
30. *Ibid*, Chapter 6, Verse44. *Ibid.* Chapter 5, Verse 25.
31. *Ibid.*, Verse 25
32. *Ibid.*, Chapter II, Verse 71.
33. *Ibid.*

5

Buddhism towards Schism and Advent of Conflicting Buddhist Schools

Buddhism emerged as a powerful religious organisation and its preaching crossed the boundary of the country and covered a number of states in the South-East Asia. People from various sides being enchanted by the Buddhist philosophies, joined it and became ardent followers of Buddhism. Buddhism produced a number of noted scholars who contributed a lot to elaborate the concept of Buddhism and its philosophies taught by Lord Buddha. Several Councils were formed from time to time that debated the issues related to it and resolved various new norms and guidelines expanding the scope of Buddhism. Dissenting viewpoints and conflicting attitudes of the leaders as well as members of the Councils resulted in schism of Buddhism. In course of time, Buddhism was divided in various schools that began to interpret basic tenets of Buddhism from their respective different angles and views with the result that the Buddha *Dhamma* appeared in different forms and styles. Thus, schism of Buddhism enlarged its meaning and scope on the one hand, and invited more critiques to judge the authenticity as well as utility of Buddhism on the other. Various schools of Buddhism that appeared after the demise of the Buddha created more confusion, however, the values of the

Buddha *Dhamma* notably expanded. In course of time, different meanings of Buddhism and peculiar style of its practice under the school of *Yogacara*, *Vajrayana* and *Mantrayana* ultimately resulted in dismantling the castle of Buddhism at least in India. This chapter discusses the advent of several Buddhist schools and examines the circumstances in which they appeared. It also analyses the merits and demerits of the new schools of Buddhism and their consequences upon the people and society.

Seed of Dissention during Lifetime of the Buddha

Even during the lifetime of the Buddha, the seed of dissention in the Buddhist's tenets may easily be discerned. There were authorities who denied accepting its authority. Since it openly attacked the *Brahmans* engaged in the process of *karmkandas* and priesthood, the most of the *Brahman* scholars and follower of Hinduism remained very much critical to emerging thought of Buddhism. Secondly, there were elements within Buddhism who disliked some of the ways prescribed by the Buddha and demanded revision in them. His cousin, Devadutta, who has been a rival to Gautam Siddhartha from the childhood, became more jealous of Buddha's name and fame. He made several attempts upon his life to finish him forever falling in conspiracy with the king Ajatasatru. He also tried to create division in the Buddhist *Sangha* by demanding stricter conditions of life for Buddhist monks, such as living throughout the year under the trees, forgoing meat and fish and refusing all invitations from faithful adherents. There were also monks like Upananda, Channa, Mettiya-Bhumajaka or Sadvargiya who would take the earliest opportunity of transgressing the rules of the *Vinaya*. There were someone who disliked the Buddha's constant instructions to do this and that. They wanted to pass easy life. Hence, they were unhappy. It is evident from the fact that hearing the demise of the Buddha, Subhadra gave a sigh of relief saying that he would now no longer have to abide by "do this, do not that."[1] When the Buddha died, there was no one to take his place except Ananda, his personal attendant, who was asked to see that the *Dhamma* and the *Vinaya* would be the supreme authority in future. This created confusion because no one was there to give final judgement on the conflicting issue.

The First Division

In the first recital of the Buddhist texts made under the presidency of Mahakasyapa, followed by not less than five hundred monks, there were someone who did not approve the resolutions on the ground that those were not in similarity what the Buddha had taught. As the years rolled down, dissentions among the monks went on rising. In the words of Bapat, "Once the monks took the liberty of bringing dissentions to the *Sangha,* they went on multiplying till the number of sects reached the figure of eighteen in the second and the third centuries after the Buddha's death. The first dissention was created by the Vajjian monks of Vaisali."[2] The main issue of dissentions was authenticity of Buddha's words and their interpretations. The monks who deviated were distinguished as the *Mahasanghika,* while the orthodox monks were distinguished as the Theravadians (*Sthaviravadians).* It was rather a division between the conservative and the liberal, the hierarchy and the democratic. In the second council the decision was in the favour of the orthodox monks. But the Theravadians refused to abide by the decision of the majority. As a result, they were expelled from the *Sangha.*

It is said that in the group of the Theravadians there were many members who were not the formal members. They have joined the *Sangha* to enlarge the number of the Theravadians. Since the orthodox group disliked their activities and conflicts began. The expelled out members, thereafter, convened a separate council's meeting in which ten thousands monks participated. In fact, it was a great congregation of monks. In the words of S. Beal, "and because in the assembly both common folk and holy personages were mixed together, it was called the assembly of the great congregation."[3]

Thereafter, in the history of the succession of the schools, it is found that the first schism in the *Sangha* was followed by a series of schisms leading to the formation of different sub-sects, and in the course of time eleven such sub-sects arose out of the Theravada, and seven from the Mahasanghika. All these branches appeared one after another in close succession within three or four hundred years after the Buddha's *parinirvana.* The Theravadians were split into *Mahisasaka, Sammitiya,*

Vatisiputuriya, Sannagarika, Dharmottariya, Sarvastivada, Dharmaguptika, Kasapiya, Haimavata, and Sankarntika. Of these the *Mahisasaka, Sammitiya, Vatisiputuriya, Saravastivada and Kasyapiya* flourished widely and became more popular. But the *Sarvastivada* sect occupied the most popular place in popularity and expansion as also in the depth of philosophical outlook. Its philosophical interpretation was the admiration of the *Brahman*ical dialecticians, philosophers and commentators. From the Mahasanghika branch of the *Ekavyavharika, Caitiyakas, Kaukitika, (Gokhulika), Bahusyritya, Prajnapptivadian, Purvasaila*, and *Aparasasaila* appeared. Among them the *Caitiyakas* and the *Bahusuritiya* contributed much towards the growth of *Mahayana* which made Buddhism so very popular that it attracted more people than it would otherwise have done. There appeared, later on, other sects also. But these different sects could not maintain their individual existence for long. Most of them either disappeared or merged with other sects shortly after their origin. Four schools *Vaivasika, Sautrantika, Madhayamika* and *Yogacara*— only survived. The details of some important schools are mentioned below.

The Theravadians

The school of the Theravada is the oldest one. Hence, it is called the most orthodox school of Buddhism. This school honoured the words of the Buddha very much and treated his personality as well as his characters as superman qualities. He was described as '*Devatideva*' which means god of gods.[4] The Buddha had taught the monks to remain away from the things that spoil character and suggested them to practice *shila*, *Samadhi* and *Prajna*. *Shila* is a good practice for human life. The word is related to good human conducts. *Shila* is related to moral concepts and it makes man morally high. It prohibits man from murder, theft, falsehood, wrong sexual behaviour and all intoxicating drinks. A monk must live the life of celibacy. He must be away from wrong statements, and wrong philosophical views. While dealing with others he must not use harsh words. *Samadhi* is *sadhana* and it helps one to keep the mind in balance and enables one to have proper insight to view the things in right direction. Through *Samadhi* one develops the quality to distinguish between right and wrong. The cultivation of *prjana* helps one to understand at one and the same time, the four Noble Truths and the Law of Dependent Origination.

The philosophy of this school is also very simple. It teaches that all worldly phenomena are subject to three characteristics. First, they are *anitya* impermanent and transient. Second, the world is full of *Dukhas.* Third is *anatma,* that means there is nothing in them which can be called one's own, nothing substantial, nothing permanent. All compound things are made up of two elements —*nama*, the non-material parts, and *rupa*, the material part. They are further described as consisting of nothing but five constituent groups. *Rupa* is the material group and four non-material qualities are *vedna* (sensation), perception (*sanjna*), mental formatives (*sanskara*, and lastly consciousness (*vijnana*). These elements were further sub-divided into so many sections and parts giving a complete detail of their meanings and influences. The number of the constituents increased gradually from two to five, then to twelve and finally to eighteen. All four elements such as *cita* (consciousness), *rupa* and *nirvana* etc., were classified into as many as eighty nine types with the result that the concept became very much vague. Following the prescribed four Noble Truths and Noble Eight-fold Paths as well as mental and physical nature of the man and the world, one may easily obtain *nirvana* where one becomes worthy man, an *Arhata*. The life of an *Arhata* is purely holy because he comes to the stage of dispassionateness. It is said that the life of an *Arhata* is the ideal of the followers of this school. It is a "life where all (future) birth is at an end, where the holy life is fully achieved, where all that had to be done has been done, and there is no more return to worldly life."[5]

The Mahisasakas School

There were two groups of this school which were prominent at two different periods. According to Pali sources, this school, along with the *Vajjiputtaakas*, branched off from the *Sthavirvadians* gave rise to the *Sarvastivadians.* This school also spread to Ceylon. *Mahisasakas* believed in the simultaneous comprehension of truths. For them the past and the future did not exist, while the present and nine *asamskrta dharmas* did. Like the Theravadians, they believed that the *Arhatas* were not subject to retrogression. However, they held that those who were in the first stage were subject to such retrogression. No *deva* or god could lead a holy life, nor does a heretic attain miraculous powers. There was no *antra-bhava* or interim existence between this life and the next. The *Sangha* included the Buddha and therefore charity given to the former was more meritorious than those given to the Buddha only. Of the eight factors of the Noble Eight-fold Path, Right Speech, Right Action and Right Livelihood were not to be considered real factors since they were not mental actions. These were therefore to be excluded from the factors of the Noble Path. Like the *Sarvastivadinas* they believed in the existence of the past, the future and the *antra-bhava.* They held that the *skandhas,* the *ayatanas* and the *dhatus* always exist in the form of seeds. The views and options what they developed proved useful, no doubt, but it were very much difficult for the common mass to grasp the hidden meaning or to understand the essence of the statements.

The Sarvastivadian School

Among the Buddhist schools which adopted Sanskrit for their literary medium, the *Sarvastivadians* came closest to the *Sthaviravadians*. With the decline of the *Sthaviravadians* in India this school bore the brunt of the battle against the Mahayanists. Acarya Vasubandhu, the writer of the *Abhidharma-kosa,* was a great champion of this school before he was converted to Mahayanism under the influence of his brother Asanga. This school flourished in India in the Punjab and the North-West Frontier Province (now in Pakistan) and Kaniska in 1st century AD. The Buddhist texts of the *Suttra* the *Vinaya* and the *Abhidharma* were engraved on sheets of copper and deposited inside *stupa* by the School. However, these engraved sheets have not yet been discovered or found. The school believed that all things exist (*sarvam asti*). The name of the school was given on that line. Like the *Sthaviravadians*, the *Sarvastivadians* were the realist among the Buddhists. They believed that it was not only the things in the present that existed, but also the things in the past and the future which were in continuity with the present. They viewed that things change their shape, colour, quality etc., but they are not finished up forever. They exist somewhere in some different shape even in subtle shape. That has existence in the present, after sometimes, disappears into the past and living in the past for certain period, it reappear in the future. Thus, this is the process of continuity or the circle of continuity continuing constantly moving and exiting in present, past and future. Like the *Vatsiputriyas, Sammitiyas* and some of the Mahasanghika, they revolted against the dominance of the *Arhats* who had attained a position of unsurpassed eminence among the *Sthaviravadians.* They maintained that an *Arhata* was subject to fall or retrogression. They also said that a continuous flow of mind might amount to concentration (*Samadhi*) of mind.

This school denied the transcendental powers ascribed to the Buddha and the Bodhisattva by the *Mahasanghikas.* It was their faith that the holy life was for gods and that even heretics could have supernatural powers. They believed in *antra-bhava*, an interim existence between this life and the next. It means they believed that the *antra-bhava* does not die even after death of the person. To understand *antr-bhava* we have to go deep into the inner heart. The inner-heart if very deep it is the base of every human activity. It is difficult to give precise definition of *antra-bhava*. It is a feeling. However, one must grasp that the *antra-bhava* is the carrier of consciousness where essence of *karmas* are deposited. It is *antra-bhava* that stands above the change and destruction. They maintained that the Bodhisattvas were still ordinary people and even the *Arhatas* were not free from the effects of past actions and still had something to learn. The *antra-bhava* carries the seed of action. According to them there were seventy five elements, seventy two of them *sanskara* compounded and three *sanskara* uncompounded which were *akasa* or space or cessation through knowledge or cessation, not through knowledge, but through the natural process of the absence of required conditions.

The Dharmaguptikas

The *Dharmaguptikas* broke away from the *Mahisasakas* with whom they differed on points dealing with gifts to the

Buddha or to the *Sangha*. This school proffered gifts to the Buddha and greatly reversed the stupas of the Buddha as it is clear from their rules of the *Vinyas*. Like the *Mahisasakas*, they believed that an *Arhata* was free from passion and that heretics could not gain supernatural powers. This school was popular in Central Asia and China, and had its own *Sutra*. *Vinya* and *Abhidharma* literature. The rules of its distinctive *Pratimoksha* were followed in the monasteries of China.

The Mahasanghika

It is universally believed that the *Mahasanghika* were the earliest seeders, and the forerunners of the *Mahayana*. They took up the cause of their new sect with zeal and enthusiasm. In a few decades, they achieved power and popularity. They adopted the existing rules of the *Vinaya* to their doctrine and introduced new ones, they revolutionised the Buddhist *Sangha*. They also made certain alterations in the *Vinaya* and *Sutra* texts. They canonised a good number of sutras, which they claimed to be the sayings of the Buddha. They rejected certain points of the canon which had been accepted in the first Council. They did not recognise the Buddhist saying, the *Parivara, the Abhidharma and parts of the Jataka.* The *Abhidharma* was compiled in the Third Council held under the patronage of the great king Ashoka. They complied afresh the texts of the *Dhamma* and the *Vinaya*. Excluding all these texts calling them additional and are not included in the canonical collection of the *Mahasanghika*. The compilation of the *Mahasanghika* was designed the Acriyavada as distinguished from Theravadas, compiled at the First Council. Yuan Chwang records that the *Mahasanghikas* had a complete canon of their own which they divided into five parts, viz., the *Sutra*, the *Vinaya*, the *Abhidharma*, the *Dharnis* and miscellaneous.[6]

During the second century after the Buddha's death, the *Mahasanghika* sect met the fate of division into *Ekavyaharika*, *Lokotara, vada, Kukhutika, Bahusrutiya* etc. Among the *Saila* schools were the most prominent and had great influence in the south India sections into which the *Mahasanghika* were divided the *Caityaka* and the so long as the Theravadian's influence remained strong, the *Mahasanghika* could not make much influence, but die to their continued hard struggle for existence and survival they made recognisable space. They established centers at Patliputra and Vaisali. They also spread their network to both the north and the south of the country. There are a number of inscriptions made by them and epigraphic evidence that reveals the truth that they had spread strong hold in the country. They were not confined only to the Magadha, but they also spread over the northern and western part of India. The general doctrines of the *Mahasanghika* with all their branches are in the *Katha-vatthu*, the *Mahavastu* and the work of *Vasumitra, Bhavya and Vinitadeva.*

Like the Theravadians, the *Mahasanghika* accepted the cardinal principles of the Buddha. The fundamentals of the Buddha are four Noble Truths and Eight-fold Nobel Paths, the non-existence of soul, the theory of *karma*, the theory of *paratitya-samputpada*, and the gradual stages of spiritual advancement. They did not differ much in this regard. In this regard this school hardly differed. According to them:

1. The Buddhas are *lokottara* (supramandane);
2. They have no *sasrva dharma* (defiled elements);
3. Their bodies, their length of life and their powers are unlimited, they neither sleep nor dream;
4. They are self-possessed and always in a state of *Samadhi*;
5. They do not preach by name;
6. They understand everything in a movement; and
7. Until they attain *parinirvana*, the Buddhas possess *ksayajnana* (knowledge of decay) and *anutpadajnana* (knowledge of non-origination).

In short, everything concerning Buddhas is transcendental. The *Mahasanghika* conception of Buddha contributed to the growth of the later *Trikaya* theory in *Mahayana*. Thus, the *Mahasanghika* conceived of the Buddha detactically and gave rise to the conception of the Bodhisattvas. According to them the Bodhisattvas are also supramandane, and do not pass through the four embryonic stages of ordinary beings. They enter their mother's wombs in the form of white elephants and come out of the wombs on the right side. They never experience feeling of lust, malevolence. For the benefits of all classes of sentient beings they are born of their own free will in any form of existence they choose. All these conceptions led to the defecation of Buddha and Bodhisattvas. *Arahathood* is not the final stage of sanctification. The other main beliefs of the *Mahasanghika* are mentioned below:

1. The five *vijananas* (sense-perceptions) conduce both to *sarga* (attachment to worldly matters) and *viraga (*non-attachment to the same state);
2. The *rupendriyas* (organs of sense) are mere flesh. They themselves cannot perceive the *vijnanas* of the organs;
3. One can eliminate suffering and obtain the highest bliss (*nirvana)* through knowledge (*prajna);*
4. A *srotapamma* (one who has entered the path of sanctification) is liable to retrogress while an *Arhata* is not. He is capable of knowing his own nature through his *cita* and *caitasika.* He is also liable to commit all kinds of offences except the five heinous crimes, namely, the murder of an *Arhata* shedding the blood of the Buddha and creating a split in the *Sangha.*
5. Nothing is indeterminate, the nature of things must be either good or bad for it cannot be either good or bad;
6. The original nature of the mind is pure, it becomes contaminated when it is stained by *upaklesa* (passions) and *agantukarjas* (adventitious defilement); and
7. After death and before rebirth a being has no existence.

Thus, it is evident that the *Mahasanghika* differs considerably from other sects in doctrinal matters as well as in their rules of discipline. The followers of the school wore yellow robe, the lower part of which was pulled tightly to the left. [7] It is also evident that most of the views adopted or introduced by the *Mahasanghika* are not new. They existed in other religious scriptures. What they described is related to the life of a sage or *yogi*. When one goes through the Hindu religious scriptures, he may find all these descriptions.

The School of Bahusrutdiyas

This School is also a branch of *Mahasanghika*. It owes its

origin to a teacher who was very learned in Buddhist lore. As for the fundamentals doctrines of the *Bahusrutdiyas* they maintained that the teachings of the Buddha concerning *anityata* (transitoriness) *dukha, sunya, anatma* and *nirvana* were *lokottara* (transcendental), since they led to emancipation. His other teachings were *laukika* (Mundane). On this point– the *Bahusrudiyas* may be regarded as the precursors of the latter *Mahayana* teachers. According to them there was no mode which led to the salvation. Further, the *Sangha* was not subject to worldly laws. They also accepted the five propositions of Mahadeva as their views. *Bahusrudiyas* are often described as 'a bridge between the *Mahayana* schools', as they tried to combine the teachings of both. Harivarman, the leader of this school, believed in *atma-nairatnya* (the absence of soul in individual) and in *dharma-nairatya* (the soulless of all things). Like the followers of the orthodox schools, he believed in the plurality of the universe which, according to him, contained eighty-four elements. Like the *Mahayanists,* he maintained that there were two kinds of truths–conventional *(samvrti)* and absolute (*pramartha*). He further maintained that from the point of view of conventional truth *atman o*r clarification of the universe into eighty four elements existed, but, from the point of view of absolute truth neither existed. From the point of absolute truth, there is total void (*surva-sunya*). He believed in the theory of *Buddha-kaya* as well as *Dharma-kaya*, which he explained as consisting of good conduct (*sila),* concentration (*samadhi*) and insight *(prajna),* deliverance *(vimukti*) and knowledge of and insight into deliverance (*vimukti janana darsana).* Although he did not recognise the absolute transcendental nature of the Buddha, he still believed in the special powers of the Buddha. He believed that only the present was real, while the past and the future had no existence.

The *Caitiyavada* School

The *Caitiyavada* School originated with the teacher Mahadeva towards the close of the second century after the *prinirvana* of the Buddha. He is distinguished from the Mahadeva, who was responsible for the origin of the *Mahasanghika*. He was a learned and delicate ascetic who received the ordination in the *Mahasanghika* School. He professed the five of the *Mahasanghika* and started a new *Sangha.* Generally speaking, the *Caityanas* School shared the fundamental doctrines of the original *Mahasanghika*. However, they differed from them in minor details. Their doctrines are as follow:

1. One may acquire great merit by the creation, decoration and worship of *Caityas* (dwelling on the mountain *Caitya*); even a circulation of the mountain *Caityas* engenders merit.
2. Offering of the flowers garland and scents to *Caityas* are like was meritorious.
3. By making gift one can acquire religious merit, and one can also transfer such merit at one's friends and relatives for their happiness.
4. Buddhas are free from attachment, ill-will, and delusion and possessed of fine elements. They are superior to the *Arhats* by virtue of the acquisition of ten powers.
5. A person having *samyak-dristi* (the right view) is not free from hatred and, as such, not free from the danger of committing the sin of murder.
6. *Nirvana* is positive, faultless state.

It is thus very much clear that the doctrines which they contained are mostly related to that of the *Mahasanghika* from which the *Mahayana* doctrine developed. They were the first school to defy the Buddha and the Bodhisattva, which ultimately led to the complete defication of the Buddha and Bodhisattva in *Mahayana*. Their conception of *Sambhoga-kaya* led to the *Trikaya* theory which is one of the prominent features of *Mahayana*. The worship of *Caityas* and the making of gifts advocated by the branches of the *Mahasanghika* School were to large extent responsible for the evolution of the popular form of Buddhism. Thus, the *Mahasanghika* became the forerunner of the school of *Mahayana* that gained notable popularity everywhere.

The *Vaivasika* School

It came into prominence in third century after the Buddha's

Mahaparinirvana. It rejected the authority of the *Sutras* and admitted only the *Abhidharma*. The seven *Abhidharma* treaties that formed the general foundation of its philosophy were commended and accepted. They admitted the reality of both mind and external objects. They also held the theory of direct realism.

The Sautrantika School

It flourished in the fourth century after the demise of the Buddha and attached great importance to the authority of *Sutras*. Its philosophy was based on the original texts containing the discourses of the Buddha rather the commentaries there on and that is why the name *Sautrantika* was given to this school. *Dharmottara* and *Yasomitra* were followers of this school. Srilabdha who was also a well-known teacher of this school composed a famous commentary on the work of this school. According to them objects outside could be inferred from their mental pictures of ideas. They denied the existence of the past and future elements, but admitted the existence of the present only.

The *Madhayamika* School

It was called Madhayamika on laying emphasis on *Madhayama Pritipada* which means middle way. In his first sermon at Benares, the Buddha preached the middle path. The school advocated neither for self-mortification nor life devoted to the pleasures of the senses. But it is different from the middle path as advocated by the adherents of the *Madhayamika* system. It is the non-acceptance of the two views concerning existence and non-eternity, self and non-self and so on. In short, it advocated neither the theory of absolutism nor that of total unreality of the world, but merely relativity. It is, however, to be noted that the middle path propounded at Banaras had an ethical meaning while that of the *Madhayamika* is to be taken in the metaphysical sense.

***Yogacara* School**

It was called *Yogacara* because it laid emphasis on the practice of *Yoga* as the most effective method for attainment of the higher truth by going through all the ten stages of spiritual progress of Bodhisattva-hood. It is otherwise known as *Vijnanavada* on accounts of its holding *Vijnanamatra* (pure consciousness) as the ultimate reality. In short, it taught objective idealism—only thought is real. The *Yogacara* brought out the practical side of the philosophy, while *Vijnavada* brought out its speculative features.

In course of time, the four schools mentioned above gradually coalesced together and their philosophical views were formulated into two schools *Hinayana* and *Mahayana*. The Buddhism that is current today has two main divisions well known as *Hinayana* and *Mahayana*. The former prevails in Ceylon, Myanmar, Thailand, Cambodia and other countries while the latter in Tibet, Nepal, China, Japan and others. *Hinayana* is designated as southern and *Mahayana* as the northern Buddhism by the western scholars. But this is untenable from the point of view of their geographical expansion. Theravadians never call themselves Hinayanists.

The Schools of Hinayana and Mahayana

Immediately after the Buddha's demise, members of his original *Sangha* sought to organise their master's teachings into a system of doctrines on which they could agree. With that they went ahead discussing the issues with their fellows. However, disagreement on the issues was so strong and unbridgeable that there was no way out except to decide and follow their respective separate ways. The two major schools that came up were known earlier the School of *Sthaviravadians* and the Schools of *Mahasanghika* which have already been discussed above. In due course of time, these two groups came to be known as Theravadians (*Hinayana*) and *Mahayana*. The former called itself Theravadians while the latter was known as the Mahayanists. Later on, a number of other small groups appeared having inclination either with the *Hinayana* or the *Mahayana*, with a result, the Buddha *Sangha* splinted into several groups holding to different interpretations of Buddha *Dharma*. Conflict over the meaning of the *Dharma* arose not only between individual monks but also between various monasteries. As it has been stated above, the groups which remained close to the orthodox view of the Buddhism were known as Theravadians. It is the group that came to be known as the *Hinayana*. The group that established their own way came to be known as the *Mahayana*. The group of the Theravaidans was termed as 'fundamentalist'. They preserved the original view of Buddhism. *Mahayana* Buddhism includes individuals and schools who subscribe to teachings that are modifications and amplifications of the themes already present in the Theravadian's heritage. *Mahayana* means 'greater vehicle of salvation' or 'expansive way.' *Hinayana*, on the other hand, was called as 'lesser vehicle' of salvation or the 'exclusive way of salvation.'

Notable thing is that both the groups and schools look to the Buddha as their primary source of truth. The Mahayanists, unlike Theravadians, recognised member of other Buddhas and Bodhiśattvas. These personalities said to be manifestation of the Absolute and, along with the Buddha, are regularly prayed to for assistance. Some are worshiped as gods. The scriptures of both groups are different. The *Mahayana* tradition accepts as authoritative. Both the schools differ in the meaning of *nirvana* also. To Theravadians, to escape from the *sansara* or the cycle of rebirth is *nirvana*. Since birth and rebirth is the major cause of *dakha*, one must obtain *nirvana* where there is neither birth nor death. It is a state marked by a complete deliverance from all pain and sorrow. But in the *Mahayana* tradition, the whole purpose of becoming a Bodhisattva is not to escape life, but to remain in life in order to help others reach enlightenment. If the Theravadians expiation of *nirvana* coupled with the *Mahayana* concept of what it means to reach enlightenment, then hypothetically the most spiritually advanced persons would never reach *nirvana* because they always forsake escape from *sansara* in order to help others. Consequently, those in the *Mahayana* tradition have had to change the definition of *nirvana* to 'the true state of spiritual perfection' rather than escape from the rebirth.

The following table clearly illustrates the dissimilarities between these two Schools that emerged from the same root.

Theravada (Hinayana)	*Mahayana*
The Buddha: Although Siddhartha was a superior man of extraordinary intellect and exceptional talent, he was nonetheless only a human being. He is not worshiped.	**The Buddha:** Siddhartha was a sacred manifestations of the absolute, or *Brahman*. His body and physical actions were merely an illusion. He is often worshipped as a god.
Deliverance: Escaping the cycle of rebirth is dependent upon entrance into a monastery. Only there, through a great self-effort can one attain disengagement from the world and its false desires. Eventually, perhaps through several lifetimes *nirvana* will be attained.	**Deliverance:** Escaping of cycle of rebirth may be obtained through self-effort, but such effort is not mandatory, nor is joining a monastery. According to some sects, one may pray to the Buddha for deliverance. His compassion and grace can save everyone, even evil persons.
Ideal: One's life goal is simply to reach *nirvana* and exit this life. Becoming one enlightened one *(Arhata)* without regard for others is the accepted attitude.	**Ideal:** The most important goal is to help others to reach *nirvana*. One who is enlightened (a Buddha) will postpone his own 'salvation' in order to assist other.
Concern: The school of Theravadians has self-concerned. It hardly bothers for others. It is more individualist, self-centered and self-seeking for salvation.	**Concern:** Mahayanist school emphasises on attainment of enlightenment and *nirvana* for self, but at the same time it thinks about others and it is ready to lead others in this regard.
Theravadians worship only Buddha and no god, *devas* or *Brahman*.	Mahayanists worship deities Bodhisattvas and gods *devas* and Brahman.
The dominant place of Theravadians Dharma is Sri Lanka, Cambodia, Laos, Thailand, Myanmar etc.	Mahayanists are mostly found in China, Tibet, Korea and Japan etc.
Religious scriptures written in Pali language called Pali Canon, written about 80 BC and called *Sutta*.	Religious scriptures written in Pali. Divided into a number of *Sutras* called *Tripitaka* which means three baskets. *(Sutta* (discourses), *Vinya* (Discipline and *Abhiddharmma* (Philosophical analysis.
Pali Canon is brief.	Sutras are in detail.
Hinayana holds psychological realism and see suffering as a real.	Mahayana holds idealism and sees suffering as an illusion.
It denies true being behind a phenomena and avoid making metap-hysical statement.	Mahayana teaches an external absolute under many names.
To Hinayanists liberation is possible through self-effort.	To Mahayanists liberation may also be obtained through blessing of god.

Thus, it is very much obvious that both the schools differ fundamentally in so far the meaning of *nirvana* and the purpose of the life is concerned. The Mahayanists have broader view while the Hymnists (Theravadians) adopt limited view. The most important thing to note here is the fact that the Mahayanists are much more inclined to the Hindu's philosophies of birth, rebirth and theory of action and *karma*. Like Hindu philosophies they believe that the Absolute is infinite from where incarnation takes place to help and assist people of this world. In other words, they believe in the concept of incarnation. To them the Buddha was an incarnation who incarnated with the basic purpose to tell mankind about pains and suffering and to release them from that. The Buddha is not a great personality, but he is God. Since God is merciful, kind and all powerful, the Buddha also possessed all these qualities. Hence, they developed the tradition to worship Lord Buddha like God. That is why a number of statues of Lord Buddha were constructed here and there which are still available. The followers of this school worship the Buddha as God even today.

1. Despite various differences in their philosophical postulates and mental attitude both the schools have similar views related to the following issues:
2. Theory of *Karma*;
3. Theory of Rebirth;
4. Transitory and impermanent nature of the *sansara*;
5. World's changing nature brings sufferings;
6. Deliverance from Rebirth and suffering takes place through change in consciousness;
7. A liberating change in consciousness can be obtained only through following the teachings of the Buddha's love and mercy;
8. Both accept the Four Noble Truths; and
9. Both accept the Eight-Fold Noble Path.

Some Special features of Mahayana and Hinayana (Theravada)

Theravada	*Mahayana*
Doctrine of the Elders.	Great Way of Buddhism.
Classical Buddhism.	High degree of diversity.
Conservative/preserves traditions, Texts of yearly Buddhism.	Emphasizes Bodhisattva—choosing rebirth to help all beings.
Emphasises renunciation (monasticism).	Buddha seen as a guide, teacher, exemplar, not God.
Goal is to escape *sansara* through realising *Nibbana*..	Buddha is dead, not active in the world. He is continuing source of blessing, even salvation.
Monks cannot marry or have family life.	Monks may marry and may lead family life.

Thus, it may be observed that The Theravada and *Mahayana* traditions share many basic principles, practices and institutional structures. However, the Theravada is more unified, coherent tradition-based on conservation of early teaching (Pali Canon). *Mahayana* is, on the other hand, more diverse, inspired by new body of scriptures and new Buddha/Bodhisattva cults. *Mahayana* Buddhism evolved in East Asia giving rise to many new traditions. Theravada preserved in Southern Asia. *Mahayana* represents itself as a 'higher' path. It has an expanded conception of the Buddha, distinctive teachings and texts and a diverse *Sangha*.

The Three Bodies Doctrine of Mahayana

The Buddha is regarded by the *Mahayana* Schools as the universal saviour and bestower of deliverance. He is master over space and time. The Mahayanists believe that there are so many Buddhas from Gautam. There is as many Buddha as grains of sand on the bank of the Ganges. Buddha appears in all regions of the world taking many forms. Like the Hindus they believe that Buddha is omnipotent and omnipresent. However, they developed the *Tripitaka* doctrine which means three bodies of Buddha.

1. The *Dharmacarya* (Dharma-Body)

It is the inner nature of the Buddha. In all the innumerable earthly Buddhas and the countless transcendental Buddhas, there is only one *Dharmacarya*. It is the absolute reality, besides which there is no other reality. *Dhamma* is the partial manifestation of natural law, namely, 'facts'. *Dhamma* is the technical form for 'factors of existence'. The *Dharmacarya* is thus base-consciousness of existence. He has direct connection with the Absolute. Such explanation reminds one the Hindu's concept of Absolute *Brahman* which are limitless, unknowable, non-explainable, but the ultimate sources of origin of creation.

2. *Sambhogakaya*: Body of Bliss

It is the transcendental Buddha that cannot be interpreted or perceived by the senses. It may be experienced spiritually. In *Sambhogakaya* Buddhas are seen as mental creations, the idea of the Bodhisattva. It is the manifestation of the Absolute. Transcendental *Sambhogakaya* Buddhas are regarded as objectively existing supramandane and subtle beings. The most transcendental Buddha is the Amida Buddha. He is said to possess paradise in which believers are reborn there. They are the teachers of the Bodhisattvas and spiritual fathers of the earthly Buddhas. They project their compassion for all beings into the world by their meditation. Again, such concept of Buddhism brings one close to the Hindu mythology which talks of the advent of the Lord Vishnu, who is the holder of the ether and first cause of creation. The Absolute *Brahman* manifests into Lord Vishnu possessing extraordinary power or energy that is all pervasive. God *Brahma*, the creator of the universe, comes out of the navel centre of the Lord Vishnu. Thus, it is quite obvious that the School of Mahayanists is closely associated with the metaphysical philosophy of Hinduism.

Vajrayana and *Tantric* Cult of Buddhism: Wisdom of Tibet

In contrast to the common view, Tibetan reports that both the exoteric *Mahayana* and esoteric *Vajrayana* were taught by Shakyamuni in secret to certain disciples.[8] The abundance of the evidence and common sense corroborates Tibetan reports that the raw materials of *Tantric* theory and practice were already available in Shakyamuni's days, but not systematically formulated, written or published until much later. From the

Indo-Tibetan perspective, the origin of the *Mahayana* and *Vajrayana* lay in the gradual unfolding of the Buddha's reform of Indian culture and society. Far from revisions or corruptions, these traditions extend the progressive role of the Theravada academy into the Indian mainstream, with rational and universal alternatives to the elite Sanskrit tradition of arts and science.[9] As centrism emerged as definitive of Buddha's thought, it cleared the way for the *Vajrayana* to emerge as the definitive paradigm of the Buddhist contemplative science. The reason for this shift helped characterise the *Vajrayana* as a contemplative science. The *mantras* were formed in poetic form. According to *Tantras*, beings and world are seen to emerge when the space of emptiness planted with poetic seeds (*bija-mantra*). In *Tantras* these seeds are planted not in the disembodied ground of a sub-conscious mind, but rather in the embodied soil of creative, bliss-void (*sukha-sunya*) states of mind, supported by the vital energy (*prana*) of a nervous system with channels (*nadi*) complexes (*chakra*) and drops (*bindu*). While this nerve system was mapped by contemplation rather than gross anatomy, *Tantric* psychology and medicine see it as made of subtle matter and ascribe to it all the normal mind/body functions, modern science ascribes to the nerve. In this the Semitic dimension of *Tantric* worldview, like the scientific phonetics of Sanskrit grammar, is not abstract or idealistic but embedded in the living context of mind/body interaction.

There are several factors that helped the way for the *Vajrayana* to emerge as the definitive paradigm of Buddhist contemplative science. One of them is inclination of some Buddhist scholars to the Indian method of *yoga*. The Tibetan Scholar Tsong Khapa attributed the efficacy of *Vajrayana* practice not to its ritualised poetic of subtle *yogic* technology, but to the distinctive process of psycho-spiritual role-modeling known as mentor-archetype *yoga* (*guru-devayoga*). Judging from its tapping, this colourful process looks like an elaborately ritualised form of spiritual ancestor worship, aptly described by Robert Thurman as 'mentor worship.'

As for its therapeutic philosophy, the esoteric *Vajrayana* is often described as fruition or effectual vehicle in contrast to the causal vehicle of the exoteric *Mahayana*. It approaches the path of philosophy from the standpoint of its fruits or consequence, namely, the enlightened experience of a spiritual master. It does this by offering the disciple a maste.'s eye-view of herself as a living Buddha within a Buddha perfected, natural social and cultural world as well as scripting his/her dialogue of enlightening speech (*mantra*) and repertoire of enlightening activities or gestures (*mudra).* Creative, imagery, poetic formulas and performative gestures provide a working linguistic construction and imaginative simulation of enlightened perception that serves as an alternative system of reference by which the disciple can critique his or her compulsive misperception of self and world.

Vajrayana Buddhism known as Tibetan Buddhism, *Tantric* Buddhism and Lamaism, is also called 'diamond way' which means it is the precious, changeless, pure and clear. It developed during the fifth to sixth century AD when Buddhism spread through northern India, Nepal and finally to Tibet. The practice of *Vajrayana* in Tibet is still discerned. At that time, the prevailing belief of Tibet was the Bon religion, a mixture of shamanism (a form of witchcraft), magic, and primitive nature worship. *Vajrayana* was born when these practices along with magical formula designed to obtain magical powers, were in corporate into Buddhism (AD 600-1200). Included in the *Vajrayana* tradition are a number of advance meditative techniques: *yoga*, special hand gestures (*mudras*), spells, and chants. It also derives many of its doctrines from *Vedantic* and *tantric* influence.

Vedanta is an Indian school of philosophy, which teaches that God (*Brahman*) and the soul (*atman*) are one. In other words, there is only one ultimate reality –*Brahman* – and the individuality we see is nothing but an illusion. The maker (*Maya)* of illusion is ignorance (*avidya).* Enlightenment occurs when one realises that "the world is not real: only the Absolute, and the *Brahman*, is real."

The *Tantras* are a series, sixth century AD scripture associated with the worship of *Shakti*, mother of the universe. They are made available only to initiates of various *tantric* religions (Tibetan Buddhism is only one of many *tantric* belief system). Study of these texts "is said to reveal clairvoyance, clairaudience, telepathy, psychometric, the power of sound, vocal expression, and the composition of music.)

The word *Tantra* basically means "loom" and refer more specifically to the threads of loom. This expresses the foundational teaching of *tantrism*–all things are interwoven into one ultimate reality. *Tantrism* is also based on a variety of sex rituals that involve (breathing) exercises, meditation, and the prolonged sexual contact as *maithuna* (sexual intercourse)".

The sexual philosophy within *tantric* Buddhism is linked to a number of ideas. There is the belief that erotic love is a profound experience that "opens the mind to a sense of away and wanders akin to religious experience." It also presents the idea that during the act of sexual intercourse, a transcending of boundary between participants occurs, leading to an experience of oneness with each other. During this masculine and feminine sexual union the difference of different sexes disappears. Body and mind of two different sexes become one. There exists the additional notion that the best way to escape blinding passion in this case sexual lust – is to "go into the act that is desired rather than to retreat from."

Perhaps the most important part of *tantric* religion, including Tibetan Buddhism, is the belief that male and female energy resides in everyone. The male energy is said to be the dynamic, powerful, and moving force. The female energy is thought of as static and docile. These two energy correspond to aspects of one's spirituality. The female side is connected to inward property such as "wisdom and realisation" and is linked to the more symbolic or intuitive aspects of understanding." The dynamic (male) side "relates to outgoing aspects such as compassion and strength," as well as to cognitive knowledge. The goal of *tantric* sex practices is to unite the two spiritual forces though physical union.

Some followers of *tantric* religion, however, believe that sexual intercourse is not necessary. They maintain that the sex acts depicted in *tantric* art and literature are only symbolic representation of a spiritual unification of both energy that can, through meditation and other practices, lead to a uniting of the male and female energy. Many of the occult aspects of Tibetan Buddhism also come from *Tantrism*. *Tantric* tradition maintains a close relationship to magic and includes "secret teaching, scriptures in code, and the practice of drawing symbols on the ground, and uttering spell to call up deities, supernatural powers that can be used for good or evil."

According to Walt Anderson, *Author of Open Secret: a Western Guide to Tibetan Buddhism,* the *Tantric*-Buddhist ideal is to yield: "Go ahead and do it, whatever it is, if you think, you must and it does not harm somebody else. But pay attention; be fully aware of what goes on in your mind and body, of how it reality feels."

This extraordinary system to avail real wisdom helps elucidate the nature and scope of *Tantric* teaching and practice. Its elegant synthesis of therapeutic philosophy, depth-psychology and spiritual-ethical pedagogy revere the interpersonal; world of *Tantric* instruction as a psychotherapeutic —psychospiritual art with no clear parallel in any tradition, ancient or modern, Eastern or Western. Its unique hermeneutic is meant less for reading arcane texts than for unlocking the living text of the human mind and body, with the aim of revealing the wish-fulfilling gems of the creative human spirit within. In India, it may be the best compared with the ultimate hermeneutics refinement of *Upanishadic* pedagogy found in the *Vedanta* system of Bharathari and *Sanskara* as well as the sublime psychospiritual poetic of Abhinavagupta. In the words of Joseph Loizzo, "In the West, it may be compared with the Sufi pedagogy of Ibn Arabi or the Kabbaka teachings of Ablufia. In its humanism, it may be compared with the modern therapeutic philosophy stemming from Nietzsche and Freud, including the esoteric hermeneutic of Jung and Kacan."[9] In contrast to all these analogies, however, *Vajrayana* pedagogy is uniquely adopted to the needs of the main stream academic tradition covering the whole range of teaching context from large scale public lectures and complex curricula to the most intimate tutorial and mentoring bonds. Nagarjuna describes the centric practice of non-duality as culminating in the "profound, awe-inspiring performance of enlightenment, whose essence is emptiness and compassion."[10] Nagarjuna's performance effectively entails shifting the reference of 'I' and 'mine' from deluded percepts of self and world to the corrected perceptions of these twin institutions. Likewise the intent of the creation stage is to rapidly cultivate this enlightened agency by conjoining both aspects of this reconstruction in a single practice that aims at developing a 'self of selflessness.' This reconstruction is guided by poetic formulas like: "I am the self whose nature is the diamond intuition of emptiness" and "I am the purity whose nature is the natural purity of all things."[11]

Creation stage meditation on an ideal partner begins in earnest in the subtle creation stage, where it serves to arouse sexual bliss as a basis for contemplating the emptiness of touch in the co-called *vajra* offering. The explicitly sexual nature of this practice is clear in its five stages mentioned below:

1. Envisioning a seminal drop at the tip of the male partner's *vajra* or *phallus*, dwelling within the lotus or vagina (*Bhaga*) of the female;
2. Imagining sexual intercourse and drawing the orgasmic release into the whole body to 'satisfy' all the archetypes of the body *mandala*;
3. Inscribing a microcosmic *mandala* complete with all 32 archetypes within the drop that has been released into the partner's womb;
4. Withdrawing those archetypes, one by one, up the *vajra* through the central channel to the heart, from where they emanate, one by one in all directions benefiting all living beings then returning to the heart; and
5. Converting those archetypes into seed *mantras* that circle the heart, then reciting them while envisioning that they radiates archetypes that travel out on exhalation, benefit beings and coalesce back into the *mantra* circle on the heart on inspiration.

Concluding Remarks

What we mean by Buddhism today is not the essence or fundamentals of this new doctrine, but a religio-philosophical system "which assimilated and adopted new ideas and beliefs from the environment in which it developed."[12] In the course of centuries, after the demise of its founder Buddhism underwent so many changes and "included within its fold so many thoughts that the original words of the Master became changed beyond recognition."[13] The history of Buddhism is the history of developments, schisms, corruptions and reforms which the system underwent as it spread all over India and beyond, and it became accepted and reinterpreted by the most diverse cultures of Asia. While reaching in Tibet, China, Ceylon, Indonesia, and Colombia etc., it lost the original concept and adopted various modifications and different interpretation. Even the advent of *Vajrayana* as well as *Mantrayana* schools that have been discussed separately in this book, made Buddhism a subject of practice having combination of wine, intoxication, women and sexual intercourse. The picture that emerged in Tibet *Vajrayana* and *Mantrayana* damaged the sanctity of early Buddhism. The practice of *Mantrayana* where union of male and female was openly allowed that also under the influence of intoxication created hatred among many of the people. Such practice damaged good spirit of Buddhism. Practice of *Tantrayana* or *Vajrayana* prevailed in Buddhism but the essence and method were different. The ladies were sexless in imagination representing the great force of the creation. She was treated as the symbol of *Sunyata* where everything merges ultimately having no existence. But the Tibetan cult of *Mantrayana* paved the way for the growth of corruption inviting many to participate and enjoy. Since the method was very much difficult and esoteric, it was difficult and tough for many practitioners to remain confined to the goal for which it was practiced.

During the life time of the Buddha, there was no conflict and controversy. Though he did not present any written document related to his teaching, his words remained as master piece to understand Buddhism and its interpretation. His followers during his life time spread what their master told them. After his demise, disputes arose in the matter of interpretations of the words of the Master "leading to the emergence of as many as eighteen sects even before the time of Ashoka. Actual dissentions, however, took place in the *Sangha* in the Second council at Vaisali when the dissenters refused to regard all *Arhtas* as perfect. Thereafter sects after sects appeared".[14]

The conflicts between the Mahayanist (Theravadians) and the Hinayanists went on increasing for superiority of their thoughts and thanking. In due course of time, the former grew stronger and expanded more.

The *Lokotaravadins* and the sails of the *Mahasanghika* branch gave importance to the worship of *Caityas,* and defied Buddha as a super divine being. This action of the *Mahasanghika* led to the evolution of the Bodhisattva doctrine which attached much importance to the *paramitas.* The idea of the *Lokottaravadins* ultimately resulted in appearance of Mahayanism. *Mahayana* and *Hinayana* are two different Buddhist cult of thinking which developed after the demise of the Buddha. This all happened due to development of different schools of Buddhist thought. The Hinayanists are said to be upholders of the traditional and conventional interpretations of the words of the founder and are branded as conservatives and 'Hina' which means lower or lesser. The eighteen section mentioned above are essentially Hinayanic. However, they never liked to be called themselves as Hinayanists. The orthodox and conservative Buddhists are always mentioned as Theravadians. The Buddhist of Myanmar, Ceylon, Cambodia Thailand, etc., belong to the school of Theravada Buddhism, where as those of China, Japan, Mongolia, Tibet, etc., follow the ideals of *Mahayana*. Something more in detail has separately been discussed in the succeeding chapter of the book about the practice of *Mantrayana* and *Sahajayana*.

Notes and References

1. Quoted in Bapat, P.V., "Principal Schools and Sects of Buddhism", in Bapat, P.V., (Ed.) *25000 Years of Buddhism,* Ministry of Information and Broadcasting, Govt. of India, New Delhi, (sixth reprint), 1919, p. 86.
2. *Ibid.,* p. 87.
3. Records of the Western Countries, Vol. II, p. 1.
4. *Catuma-Sutta*. Also see *Majjhima-Sutta*, No. 67.
5. Quoted in Bapat, P.V., "Principal Schools and Sects of Buddhism", in Bapat, P.V., *(Ed) 25000 Years of Buddhism, op. cit.,* p. 92.

6. Watters, *On the Travels of Yuan Chwang*, Vol. II, p. 160, Kem Manual of Indian Buddhism, p. 4.
7. R. Kimura, *Introduction to the History of Early Buddhist School*, in Sir Asuthosh Mukherjee *Silver Jubilee* Vol. III, Oriental, pt 3, p. 126.
8. Biswanath Banerjee, "A Peep into Modern Buddhism", in Debvi Das Chatterjee, (ed.), *Homage to Bhikhu Jagdish*, Kasyap, Nav Nalanda Vihar, 1986, p. 25.
9. Joseph Liozzo, *Vajrayana Buddhism in Tibetan Perspective*, Colombia University Center for Buddhist Studies, New York. p. 31.
10. *Ibid.*
11. *Ibid.*
12. Biswanath Bannerjee, "A Peep into Modern Buddhism", in Debvi Das Chatterjee, (ed.), *Homage to Bhikhu Jagdish*, Kasyap, Nav Nalanda Vihar, 1986, p. 25.
13. *Ibid.*
14. *Ibid.*

6

Buddhist's Doctrines of *Sunyata* (Emptiness), *Karma* and Re-birth

Emptiness (*Sunyata*) is the key-concept of Buddhist philosophy, found in the ontology of *Mahayana* Buddhism. The phrase "form is emptiness, emptiness is form" is, perhaps, the most celebrated paradox associate with the Buddhist philosophy. It is the supreme *mantra*. The expression originates from the *Prajna Pramita Hirdaya Sutra*, communally known as the *Heart Sutra*. It contains the writing of philosophical essence in about six hundred scrolls that makes up the *Maha Prajna Pramita*. The *Heart Sutra* is the shortest text in this connection. It belongs to the oldest *Mahayana* texts and presumably originated in India around the time of Jesus Christ. This chapter thoroughly discusses about the Buddhist concept of *Sunyata* and critically examines its philosophical significance and also its relevance in the world of metaphysics.

Sunyata or emptiness means nor form, nor feeling, nor perception, nor impulse, nor consciousness, nor eyes, ears, nose tongue, body, and mind; nor form, sounds, smells, tastes, touches or object of mind; nor sight element, and so forth. There is nor ignorance, nor extinction of ignorance. There is neither decay nor death. There is nor extinction of decay and death. There is nor suffering, nor origination, nor stopping, nor path. There is nor cognition, nor attainment and non-attainment. In *sunyatc,* a Bodhisattva resides there because of his non-attainment through having relied on the perfection of wisdom. He dwells there without coverings. In the absence of thought, he does not tremble; he has overcome what can upset him; and in the end he attains to *nirvana.* Thus, it is clear that a Bodhisattva, while reaching to the stage of *sunyata* is not affected by any thought, any action, any thinking, any worldly essences and anything. He stands or lives without attachment. Things are around him, but to him it seems that there is nothing except himself. This is in the Buddhist term, in fact, a state of *nirvana* which means go above the attraction of the mundane world and its influences. *Nirvana* means to remain in absolute emptiness where there is nothing except all pervasive tranquility. All those who appear as Buddhas in the three periods of time, are fully awaken to the outmost, right and perfect enlightenment because they have relied on the 'Perfection of Wisdom.' Therefore, one should know the *prjnapramita* as the great spell, the spell of great knowledge the outmost spell, allayer of all suffering, in truth for what could go wrong.

The Perfection of Wisdom refers to the wisdom that directly and intuitively understands the ultimate nature of phenomena. The Bodhisattva knows that the "emptiness is form and form is emptiness." He has done away with views, ideas and perceptions and looks upon reality without any obstructions of mind. He is stable and firm. Bodhisattva, from the *Vedantic* point of view is a seer, who has reached to the stage of *Brahman* where there is no manifested world. If there is anything, it is perfect wisdom (supreme idea) from which manifestation emerges. It is, in fact, the primal source of creation and abode of complete annihilation of creation. Like Plato's absolute idealism the Buddhist *Sunyata* is the blank of space of origin and merger.

Sunyata (Voidness)

The philosophy of *Sunyata* is the product of the Buddhist school of *Madhyamika* that is related to *Mahayana*. This school was propounded by Nagarjuna in 2nd century AD He denied the real existence of the principal manifestations and categories of the empirical reality such as birth and destruction, causality, time, the sensorial activity, the elements that constitute man, passion and its subject, action and its agent, suffering, the consequences of actions (*karmas*), the reincarnation cycle, the ego, the Buddha, the saving truths taught by Buddha, the liberation from the reincarnation cycle (*Moksa)*, being and non-being etc. This school denies the true existence of the empirical reality in its totality. To the school of *Mahayana*, the empirical reality includes all beings and things. It is all an appearance, a phenomenon, which lacks a true existence, which is like a dream, a mirage, and an illusion, created by magic. In reality they have temporary existence. What they appear in reality is not reality. That is void. In the philosophy of *Vedanta* what manifestation or creation appears is nothing, but the product of *Maya* that itself is non-existing. Things that appear to be are illusions because they have no independent base. They are reflection of Divine energy like the rays of the sun. They are subjects of destruction. They appear for the time being and disappear into the primal cause. Thus, nothing is permanent.

The empirical reality is designated by the Madhayamika School with the name 'envelopment reality' or 'concealment reality. This is all because the empirical reality affectively envelops, conceals the true reality. Nagarjuna affirms the non-existence of the empirical reality because there is nothing in it that exist *in se et per se*. That, which has its existence to our sense organs, exists not as it is, but in the enveloped form. The real essence of existence is concealed. Everything in it is conditioned, relative, dependent and composed. The conditionality, relativity, dependence and the fact of being compose constitute the nature, the form and being of the empirical reality. The doctrine that developed in this relation is called *Pratityasamutvada* (dependent origination or universal relativity). This doctrine negates the empirical reality. There is true reality, but it is covered and concealed. To see that a different eye is needed that can be obtained through *sadhana* only prescribed in Buddhist philosophy. The same fact has been described in the Hindu religious scriptures. The *Bhagvad Gita* prescribes that no one can perceive the ultimate reality except those who have divine eyes; and to have divine eyes one must concentrate the truth through the methods prescribed for *Yoga*. *Yoga* is *sadhana*.

It is notable that the Madhayamika School neither affirms the universal reality nor rejects the real existence of the world in a dogmatic way. It has to establish and demonstrate its thesis against other philosophical and religious, Buddhist and non-Buddhist schools, which adopt realistic and absolutist position.

Emptiness and Nihilism

The western scholars who developed deep interest in the Buddhist philosophies regarded that the Buddhist concept of Emptiness is equivalent to the concept of nihilism, but it is not so. Both Emptiness and nihilism are different and they differ in their basic conception. What is nihilism? Nihilism is the branch of philosophy dealing with the transcendental concept of absolute reality concluding that there is no such absolute truth that exists somewhere. Since nothing definitely and confirmedly can be said about transcendental truth or absolute truth, it is futile to talk about it. According to it, ultimate reality, if there is anything like it, is unknowable. Their apprehension is that nothing exists like supreme reality, that nothing meaningful can be communicated about the transcendental world. Since the senses of human faculty is unable to comprehend such absolute truth (if it exists), it is all meaningless to talk about it and derive conclusion related to it. It is convenient to accept that there is nothing. So, nothingness is the basic concept of the nihilist philosophy regarding existence of God or ultimate truth. They are skeptical about this truth. On the other hand, the Buddhist philosophical concept of ultimate truth is quite opposite to that of nihilism. It thinks that ultimate reality is there and it is knowable. There is a clear-cut ontological basis for phenomena and that we can communicate and drive useful knowledge from it about the world. So, emptiness of Buddhism cannot be confused with nihilism. Emptiness is not non-existence and it is not non-reality. There is, in fact, 'something 'that exists permanently, but it is impossible to understand that 'something' because it stands or exists beyond the catch of human sensual organs.

Idealism and Buddhist's Concept of Emptiness

The philosophy of idealism propounded by Socrates and his disciple Plato believes that there is absolute idea that exists everywhere without any form. It is the basic cause of all material worlds. Idea that is abstract is imperishable and pure. It is the root cause of knowledge. The things whatsoever we see or perceive are reflection of supreme ideas. The essence has no inherent existence. It is not to be found in physical object. Essence is neither physical nor mental. It cannot be found in the world, not in the mind, and certainly not in any heavenly realms, as Plato imagined. A cup or a horse is there because the figure of the cup and the horse is in idea. If there is no idea, how the things may take the material shape. So, idea is primary and the matter is secondary. Idea is permanent but material things are changeable. Existence of material shape relies upon mental idea. So, the existence of metaphysical world or transcendental world cannot be denied. The Buddhist concept of emptiness is quite nearer to the ideal concept of reality. The Buddhists believe that reality is there but without any form. It is empty. To say that there is nothing which is not wise. Here emptiness does not mean nothingness but 'something' without form as an idea exists without form. In the emptiness, there is essence as there is wisdom in the idea. The essence of the emptiness, according to the Buddhist philosophy, exists in the mind whereas the idea, according to the idealist remains in soul. There is a body and mind in existence of mankind. In the mind there is sensation, feeling, cognition ideas etc. Analysis of the brain brings the fact to the light that there are nervous system, axons, synapses and neurotransmitters. However, none of these constituents describe the essence of the person, the mind, or the brain. The essence remains elusive. A cup containing nothing is apparently empty, but it still has 'something' inside. This 'something' is vague that cannot be explained in words.

The Buddha believed that the world is congregation of things and so body also. There is nothing that exists alone. Substances existing in different form cause creation. The *Heart Sutra* expresses the same idea by stating the 'emptiness' of the five *Sakandhas*, i.e., the emptiness of the body, sensations, perceptions, mental formations and consciousness. Aggregation of these five elements results into a body. When one talks about the essence of a person, it is related to five *skandhas*. We talk of experience. What is experience? In reality one experiences objects and phenomena through the senses. This is the one form of experience. One also experiences feelings, moods, thoughts, and emotions. The former can be called sensory experience and the latter mental experience. Upon contemplating the distinction one may find that there is no clear boundary between sensory and mental experience. As soon as one perceives a physical object, the corresponding mental experiences are immediately triggered. First one thinks 'apple'. This is identification. Following this thought, a number of things we associate with apples may come to mind, for example, 'sweet, edible, green, red, healthy, delicious, and juicy' and so on. These associations may be followed by the build-up of consuming the apple now or later. All these mental experiences are caused by, yet independent of the original object. If the apple is withdrawn, the memory of it may be able to sustain the chain of thoughts for a short time, yet it will eventually cease and there will be nothing except emptiness.

Inherent Existence

The *Mahayana* school of Buddhism developed the doctrine of 'dependent ordination' which means nothing is absolute alone. Existence either in physic or without physic is not alone. Something exists in combination of several elements. It may be inferred that mental experience requires sensory experience or respectively memory of sensory experience. Sensory experience in turn requires the body. If one carries through a thought experiment and examined whether each of the *skandhas* is able to exist without the other four, one finds that this is not possible. The latter four aggregates all depend on the body. Without the brain and the nerve system there is no consciousness, no sensation, nor perception and no mental formulations. On the other hand, we cannot imagine the body to function without the mind. The body and the mind depend upon each other. So, the five *skandhas* depend upon each other. That is congregation. It may be concluded that none of the *skandhas* is absolute or may stand alone.[1] Body, sensations;

perceptions, mental formation and consciousness are interrelated. Experiences emerge after the interaction of five *sakandhas* just as object, experience are conditioned by the inter play of multiple phenomena. Experience has no inherent existence either. The percept is the mental expression; the subject is the owner of it, the thinker; and the object is that which causes the mental impression. This three-fold divisions seem so natural to us that it reflected in the grammar of most human language. We perceive the separation of subject, percept and object as real, because mind attributes an owner to experience and thought. This owner is 'self', the subject, the centre of consciousness, the supposed psychological entity. Surprisingly, this identity remains completely undetectable. Body, feeling, precipitation and mental formation are not the self. Consciousness is not the self either, otherwise it would follow that the self-temporarily ceases to existence during unconsciousness, for instance during the deep sleep.

Is it true that self is independent of supporting the surrounding world? According to Buddhism, obviously it is not. The self cannot exist in mental vacuum, a world devoid of sense impressions, thought and mental images. It seems there is no basis of an independent entity. It seems more that the self is an emergent phenomenon arising from the application of complex interpretative schemes to perception. In particular, it arises from the conceptual division between subject, object and percept. Through introspection it is possible to realise that the 'self' is not fundamental. It is created by the mind through identification and discernment. The 'self is itself a mental formation—a product of mind. It is therefore, empty of inherent existence.[2]

The Emptiness of Matter

In ancient Greece it prevailed that matter is composed of indivisible small elements with certain characteristics such as, the characteristics of earth, water, air, and fire. The Greek philosophers called these elements atoms and they held that atoms are solid and fundamental, like microscopic billiard walls. It was Earnest Rutherford, who invalidated the billiard ball theory by conducting an experiment, which represented that atoms have an internal structure. He established that an atom has a nucleus containing most of its mass and the electrons orbit of the nucleus. He further established that the nucleus of an atom is only about one-ten-thousandth of the diameter of the nucleus itself which means that 99 per cent of the atoms volume consists of empty space. This is the first manifestation of emptiness at the subtle level of matter. Not long after Rutherfold's discovery related to atom, physicists found that the nucleus of an atom likewise has an internal structure and that the protons and neutrons making up the nucleus are composed of even smaller particles, which they named quarks after a poem of James Joyce. Interestingly, quarks are hypothesised as geometrical points in space, which implied that atoms are essentially empty. This is the second manifestation of emptiness at the subtle level of matter.

The terms 'quark' and 'point in space' still suggest something solid, since they can be imagined as irreducible mass particles. Quantum field theory does away even with this finer concept of solidity by explaining atoms in the terms of field properties. Quantum Electrodynamics (QED) and experimental observation has produced an amasing successful theory of matter by combining quantum theory, classical field theory, and relativity. No discrepancies between the predictions of QED, sub-atomic particles are indistinguishable from fields, whereas fields are basically properties of space. In this view, a particle is a temporary local densification of a field, which is conditioned by the properties of the surrounding space ergo; matter is not different from space. This is the third manifestation of emptiness at the subtle level of matter.[3] It substantiates the Vedic philosophy as well as the perception of the idealistic view that mater is nothing but reflection of unseen or unmanifested energy of empty space.

Existential Character of Buddha's Philosophy

The root of the Buddha's theory of *Sunyata* or emptiness is rooted in the philosophy of existentialism. Hence, it is wise to have a cursory look over it. It is obvious that the Buddha's theory of emptiness or *sunyata* is the base of his philosophy. He did not believe that there is something or the identity that exists independently being the basic cause or fundamental cause of creation and its governor. Like Hindu's *Shankhya* philosophy he believed that things come out of great emptiness (*sunya*) and ultimately merge into it. The space that is boundless is void, but it is the origin place of all elements. When one makes a study of the Buddha's philosophy, its similarity with existentialism becomes clear. The modern existentialist attitude to philosophy is much related to the Buddha's philosophy of existentialism. The Buddha is concerned to the questions who created universe and whether there is God. The speculation in existence of God is irrelevant to the Buddha. Since he did not speculate about existence of God and soul, these questions have no meaning here. The existentialists believe that no amount of speculation has led philosophers to any conclusion so far as these questions are concerned. Plato, Aristotle, Locke, Berkeley, Hume, Descartes, Leibnitz, Kant, Hegel and host of other great philosophers have failed to find answers to these puzzling questions. They speculated but they never arrived at the uniformly accepted ultimate truth. They differed in their conclusions. These, in the words of Angraj Chaudhary, "remain arm-chair speculations, which have no bearing on and relevance to the immediate problems of mankind,"[4]

Like existentialists, the Buddha thought it wise to have his concerned with the human problems of the present life, not with the questions related to ideologies or idealism that have no definite answers to mysterious truth. The questions like whether the world is eternal or not, whether the world is an ending thing, or whether the life principle is the same as the body or different, whether the *Tathagata* is or not or both or neither after dying" are useless because they are "not calculated to profit; they are not concerned with the Norm" (*Dhamma*). They do not rebound even to the elements of right conduct, "nor to detachment, nor to purification from lusts, nor to quietude, nor to tranquilisation of heart, nor to real knowledge, nor to the insight nor to the *Nirvana*."[5] To the Buddha, the question that agitated his mind and heart was how to help man to get rid of sufferings that are constant in the world. He took all these ideal questions as absurd because these were irrelevant to man's real life in this world. So, he devoted his whole life to find out the ways to liberate mankind from the problems of sufferings and pains. He knew that man confronted by a large number of serious and immediate problems and the slightest negligence of which will spell out a catastrophic disaster unheard of in the history of human civilisation. To investigate into the transcendental world and look into the world of metaphysic was secondary to the Buddha. His consideration was totally confined to the world of existence.

The existentialists profoundly realised that the growth of industrial revolution and man's inclination towards material prosperity has alienated him not only from the family and social life but also from himself. So, existentialism appeared as a protest against "various forms of dehumanisation" that appeared as a result of "industrial technology, rationalism, materialism and objectivism." Like that the Buddha felt that the growth of ritualism and *Brahman*ism to avail material facilities by worshipping various gods and goddesses had made man the blind followers of blind religion deviating him from the real path of the human life. So, he propounded the religion based on scientific belief as well as a religion that could help man to get rid of existing problems of mankind forever. Existentialism, in fact, is an essentially a man-centered philosophy and individualistic one that emphasises human existence and its peculiar qualities more than the physical world. First is man, then anything is there. Nothing is above man.[6] Man is nothing else, but what he makes himself.[7] Sartre further says, "man is at the start a plan which is aware of itself, rather than a patch of moss, a piece of garbage, or a cauliflower; nothing exists prior to this plan, there is nothing in heaven; man will be what he will have planned to be."[8] Like that the Buddha said again and again that man is wholly responsible for what he does and is also equally responsible for what he becomes. Good and bad actions done by him produce their results which create his self.[9] His self therefore is created and caused by his own actions. According to him man is his own master.[10] Unlike Hindu philosophy, the Buddha thought that there is no fate; and if there is any fate, man himself is the creator of his own fate. Action produces results and it is man who does action.

According to the Hindu religious philosophy, man is bound

to perform prescribed action under the influence of three natural energies—*Sattvas*, *Rajhas* and *Tamsas*. That is prevalent everywhere in the nature including the human nature. The nature of each living being is the product of his past actions that are stored in his consciousness which remains alive even after his death. Consciousness, in fact, is the bed-rock of actions. The idea of actions emerges from consciousness which contains impression of good as well as bad impacts of one's past lives. In this regard, the *Bhagvad Gita* says:

None, verily, even for an instant, ever remains doing no action; for everyone is driven helpless to action by the energies born of nature. (*The Bhagvad Gita*, Discourse—III, 5)

It further says:

> Actions are wrought in all cases by the energies of Nature. He whose mind is deluded by egoism thinks 'I am the doer.' (*The Bhagvad Gita*, Discourse—III, 27)

Though apparently Buddhism is inclined to philosophies of existentialism, but inwardly they differ also. To the Buddha the self is related to the spiritual and individual principle, while latter's notion of self is related to social aspect. Moreover, the school of existentialism is mostly related to material society whereas the Buddhas thought has concerned with spiritualistic that ends with attainment of *nirvana*. Existentialists discard metaphysics while the Buddha adopted the middle way of spiritualism. Moreover, the Buddha finds the remedies of human sufferings in improvement of his individual thinking and actions towards right directions. He is not pessimistic. He did not believe in non-action or quietism. He believed that man could get rid of problems by himself provided he followed the path prescribed by him. He maintained that man has an infinite capacity to work out his own salvation. He can make himself what he wants to be. Devotion to God and prayer to Him are not certain to yield desired fruits, but actions on the right path certainly yield good fruits. The Buddha believed on this line. So, his emphasis had been on the problems that had been surrounded mankind from the beginning of creation. He wanted to correct the human actions first and then thinking. Without good conducts right thinking is not possible and without right thinking human problems cannot be resolved. No one may attain *Nirvana* until he or she behaves properly and thinks judiciously.

Madhayamika School and Dependent Origination (Universal Relativity)

The philosophical school of *Madhayamika* of *Mahayana* Buddhism denies the true existence of empirical reality in its totality. For this school, the empirical reality includes all beings and things. What appears is only an appearance, a phenomenon, which lacks a true existence, which is like a dream, a mirage, and an illusion, created by magic. Thus, it is quite near to the philosophy of non-dualism here. The great majority of the *Karakas* of the *Madhyamakasastra* composed by Nagarjuna (2nd century A.D.), the founder of the Madhayamika school, is festinated to deny the real existence of the principal manifestations and categories of the empirical reality: birth and destruction, causality, time, the sensorial activity, the elements that constitute man (*dharma*), the consciousness of actions, the reincarnation cycle, the ego, the Buddha, the Saving truth taught by Buddha, the liberation from there incarnations cycle (*moksha*) being and non-being etc., in the same way, a great part of intellectual activity of Nagarjuna's school had an identical aim.

The empirical reality is designated by the Madhayamika School with the name 'involvement reality' or 'concealment reality'. This is as an appropriate term because according to the Madhayamika conception, the empirical reality affectively envelops, conceals the true reality. (*pramarthasatya).*

Mahayana school is divided into two systems of thought—the *Madhayamika* and the *Yogacara*. It was called *Madhayamika* on laying emphasis on *Madhayama Pritipada* which means middle way. In his first sermon at Benars (Banaras) the Buddha preached the middle path. The school advocated neither for self-mortification nor a life devoted to the pleasures of the senses. But it is different from the middle path as advocated by the adherents of the *Madhayamika* system. It is the non-acceptance of the two views concerning existence and non-eternity, self and non-self and so on. In short, it advocated neither the theory of absolutism nor that of total unreality of the world, but merely relativity. It is, however, to be noted that the middle path propounded at Banaras had an ethical meaning while that of the *Madhayamika* is to be taken in the metaphysical sense.

The Madhayamika School is said to have originated with the teacher Nagarjuna in the second century A. D. It presents in a systematic manner the philosophy of the Madhayamika School. It teaches that *sunyata* (the indescribable absolute) is the Absolute. There is no difference between *samsara* (phenomenal world) and *nirvana* or *sunyata* (reality). *Sunyata* or the absolute corresponds to the *nirguna Brahman* of the *Upanishads*. In the invocation in verse at the beginning of the work, Nagarjuna gives the fundamentals of his philosophy in a nutshell. He describes Dependent Origination (*Pratitya-smputpada*) by means of eight negatives. There is neither origination nor cessation; neither permanence nor impermanence; neither unity nor diversity; neither coming-in nor going-out; in the law of *Pratitya-smputpada*. Essentially there is only non-origination which is equated with *sunyata*. Elsewhere he also states that *Pratitya-smputpada* is called *sunyata*. Hence *sunyata* referring as it does to non-origination is in reality the middle path which avoids two basic views of existence of things or a kind of relativity. Dr Radhakrishanan writes: "By *sunyata* therefore, the Madhayamika does not mean absolute non-being, but relative being."[11] The *Madhayamika* wing holds *sunyata* to be the central idea of its philosophy and is therefore designated *sunyatavada*. The *Madhyamika-karika* further deals with two kinds of truths: *samvrti* (conventional or empirical truth) and *paramartha* (higher or transcendental truth). The former refer to ignorance or delusion which envelops reality and gives a false impression, while the latter is the realisation that worldly things are non-existent like an illusion or echo. Transcendental truth (*Pramartha–satya*) cannot be attained without restoring to *smavrti–satya* (conventional truth). *Samvrti-satya* is only a means while *Pramarth-satya* is the end. Thus, viewed from the relative standpoint, *Pratitya-samputpada* explains worldly phenomena, but looked at from the absolute standpoint (*paramartha*). It means non-origination at all times and is equated with *nirvana* or *sunyata*.

Nagarjuna affirms the non-existence of the empirical reality because there is nothing in it that exist *in se et per se*. Every existence has its conditions. Nothing is purely independent. Existence of a being or a thing depends upon other things. So, existence is relative, dependent and composed. The conditionality, relativity, dependence and the fact of being composed, constitute the nature, the form and being of the empirical reality. The empirical reality exists so long as its constituent parts exist together. The term *pratitya-samutpada* literary means 'dependent origination' and Stcherbatsky translates it as pertinently by 'universal relativity' designates that nature is a form of beings. And it is this characteristic which allows the negation of the empirical reality by the dialect of Nagarjuna's school. To make it more obvious, it may be said that, according to Nagarjuna, what exists to our experience is temporary existence or existence in concealment. The term concealment denotes various contemporary elements supporting existence of a thing. As soon as the supporting elements disperse, the thing disappears or the existence of the thing goes away. If the empirical reality were composed by substances or if an ultimate substance was its essence and fundamental, the abolishing analysis, practiced by the Madhayamika School, would stop, frustrated, before that unshakable basis.

The Madhayamika School does not affirm the universal relativity and does not deny the real existence of the world in a dogmatic way. It has to establish and demonstrate its thesis against other philosophical and religious. Buddhist and non-Buddhist schools, which adopt realistic and absolutist positions. Its problem is neither to discard the theory of absolutism in totality nor to support it fully, but to express it in a different way. And it is that different way which came to be known as the doctrine of dependent origination (*sunyata*). The thesis that is developed by the followers of the Madhayamika School, in fact, relies upon the philosophy propounded by the early Buddha, but its presentation is in different manner. The school uses reasoning and logical argument. The arguments developed by the *Madhayamika* thinkers to defend their own negative conception and to destroy contrary thesis are contained specially in the great commentaries that accompany the works of

Nagarjuna and of other masters that followed him among those commentaries. It is necessary to mention the most valuable commentaries of Candrakriti on Nagarjuna's *Madhayamika-sastra*. This commentary reveals the parallel use of Buddha's word and logic. Generally the great masters of the *Madhayamika* school, like Aryadeva, Buddhapalita, Candrakriti, Santidev, Prajanakaramati, who were faithful to the school founder, adopt the *prasangika* or *reductio ad absurdum* method. They do not adduce arguments of their own invention. They limit themselves to show the contradictory and absurd consciousness that derive from the thesis and arguments of the rival schools. For instance, if one of these schools affirms the real origination of beings and things, the *Madhayamika* will indicate that, in that case, origination should be either out of one self or out of another or without any cause, and will show that all these alternatives are logically impossible, implying for that aim, as basic principles of his own argumentation, the adversary's to his own principles.[12]

The Madhayamika School utilises the analysis of the empirical reality in order to get results which destroy the rival doctrines and which found its own world conception. The treaties *Hataralandmapraakarna*, Karakas and commentary, give us an example of this procedure. The author investigates the empirical reality and finds that it is composed only by entities which, on being analysed, happened to be mere appearances after appearances, which cover or conceal other entities and so on. The process of concealment of entities continues till it comes to *sunyata* or the final cover that is too subtle to further analyse. It has already been stated that an atom which is the smallest non-visible or microscopic particle contains electron and proton in its nucleus where there is 99.99 empty spaces or *sunya*. So, finally there is no reality except *sunya.* All beings or things come out from this *sunya* and ultimately merge into this *sunya.* So, ultimate result is void.

Thus, the true reality in the Madhayamika School is concealed by empirical reality. That reality is completely outside the pale of human world and human thought, and it is absolutely 'heterogeneous'. Nevertheless, in order to speak about true reality, when it is expressed in words and ideas, present itself under a deformed image, because it is submitted necessarily to the categories of space, time, cause, existence, non-existence, unity, multiplicity, etc., that belong to empirical reality and have nothing to do with true reality. It is necessary always to have in mind this unavoidable deformation of true reality, as it is understood by Nagarjuna when he speaks about it.

The True Reality Comes Forth through the Abolition of Empirical Reality

Madhayamika School denies the real existence of empirical reality because it is neither independent nor stable. The elements that constitute a being are different and united for the time being. As soon as they disperse due to any reason the reality that stands also disperse. So, where is the real reality? What appears or belong to the empirical reality is only an apparent 'phantasmagoric' and inconsistent existence. As a result of the abolishing process realised by Nagarjuna's school there remains 'something' completely different from the empirical manifestations, categories and characteristics. This so-called 'something' that remains after the abolishing of analysis is outside the concept of being and non-being. It means that that is void and about which neither anything can be imagined nor explained. If somebody attributes to this 'something' any characteristics that belong to empirical reality, Nagarjun's disciple would apply the same destructive dialectic that he applied before, in an analytical and abolishing process which never finds an ultimate, autonomous reality, truly existing. That 'something' that remains as 'residue' of the total negation of empirical reality, in which there is nothing that belongs to it and which cannot be either grasped by the mind or expressed by the word. So, that 'something' is the true reality and also the true nature of empirical reality. This notion of Madhayamika School resembles to the Vedic view related to Absolute reality that is "*na iti, na iti...*" (This is not, this is not). Thus, the Madhayamika School designates true reality as *sunyata,* voidness, *sunya*, void etc. They are simple metaphors, perhaps the most appropriate to indicate the 'residue' that remains after the abolition of empirical reality—a 'residue' that neither it was nor it is, and referring to which nothing can be thought, nothing can be said. That is why the Buddha remained always silent whenever he was asked explaining about God or Absolute Reality. Silence is the only explanation of Absolute Truth.

Sunyata and the Divine and the Sacred

The *Sunyata* refuses the notion of divine and sacred. It is all because those are notions that belong exclusively to empirical reality. It also refuses notions that belong to the same level. However, it does not mean at all that the divine and sacred are absent from Madhayamika Buddhism. Buddhas and Bodhisattvas are their most respectable and honourable coins. Buddhas and Bodhisattvas are divine because they are symbol of wisdom and purity.

One of the causes which contribute the most to render difficult understanding of the *sunyata* doctrine of Buddhism is the application of the word 'absolute' to designate it. Rigorously it is licit to designate the *sunyata* with the expression 'the absolute', but only so far as the *sunyata* is totally something different from empirical reality. However, the expression 'the absolute' represents the outmost degree of abstraction and of elimination of intellectual connotations. It is loaded with religious shades and resonance. To designate the *sunyata* as 'the absolute' exposes one to the danger of transporting it, unconsciously, to the religious level, of defying it, of giving it a sacred status. The *sunyata* can be equated with the term 'absolute', if one does not forget that it indeed is an 'Absolute', but an absolute that has in itself nothing of divinity, is a completely unsacred absolute.[13]

The Buddhist theory of *Sunyata* propounded by the school of Madhayamika constitutes the most radical and rigorous conception, elaborated in India, of an absolute in all fullness of the world, without any concession to the religious feeling of man or to his religious needs. *Brahman*, the absolute imagined by the *Vedanta*, in the most decorated form which gives us the non-dualistic *Vedanta*, admits in itself the notion of 'being', 'consciousness', 'blissfulness', and even of 'divine' and 'sacred'. The *Vedanta*'s notion of absolute *Brahman* falsifies other existence, no doubt, but it confirms the final reality. According to it, the Absolute *Brahman*, though having no form, is the final cause of creation of the universe. The creation is the manifestation of that absolute power. But in the case of Nagarjuna's conception of *Sunyata,* there is either full negation of such power or complete denial of any powerful form except complete void or emptiness. The *nirvana* in the Buddhist concept is to rise above all feelings thinking, consciousness, activities, involvement, etc. In other words, to reach *nirvana* means to merge completely into *sunyata* where there is nothing; neither feeling nor sensation; neither intelligence nor consciousness; neither coming-in nor going-out; neither existing nor non-existing; neither experience nor non-experience. However, it is not nothingness at all. There is 'something' and that 'something' is beyond human understanding and indescribable. The Buddhism in this sense approaches the non-theist *Samkhya* which considers that the *Purusa* (individual spiritual principle), the only absolute that this school accepts, has nothing in itself of divinity. In the words of Tola and Dragonetti:

> While constructing his notion of *Sunyata*, Nagarjuna reveals not only a remarkable intellectual rigour, as he presents the *Sunyata* deprived of any element that does not accord with the most extreme abstraction, but also reveals no less remarkable audacity. His abolishing analysis of the empirical reality does not limit itself to the common being and things of the world; it attacks also, with the same severity, the most valuable and respectable beliefs and doctrines of the Buddhist church to which he and his school belongs. With the same implacable logic and in the same way in which Nagarjuna denies movement, birth and destruction, etc., he denies also Buddha's person, his teachings, the action that enchains one to the reincarnation's cycle, the reincarnations themselves and the liberation (*moksha).*[14]

Lastly, it may be said that the Nagarjuna's doctrine of *Sunyata* neither rejects the theory of Absolute truth in totality nor approves the absolute reality. It follows the middle path which means it affirms like nihilists, that there is nothing in the last resort of reality on the one hand, and agrees to the *Vedantic* view that what ultimately exists that is beyond our reach because human wisdom or sensory organs can never apprehend that. The microscopic analysis and observation of existing reality brings one to the conclusion that what we talk of reality is concealed or dependent because of its association or covering with constituent elements. When these are analytically separated, nothing is left to be analysed because either our sensory organs are not in a position to penetrate into that subtlety or there is nothing to be examined or analysed further. So, the doctrine of *sunayata* comes closer to the *Vedantic* philosophy that there exists *Mahasunya* having no limit. The state of *Mahasunya* is the final abode of beings and non-beings to emerge and merge or to manifest and defuse. Nagarjuna arrives to this conclusion through logical conviction, not through intuitive knowledge. So, his doctrine of *sunyata* is more logical and empirical. His approach is scientific and pragmatic.

Doctrine of *Karma*

The concept of *karma* and rebirth is very much common in the Hindu religious scriptures. *Karma* means action, the activity which keeps man engaged throughout the life. *Karma* is the means to avail what one wants. It is the means to reach near the goal and get it. Nothing happens in the world without activity. Every creature in this world is bound to perform duties. Doing right *karma* one may avail the heavenly pleasure on the one hand, if *karma* is performed falling into the trap of lust, greed and wrong desires, it will propel him towards hell where there is darkness, pain and troubles. *Karma* is constant in the heart of every creature. No one can escape from *karma*. Describing the nature of *karma* the *Bhagvad Gita* states:

na hi kascit ksanam api
jatu tisthaty akarma-ket
karyate hy avasah karma
sarvah prakrit-jair gunaih

"Everyone is forced act helplessly according to the qualities he has acquired from the modes of material nature; therefore no one can refrain from doing something, not even for a moment." (*Bhagvad Gita,* Chapter 3, Verse 5.)

Thus, it is evident that one is bound to perform *karma* as per one's nature, and the nature is the product of his *sanskara* that itself is the product of the essence of past performances done in the past life. The circle of birth and death is endless and it continues till one avails *nirvana* or *moksha*. It is *sanskara* or nature that tempts one to do this or that with the intention to get the desired fruits. So, the root of the nature of beings is strongly rooted in their hearts. They are born with the marked purpose to achieve and enjoy what they failed to achieve and enjoy in the past life. Since the lust and desire are endless, the circle of birth and *karma* continues. Both Hinduism and Buddhism suggest to get rid of the circle of birth and death through availing *nirvana* or *moksha*. *Nirvana* is only possible when all desires are dropped for ever. The Hindu religious scriptures provide various ways and means to avail *moksha* such as through *Karma-yoga*, *Janan-yoga*, *Dhyana-yoga* and *Bhakti-yoga* while Buddhism prescribes attainment of *nirvana* through correcting vision, thinking, action, doing *sadhana* and *Samadhi*. The Buddha propounded Four Noble Truths and Eight-fold Noble Path that help one to achieve *nirvana*. In both ways until *karma* is reformed and performed in right direction suppressing or eradicating selfish wills, desires etc., it is impossible to get *nirvana*. So, *karma* has great significance in human life. Man has reasoning capacity. Reason situated in the inner-most part of the heart is light that has been covered by lust, greed, desire, hatred, jealousy, selfishness, violence etc. Until these covers which have darkened and enveloped the reason are removed, one will continue to perform in darkness resulting in harmful consequences to both the performer and the society. Buddhists call this right consciousness while the Hindu's religious scriptures name it soul. So, *nirvana* or *moksha* means to release consciousness or soul from the captivity of ignorance.

All living-beings are alike and yet amongst all the living-beings there are many differences. For instance, some are wealthy, some are less wealthy, some are strong and healthy, others are weak and suffering from vital diseases, some are wise; some are fools and so on. These differences may be marked among other living-beings like birds, animals, insects etc. They all differ in their nature and quality. Even among the fauna and flora one may easily discern differences in their qualities and utilities. These differences are due to *karma*. What we share desire, ill-will and ignorance— are common to all living beings, but the particular condition in which we find ourselves is the result of our particular *karma* that conditions the situation in which we may be healthy, rich and so forth. These circumstances are decided by *karma*. It is in this sense that *karma* explains the differences amongst living beings. It explains why some beings are fortunate while others are less fortunate. Why some are born with silver spoon in their mouth while some are born in the poor family having not even essential requirements to support life. The Buddha has specifically stated that *karma* explains the differences between living being. Good *karma* creates good circumstances and bad *karma* creates bad circumstances in the present life and contains the seeds of goodness and badness for the future life also. Not only Buddhism but all religions put emphasis on performance of good *karma* and avoid bad *karma*. A good *karma* is good to both the performer and the society while a bad *karma* is injurious and harmful to him and others.

Law of Karma

Karma has its own laws. Each and every action is bound to yield fruits; everyone is bound to eat the fruits produced by his own *karma*. The essence of *karma* does not die; it remains active somewhere in the heart (conciseness). *Karma* yields fruits when it is ripen. So, it is said that one has to harvest what he sows. There is the theory of *Karma-vipaka* or *karma-fala* that is intentional action and its fruits. In the most basic sense the law of *karma* in the moral sphere teaches that the similar action will lead to similar result. If one plants a mango seed, the plant that springs up will be a mango fruit. In the law of *karma* if one does wholesome action, eventually he will get a wholesome fruit, and if one does an unwholesome action, eventually he will get an unwholesome, painful result. It is what we mean and we say that causes bring about effects that are similar to the causes.

Buddhism talks of two varieties of *karma kushala* and *akushala*. The former means intelligent or skilful. This helps us to understand how these terms are being used, not in terms of good and evil, but in terms of skilful and unskillful. In terms of intelligent and unintelligent, in terms of wholesome and unwholesome. *Karma* is wholesome in the sense that those actions which are beneficial to oneself and others, those actions that spring not out of desire, ill-will and ignorance, but out of renunciation, loving kindness and compassion and wisdom. The *Bhagvad Gita* states that the action which is done to fulfill personal desires coming out of greed and lust bind one, but if the *karma* is performed being detached from the fruits and in the interest of the whole society, does not bind the performer. It is said:

Jneyah sa nitya-sanyasi
Yo na dvesti na kankasati
Nirdvandvo hi maaha-bhava
Sukham bandhat pramucyte

(*Bhagvad Gita,* Chapter 5, Verse 3)

"One who neither hates nor desires the fruits of his activities is known to be always renounced. Such a person, free from all dualities, easily overcomes material bondage and is completely liberated, O mighty-armed Arjuna."

It is further said:

Brahmany adhyaya karmani
Sangam tyaktva kariti yah
Lipyate na so papena
Padma-patramevambhasa

(*Bhagvad Gita,* Chapter 5, *Verse 10*)

"One who performs his duty without attachment, surrendering the results unto the Supreme Lord, is unaffected by sinful action, as the lotus leaf is untouched by water."

Thus, it is crystal clear that the action that is performed without any lust or attachment in the interest of others does not bind one. Even a dirty or evil action is performed with the purpose to help others is pious because it is done to help others. Lord Buddha fully understood the meaning of action. So, he recommended good actions devoid of selflessness. He taught people morality that is related to goodness. He suggested the followers to be away from desire, lust, hatred, violence, theft, robbery, telling lie etc., and always act in the interest of the society. A wise-man is he who understands effects of *karma* and performs good *karma* that is *kushala*.

The Buddha says, so long as an unwholesome action does not bear it fruits of suffering, a foolish person will consider that action good. But when that unwholesome action bears its fruits of suffering then he will realise that the action is unwholesome. Similarly, so long as a wholesome action does not bear its fruits of happiness, a good person may consider that action unwholesome. When it bears the fruits of happiness, then he will realise that action is good. So, one needs to judge wholesome and unwholesome action from the point of view of long-term effect. Some action bears fruits immediately while some action takes time. Action bears fruits even in the coming life.

The unwholesome actions which are to be avoided relate to the three doors or action, and these are body, speech and mind. The three unwholesome actions that are to be avoided are killing, stealing and sexual misconduct. These are related to the body. The four unwholesome actions related to speech which are to be avoided are lying, slander, harsh speech and malicious gossip. The three unwholesome actions of mind which are to be avoided are greed, anger and delusion. By avoiding these ten unwholesome actions one will avoid one's consciousness. The fruit of these unwholesome actions can take various forms. The fully ripen fruits of the unwholesome actions consists of rebirth in the lower realms, in the realms of suffering hell, hungry ghosts and animals. If these unwholesome actions are not sufficient to result in rebirth in these lower realms, they will result in unhappiness in this life as a human being. The fruits of actions results in similar action. If one commits murder to someone angrily, in the next life he would also be killed by the murdered person. If the murder has been committed unknowingly, the murderer shall have to be deprived of his nearest relatives in the next life. Generous action results in wealth and prosperity. Hearing of the *Dhamma* results in wisdom.

Kinds of *Karma* and its Fruition

Karma, be it wholesome or unwholesome, is modified by the conditions under which the actions are performed. In other words, a wholesome action or unwholesome action may be more or less strong depending upon the conditions under which it is done. The conditions which determine the weight or strength of *karma* may be divided into those which refer to the object—the being to whom the action is done. So, the conditions that determine the weight of *karma* apply to the subject and object of the action. If we take the example of killing, in order for the act of killing to have its complete and unmitigated power, five conditions must be present—a living being, the unawareness of the existence of a living being, the intention to kill the living being, and the consequent death of the living being. The subjective conditions are the awareness of the living being, the intention to kill and the action of killing. The objective conditions are the presence of the living being and the consequent death of the living being. There are five conditions that modify the weight of *karma* and they are persistent, repeated action, action done with great intention and determination, action done without regret, action done towards those who possess extraordinary qualities, and action done towards those who have benefitted one in the past.

The effects of *karma* may be evident either in the short-term or in the long-term. *Karma* may be divided into three varieties related to the amount of time that is required for the effects of these actions to manifest themselves. *Karma* can either manifest its effect in this very life or in the next life or only after several lives. When *karma* manifests its effects in this life, we can see the fruit of *karma* within a relatively a short length of time. This variety of *karma* is easily verifiable by common persons. For instance, when someone refuses to study, when someone indulges in harmful destructions like consuming alcohols and drugs, when someone starts stealing to support his harmful habits, the effect will be evident within a short time. One cannot see the long-term effect of *karma* but the Buddha and his prominent disciples who have developed their minds are able to perceive directly the long-term effect. For instance, when Maudgalyayam was beaten to death by bandits, the Buddha was able to tell that this incident was the effect of something Maudgalyayam had done in a previous life when he had taken his aged parents to the forest and having beaten them to death. The effect of this unwholesome action done by many lives before was manifested only in his last life. *Karma* accompanies like a shadow. The Buddha had said that nowhere on earth or in heaven can one escape one's *karma*. So, when the conditions are appropriate, dependent upon mind and body, the effects of *karma* will manifest themselves automatically. This is the law of *karma*.

Besides the two varieties of *karma*, wholesome and unwholesome, there are neutral and ineffective *karma* also. Neutral *karma* is *karma* that has no moral consequences either because the very nature of the action is such as to have no moral consequences or because it is done involuntarily and unintentionally. For instance, sleeping, walking, breathing, eating, handcraft or so forth in them has no moral consequences. Similarly, unintentional action is ineffective *karma*. In other words, if one accidently steps on an insect, being unconscious of its existence, this also constitutes neutral *karma* because there is no intention or intentional element is not there.

Philosophy Behind Rebirth

The philosophy of rebirth is as old as our civilisation. Almost all the major religions of the world talk of rebirth and teach people to get rid of the circle of births. In fact, the concept of *nirvana* or *moksha* is related to birth and rebirth. In the universe every creature is born, it grows, flourishes and ultimately dies. There is no one on the earth who can escape birth or rebirth. According to the Hindu philosophy life is continuation. It never ceases because it is related to immortal soul. Life appears and disappears with death and birth respectively. It is a vital concern of all beings. Life is energy which enables one to live and act. It is a journey which has to pass through several milestones. It is consciousness through which one thinks, decides and acts. Life is the base of body, mind, consciousness and what not. It is the life that takes birth after each and every death. It is said that there are three bodies physical, subtle, and causal. After the decay of physical body, other two bodies remain in existence containing the essence of *karma*. Desires which are unfulfilled in the present life follow after death and cause rebirth.

Rebirth cannot be confirmed scientifically. There is no convincing scientific theory to prove rebirth. So, it is totally a faith. All religions talk about rebirth or cycle of rebirth. Buddhism, too, has strong belief in rebirth. The Buddha while attaining his enlightenment came to know about his past lives. He remembered even the names of his past lives. Like him some of his prominent disciples, like Aanda, remembered their past lives. There is enough literature that talks of past lives. However, nothing is there to convince scientifically or rationally about rebirth. Some discoveries have been made in this regard. Psychologist and parapsychologists have also made various investigations about rebirth. These investigations confirm rebirth. So, the belief regarding rebirth is very much common. One scholar who has been particularly active in this area in recent years is Professor Ian Stevenson of the University of Virginia in USA. He has published findings on more than twenty cases of rebirth. There are persons who have the memory related to their past lives. For instance, Bridey Murphy narrated her memory of past life in a country which she had never visited in the present life. All these investigations and expressions of rebirth by different persons make the belief of rebirth stronger today. However, there are many who do not have any faith in rebirth.

In Hinduisms, rebirth is a cycle that continues ceaselessly. Physics change or disappear, not soul because it is permanent having no shape. One who is in the cycle of rebirth dies and takes birth again and again in different bodies according to one's past *karmas*. The Hindu religious scripture talk of the kinds or varieties of creatures which are divided into eighty-four thousands. A *jiva* (living being) has to travel in these kinds of life according to his/her performances of the life. One gets the body as per one's own *karma*. The human form is the most prominent type of body because one may avail enlightenment or *moksha* only in this life getting permanent relief from the cycle of death and rebirth. In Buddhism, rebirth is part of the continuous process of change. In fact, we are not only reborn at the time of death; we are born and reborn at every moment. This too, like many other Buddhist teaching, is easily verifiable by references to our own experience and by reference to the teaching of science. For instance, the majority of cells in the human body die and are replaced many times during the course of one's life. Cells die and reborn and the process continues. Even in our mental process memories, knowledge appears, reappears, and disappears moment by moment. That means these memories and experience take birth, die and reborn. Buddhism teaches that there are various realms, spheres or dimensions of existence. There are thirty one planes of existence. The six realms are very important. These may be divided into two groups, one of which is relatively fortunate and the other relatively miserable. The first group includes three of the six realms and they are the realms of the gods the realm of the demi-gods and the realm of human beings. Rebirth in these fortunate realms is the result of wholesome *karma*. The second group includes the three realms that are called the realm of woe and they are the realms of animals, the realms of hungry ghosts and the realm of hell beings. Rebirth in these states of woe is the result of unwholesome *karma*.

The Buddhist theory of rebirth is much similar to that of Hindu *Dharma* that talks of various kinds of births taking place accordance with *karma*. Those who do good *karma* are entitles to get higher realm of rebirth including the realms of gods, semi-gods, *gandharvas*, etc., who enjoy heavenly pleasures. On the other hand, those who are constantly engaged in bad *karma* go to hell after death and suffer a lot. Good *karma* and bad *karma* represent the notion of *punya* and *papa* (sin) in the Hindu *Dharma*. When the essence of good *karma* is over, one takes rebirth enjoying equally good life. Thus, the theory of Hindu *Dharma* related to rebirth is based on performance of *dharma* which means duties.

Like Hinduism, Buddhism also talks of various kinds of hells. The hungry ghosts suffer chiefly from hunger and thirst and also from heat and cold. They are completely bereft of the subjects of their desire. It is said that when the hungry ghosts perceive a mountain of rice or a river of fresh water, and rush towards that vision, they find the mountain of rice is only a heap of pebbles, and the river of fresh water only a river of ribbon of blue. Similarly, it is said that in the summer even the moon is hot, while in the winter even the sun is cold for them. The foremost cause of rebirth as a hungry ghost is avarice and miserliness born of greed. As with the hells the beings in this realm are not condemned to eternal existence in the form of hungry ghosts, for when their unwholesome *karma* is exhausted, they will be reborn in a higher realm.

Again, in the realm of animals (*Tiryak*) the living beings suffer from a variety of unhappy circumstances. They suffer from the fear and pain that is the result of constantly killing and eating one another. They suffer from the depredation of man who kills them for food or for their hides, horns or teeth. Even if they are not killed, domestic animals are forced to work for man and are driven on by hooks and whips. All these are a source of suffering. The principal cause of rebirth as an animal is ignorance. In other words, the blind, heedless pursuit of one's animal like desires, their occupation with eating, sleeping and sexual desire and the disregard of developing one's mind to the practice of virtue and so forth lead one to be reborn as an anaemia. There is a relationship between hatred and rebirth in the hells, and between greed and rebirth in the realm of hungry ghosts, and between ignorance and rebirth in the realm of the animals.

Buddhism talks about demi-gods (*Asuras*) who are more powerful physically and are more intelligent mentally than human beings. Yet they suffer because of jealousy and conflict. Mythologically, it is said that the *Asuras* and gods share a celestial tree, the former are custodians of the roots of the tree. They are envious of gods and constantly attempts to take the fruits of the tree from gods. As a result of this, they fight with the gods, and are defeated by the gods and suffer greatly as a consequence. Because of this constant jealousy, envy and conflict, existence amongst the *Asusras* is unhappy and unfortunate. As with the other realms, there is a cause of rebirth amongst the demi-gods. On the positive side, the cause is generosity. On the negative side, the causes are anger, envy and jealousy.

The sixth realm that is the realm of gods (*Devas*) is the happiest amongst the six realms. As a result of having done wholesome actions, of having observed the moral precepts and having practiced meditation, living beings are reborn amongst the gods where they enjoy sensual pleasure or spiritual pleasure, or tranquility depending upon the level within the realm of the gods in which they are born. Nonetheless, the realm of the gods is not to be desired because the happiness of the gods is impermanent. No matter how much they may enjoy having their existence as a god, when the deposit of their *karma* is exhausted, when the merits of their good conduct and the power of their experience in meditation are exhausted, the gods fall from heaven and are reborn in another realm. This moment, at the moment of their death, it is said that gods suffer even more mental anguishes than the physical pain suffered by beings in the other realms. The negative factor associated with birth in the realm of gods is pride. Confirming about the fate of deluded and misguided people, *the Bhagvad Gita* declares:

These cruel haters, worst of men, I hurl these evil-doers forever in the worlds into the wombs of the demons only. Entering into demoniac wombs, the deluded ones, in birth after birth without ever reaching Me, O son of Kunti, pass into a condition still lower than that. *Bhagvad Gita*, Discourse XVI, Verse 19-20)

Significance of Human Life

The notable fact is that no beings want to be reborn in the lower realms where there is nothing except acute sufferings and scarcities. But their *karmas* either knowingly or unknowingly are such that they have to face the fruits of actions. Secondly, their staying in a particular realm is not permanent. They get release from the existing realm by the mercy of God and they are given chance to be born in the realm of human beings so that they may get permanent release from the circle of rebirth by performing meditation and obtaining real knowledge or realising absolute truth. Even gods or semi-gods have to be reborn. The status of their pleasure and happiness is impermanent. They come down. They enjoy heavenly life so long the essence of their good *karmas* is in deposit. Thirdly, except the realm of human being, in both the lower and upper realm the beings have to either suffer or enjoy. They cannot perform actions because they have no physical body. To come out from the ceaseless circle of death and birth depends upon meditation and attainment of enlightenment.

The human realm is the most favoured of the six realms because as a human being one has the motivation and the opportunity to practice the *Dharma* and to achieve enlightenment. One has this motivation and opportunity because the conditions conducive to practicing the path are present. In the human realm, one experiences both happiness and suffering. The suffering in this realm, though terrible, is not as great as the suffering in the three realms of woe. The pleasure and happiness experienced in the human realm is not so great as the pleasure and happiness experienced in the heavens. Human being has sufficient intelligence to understand reality. They have been given light (*Budhi*) in their heart to know what is right and what is wrong. Moreover, they have intellectual capability to avoid wrong path and follow the path of goodness. It is only greed, avarice, lust, envy, jealousy etc., that misguide man and force to move towards wrong path. Falling in temptation man commits sins that result ultimately in falling down in the lower realms of life whether they have to reap the fruits. It is said that one being gets human body not by his own good *karma* but by mercy of God who gives one chance to obtain *moksha*. So, the significance of human body has been greatly mentioned in all *dharma* of the world. The human life must not be spoiled in indulging into lusts and wrong desires for attainment of temporary so-called pleasures and prosperity.

The Buddha spoke about the rarity and the precious nature of opportune birth amongst human beings. He used a simile to illustrate this point. Suppose the whole world were a vast ocean, and on the surface of this ocean there were a yoke floating about, blown about by the wind, and suppose at the bottom of the ocean there lived a blind tortoise which came to the surface of the ocean once every hundred years. Just as difficult as it would be for that tortoise to place its neck though the opening in that yoke floating about in the ocean, just so difficult is to attain opportune birth as human beings. Elsewhere it is said that as if one were to throw a handful of dried peas against a stone wall, and just as if one of these peas were to strike in a crack in the wall, so to be born as a human being with the opportunity to practice the *Dharma* is similarly difficult.

It is, thus, ample clear that the cause of rebirth is wholesome and unwholesome *karmas* performed or to be performed by human beings. Every action is enshrined in hearts with the fruits of *karma*. The doers have to enjoy the fruits either willingly or unwillingly. Different realms of beings mentioned above are different abodes in the universe where the beings have to reside as per the fruits of their *karmas*. There is no release at all because that is the eternal law of the nature. One is bound to travel from one realm to another. Realisation of pain and pleasure available in various realms is there but there is no escape. In lower realms beings realise and repent but have nothing to do except to face the circumstance and bear the fruits. Even in the realms of gods and semi gods, too, there is realisation that the status of pleasure would disappear one day and beings availing such pleasant realms shall have to meet the end because nothing is permanent. But they, too, can do nothing except facing the fate. It is only the human life where something decisively can be done to get permanent release from such circumstances. Hence, it is wise for every human being to think of the reality and at least protect himself from falling into the endless currents of lusts, avarice, hatred, jealousy, violence etc. The wisest is one who tries to end the circle of death and birth by availing enlightenment. The Buddha has set the ways how to get enlightenment and become a Buddha. It has rightly been said that "Action done with a pure mind motivated by generosity, love and so for the result in happy mental states or states of existence like the human realm and the realm of gods. But actions done with impure mind affected by greed, ill-will and so forth result in unhappy lives like those of the hungry, ghosts and hell beings."

Rebirth and Transmigration

Rebirth and transmigration are two different things. Buddhism consistently speaks of rebirth and not transmigration. This is because in Buddhism there is no belief in an abiding entity, in a substance that transmigrates. Buddhists do not believe in a self that is reborn. When a sprout is born from a seed, there is no substance that transmigrates. The seed and the sprout are not identical. Similarly, when one lights a candle from another candle, no substance travels from one to the other, and yet the first is the cause of the second. When one billiard ball strikes another, there is continuity, the energy and direction of the first ball is imparted to the second. It is the cause of the second billiard ball moving in a particular direction and a particular speed. When one steps twice into a river, it is not the same river and yet there is continuity, the continuity of cause and effect. So, there is rebirth, but not transmigration. Continuity is a circle of change of things. They appear and disappear but the process of change continues. There is moral responsibility, but not an independent, permanent self. There is dependent continuation or origination. The existence is there due to supporting constituent elements of a thing. Since these elements are the subjects of change, the things appear and disappear moment after moment, but the process continues. A child grows up into young and a youth becomes old but the process of change is constant there. So, the rebirth is continuous process of change. It has its own causes that result into decay and rebirth.

References

1. Thomas, Knriem, *Introduction to Buddhism,* p. 17.
2. *Ibid.*
3. *Ibid.,* pp. 17-18.
4. Angari Chaudhary, "The Existential Character of Buddha's Philosophy", in Devidas Chatterjee (ed.), *Homage to Bhikhu Jagdish Kashyap*, Nav Nalanda Mahavihar, 1986, p. 305.
5. Quoted in *Ibid.,* p. 306.
6. *A Handbook in Social Philosophy*, p. 137.
7. For detail study of philosophy of existentialism and man see, Jean-Paul Sartre, *Existentialism,* pp. 18-22.
8. *Ibid.,* p. 18.
9. *Ibid.,* p. 19.
10. *Piya Sutta, Samyutta Nikaya*, Vol. I, p. 71 (Nalanda Edition).
11. *Atta hi attano natho* (self is the lord of self), *Dhammapada*, Verse 160.

12. Dr Radhakrishanan, *Indian Philosophy*, Vol. I, p. 661.
13. Fernando Tola and Carmen Dragonetti, "Nagarjuna's conception of Voidness" in Devidas Chatterjee (ed.), *Homage to Bhikhu Jagdish Kashyap*, pp. 67-68.
14. Devidas Chatterjee (ed.), *Homage to Bhikhu Jagdish Kashyap, op. cit.*, p. 72.
15. *Ibid.*, p. 74.

7

Vajrayana and *Tantric* Cult of Buddhism

The philosophies of *Vajrayana* and *Tantric* cult of Buddhism is very much conflicting and vague. This appeared with the marked purpose to reach to the ultimate theory not through following the ideal as well as ethical precepts, but through shortest practical way. The methods and ways what the propounders and followers of this school developed and applied are esoteric and not approvable by many. The school permitted the use of women, wine, meat and meditation to apprehend reality and achieve *shidhi*. Their philosophies are related to the popular cult of *Siva-shakti* and also to the world of mundane. *Vajrayana* is the way to reach to reality being firm while moving on the way without fluctuation and diversion. The path is so difficult and sloppy that the person having weak personality may fall down or deviate from the right path to the wrong path. The word '*Vajra*' means hard, as hard as the god Indra's weapon called *Vajra* (thunder volt). The propounders and the followers of this school also developed certain kinds of *mantras*, *mudras* and symbols that help the followers to reach the goal easily. This chapter critically discusses and examines the advent, growth, way of practice and consequences of the *Vajrayana*, *Mantrayana* and *Sahajayana* including the process of *tantrism*.

Impact of the Ancient Indian Philosophy on *Vajrayana* and *Mantra Tantra*

Since the school of *Vajrayana* is much related to the ancient Indian religious thoughts specially in respect of the theory of absolutism, *Sankhya Darshan* and non-dualism of Sanskara, it would be better to have a cursory view upon the prevailed Hindu's religious faiths and practices to make the study more authentic. The reaction against Vedic rites began early in the *Upanishadic* period and reached its climax with the *Samakhya* school led by Sankaracharya. The Vedic rituals were based on the principle of superiority and inferiority on the basis of caste and *varna-dharma* system.[1] The *Bhagvad Gita* also speaks of the futility of sacrificial rites on the ground of their perishibility.[2] The *Bhagvad Gita* and the *Bhakti* movement, according to Shri R.G. Bhandarkar, owe their origin to the stream of thought which began with Upanishads and culminated in the rise of Buddhism.[3] The *Gita* put emphasis on *Sankhya*, *Karma* and *Bhakti*, but favoured *Bhakti* as the most suitable way of salvation. At the moment, in the words of Bapat.

> When the Buddha appeared on the scene, he discovered to his dismay that the spiritual and intellectual life of the community (Hindus) was under the sway of small number of *Brahmans*. This made him undertake the lifelong mission of throwing open to all communities the privilege of renunciation or *pravrajya*. He invited people to join his religious order, irrespective of whether or not the underwent preliminary conditions such as *upanayana*, initiation in Vedic studies, as prescribed for *Brahmans*, thereby widening the scope of the religious life called *Brahmacarya*."[4]

Advaitism (Non-dualism)

The philosophy of Advaitism is basically related to the fact that there is only one *Brahman*, Absolute, all pervasive, all powerful, eternal, invisible, inconceivable, and *nirnkara*. Except Him there is nothing. Whatsoever appears to exist to our senses is unreal because they do not have permanent existence. They are mere reflection coming out of the Absolute and ultimately they merge into it. The mundane world is manifestation of the

Absolute *Brahman*. The manifestation is not permanent. Rather it is temporary in the sense that it is disappearing, moment after moment. It is the creation of or the product of *Maya* (illusion) that is not real, rather it is false, due to its impermanent nature. The world is illusion because of its perishable nature. There is only one God, Supreme and Absolute. A great champion of this school Sankaracharya took this weapon of the illusion theory and used it against his rival realists, the *Naiyayikas* and the *Vaisesikas*. *Samkar's* stand in advocating the unreality of the world, however, is logical and independent, for according to the Upanishads there existed previously only the *Brahman* or *Atman*, and things other than that were unreal and diseased *(antam)*.[5] Such a declaration makes it obvious that nothing but the *Brahman* or *Atman* is real. The rest is *Maya*. The term *Maya* has two meanings–*prakriti* and illusion or illusory objects. *Maya*, in the former sense, is common to the Upanishads and the *Gita* and in the latter sense it is peculiar to the Buddhists and the advaitins. The earlier Buddhist doctrine, did not mention about *Maya* doctrine.

This view of Absolute could not attract many more due to its vagueness, confinement to the class of *Brahman*ism and non-apprehensible by ordinary people who lacked the proper knowledge to understand it. At this very moment, the Madhyama philosophy of Buddhism appeared. Nagarjuna, one of the greatest thinkers of India, systemised the theory related to absolutism. The Buddha followed a moderate path avoiding the two extremes indulgence in sensual pleasures and the habitual practice of self-modification. Buddhism must be understood in the terms of way of life and a cultural movement. Its philosophy is not merely an exercise in abstraction but intellectualisation and rationalisation of the movement and the way of life. That is why it attracted more common people. When an attempt was made to interpret and discover the true import of the path, Nagarjuna came forward with his own interpretation and called it Madhayamika or moderate. The central idea in his philosophy is *prajna,* wisdom or ultimate knowledge derived from an understanding of the nature of things in their true perspective, viz., *sunyata*. *Sunyata* for him is a synonym for 'dependent origination'. So, the dictum:

'everything is void' *(survam sunyam)* must be taken to mean that everything has a dependent origination and is hence non-substantial. Here 'everything' stands for all things, *dharmas*, internal and external. So, everything for him is devoid of any substantiality and becomes illusory. When this is realised the *dharmadhatu* or the monistic cosmic element becomes manifest.

The formation of the non-origination theory by Nagarjuna is logical corollary of his doctrine of relativity (*sunyata*). The non-origination theory, as applied to the phenomenon world, was unknown in Advaitism before Gaudapada. The *Upanishads* speak several times of *Atman* and *Brahman* as inborn (*aja)*, imperishable (*avyaya*) *ananta* (endless), eternal (*nitya)*, but no where do they speak of the external world. Nor we do find anybody, before Gaudapada in the galaxy of Advaitins, who pleaded for the non-origination of things in general as did Gaudapada in his *Karkia*. Therefore, there is no denying the fact that Gaudapada must have taken the idea from Nagarjuna and adopted it suitably to provide the Advaita doctrine with a firm foundation.[6]

The second important *Mahayana* school is that of the *Yogacara*, followed by mentalists. They did not make any undue claims for the non-origination theory notwithstanding the fact that they too held the world to be unreal. Thus, both the *Madhayamika* and the *Yogacara* schools maintained the *Maya*-like nature of the world. The Advaitins, likewise, adhered to the *Maya* doctrine in order to sustain their belief in Advaitism. Shankaracharya's theory of Advaitism got more popularity and became the most reliable source of the school all over India. He revived the existing cult of Brhaminism.

Vajrayana Buddhism and Tibet

Tibetan Buddhism is a syncretic result of three major influences mentioned below:

1. *Mahayana Buddhism via Padmasambhava*—This carries the core doctrine of historical Buddhism with a heavy emphasis on *Karuna* and the role of the Bodhisattva.
2. *Tantrayana Buddhism/Tantric Hindu Darshana*— It emphasises the role that one's body and senses can play in the awakening of the mind. It is *tantric* tradition that brings us near to the *Kamasutra.*

3. *Bon the Indigenous Religious Tradition of Tibet*— It puts emphasis on mystical and animistic nature of the world.

Vajrayana Buddhism known as Tibetan Buddhism, *Tantric* Buddhism and Lamaism, is also called 'diamond way' which means it is the precious, changeless, pure and clear. It developed during the fifth to sixth century AD when Buddhism spread through northern India, Nepal and finally to Tibet. The practice of *Vajrayana* in Tibet is still discerned. At that time the prevailing belief of Tibet was the Bon religion, a mixture of *shamanism* (a form of witchcraft), magic, and primitive nature worship. *Vajrayana* was born when these practices along with magical formula designed to obtain magical powers, were in corporate into Buddhism (AD 600-1200). Included in the *Vajrayana* tradition are a number of advance meditative techniques: *yoga*, special hand gestures *(mudras)*, spells, and chants. It also derives many of its doctrines from *Vedantic* and *tantric* influence.

Vedanta is an Indian school of philosophy, which teaches that God (*Brahman*) and the soul (*atman*) are one. In other words, there is only one ultimate reality –*Brahman* – and the individuality we see is nothing but an illusion. The maker (*Maya*) of illusion is ignorance (*avidya*). Enlightenment occurs when one realises that "the world is not real: only the absolute, and the *Brahman*, is real."

Key-features of *Vajrayana* Buddhism

Following are the key-features of *Vajrayana* Buddhism:

1. There is an emphasis on the unity of wisdom (*prajna)* and compassion (*karuna*) as the ideal. Two symbols of this unity are found in the *Yab Yum* (the sexual union of male and female) and the *doreje* and *vajra*. (vagina and penice).

2. As with *Mahayana*, the *Prajnaparamita* is the philosophic foundation of Tibetan Buddhism. However, they have added to this work a collection of writings called the *Sadhanas* which are derived from *Tantric* texts. These *Sadhanas* prescribe various meditation exercises which distinguish *Vajrayana* dramatically from Theravada Buddhism.

3. The goal of Tibetan Buddhism is to become awaken or to experience Tharpa. Awakening is seen the opening of consciousness to the ultimate reality of emptiness. This process is not the slow scholarly route of the Theravada School which seeks to deny the ultimate reality of the body and substantial world. Instead, it is a dynamic process. 'Grappling with life' and involving the spirit, the mind and the body. Because of this, a diverse number of practices evolved which were designed to assist one in these efforts.
4. The emphasis on the humanity of the historic Buddhas (the Five Celestial Buddha) and Bodhisattvas was laid. Two are the Amitabha Buddhas who reigns over Sukhavati (the pure land of the western paradise and Avalokitesvara the Bodhisattva of Infinite compassion).

Visualisation in Buddhism in the Tibetan form is identification with a particular or Bodhisattva in order to attain the quality that it manifests. *Mantras* represent a force or deity and the chanting of the *mantra* is a way of connecting the practioner with that fore deity. The well-known *mantra* is *'Om mani padme hum'* which is translated as 'Om' the sound of creation, *padme* the jewel in the lotus, *'hum'* closure. The Tibetans have developed a tradition of singing that involves producing the lowest possible notes in the vocal range while simultaneously singing high overtones. *Mudras* are postures or hand gestures representing various deities and virtually every state of consciousness. *Mandalas* in *Vajrayana* Buddhism are symbolic representations of themes in meditations. Central *mandala* is the *kalcakra* which is a representation of perfection and, are usually swept up immediately upon completion to remind one of the impermanence of all things.

The *Tantras* are a series of AD sixth century scripture associated with the worship of *Shakti*, mother of the universe. They are made available only to initiates of various *tantric* religions (Tibetan Buddhism is only one of many *tantric* belief system). Study of these texts is said to reveal clairvoyance, clairaudience, telepathy, psychometric, the power of sound, vocal expression, and the composition of music.

The word *Tantra* basically means "loom and refer more specifically to the threads of loom. This expresses the foundational teaching of *tantrism*—all things are interwoven into one ultimate reality. *Tantrism* is also based on a variety of sex rituals that involve (breathing) exercises, meditation, and the prolonged sexual contact as *maithuna* (sexual intercourse)".

The sexual philosophy within *Tantric* Buddhism is linked to a number of ideas as it has already been stated and explained in this chapter. There is the belief that erotic love is a profound experience that "opens the mind to a sense of away and wanders akin to religious experience." It also presents the idea that during the act of sexual intercourse, a transcending of boundary between participants occurs, leading to an experience of oneness with each other. There exists the additional notion that the best way to escape blinding passion—in this case sexual lust – is to "go into the act that is desired rather than to retreat from it."

Some followers of early *Tantric* religion believed that sexual intercourse is not necessary. They maintain that the sex acts depicted in *Tantric* art and literature are only symbolic representation of a spiritual unification of both energy that can, through meditation and other practices, lead to a uniting of the male and female energy. Many of the occult aspects of Tibetan Buddhism also come from *Tantrism*. *Tantric* tradition maintains a close relationship to magic and includes "secret teaching, scriptures in code, and the practice of drawing symbols on the ground, and uttering spell to call up deities, supernatural powers that can be used for good or evil."

This extraordinary system to avail real wisdom helps elucidate the nature and scope of *Tantric* teaching and practice. Its elegant synthesis of therapeutic philosophy, depth-psychology and spiritual-ethical pedagogy, reveres the interpersonal world of *Tantric* instruction as a psychotherapeutic–psychospiritual art with no clear parallel in any tradition, ancient or modern, Eastern or Western. It's unique hermeneutic is meant less for reading arcane texts than for unlocking the living text of the human mind and body, with the aim of revealing the wish-fulfilling gems of the creative human spirit within. In India it may be best compared with the ultimate hermeneutics refinement of *Upanishadic* pedagogy found in the *Vedanta* system of Bartrhari and *Sanskara* as well as the sublime psychospiritual poetic of Abhinavagupta. In the words of Joseph Loizzo, "In the West, it may be compared with the Sufi pedagogy of an Arabi or the Kabbaka teachings of Ablufia, in its humanism; it may be compared with the modern therapeutic philosophy stemming from Nietzsche and Freud, including the esoteric hermeneutic if Jung and Kacan."[7] In contrast to all these analogies, however, *Vajrayana* pedagogy is uniquely adopted to the needs of the mainstream academic tradition covering the whole range of teaching context from large scale public lectures and complex curricula to the most intimate tutorial and mentoring bonds. Nagarjuna describes the centric-practice of non-duality as culminating in the "profound, awe-inspiring performance of enlightenment, whose essence is emptiness and compassion."[8] Nagarjuna's performance effectively entails shifting the reference of 'I' and 'mine' from deluded percepts of self and world to the corrected perceptions of these twin institutions. Likewise the intent of the creation stage is to rapidly cultivate this enlightened agency by conjoining both aspects of this reconstruction in a single practice that aims at developing a 'self of selflessness.' This reconstruction is guided by poetic formulas like: "I am the self whose nature is the diamond intuition of emptiness" and "I am the purity whose nature is the natural purity of all things."[9]

Features of *Mantrayana* in *Vajrayana*

The ways and means that new Buddhists adopted were not their own. Rather they borrowed them from practices of Hinduism where *mantra* and *tantra* were playing dominant role in the society. Practice of *Tantrism* in the Hindu society at that very period was very much popular. Such practices had their roots in the Veda called as *Sama Veda* where a lot has been mentioned about poems, chhandas, songs and *mantras*. What has been said by the Buddhists about the *Vajrayana* means a way and posture for sitting to obtaining knowledge should be as stronger as *Vajra* (a hard and strong weapon used by god Indra). *Vajra* means 'firm substantial, indivisible, invincible, and impenetrable and cannot be burnt or destroyed'.

The name of the *Vajrayana* is derived from the word *bodhicitta* which is considered as the *Vajra*. It means in *sadhna* one must sit strongly and tightly to realise truth. The truth reflects in the *cita* (consciousness), so it is *bodhicitta*. (Awareness in consciousness). After intense practice in *Vajra mudra* the *bodhicitta* of a *sadhaka* (practitioner) may attain the state of tranquility. In other words, a *sadhaka* realises the *bodhi* (knowledge) when his *bodhicita* attains the state. A *sadhaka* realises the *Vajrasattva* when he realises that all existence is nothing but *sunyata*. In its pure nature and he himself becomes the Vajrasattva through this realisation. The Vajrasattva is called Mahasattva who is full of infinite knowledge and who is engaged in the right form of religious observance.

Through the practice of *Vajrayana* one realises Bodhisattva that is realisation of self. Though the Buddhist denies the existence of self, but they have adopted it in different way. According to the Hindu *Vedantic* philosophy self is immortal and imperishable, the base of *cita* and ego. *Vajrayana* philosophy puts emphasis on realisation of *Bodhicitta* which means awareness of inner-consciousness. In Hindu philosophy, inner-consciousness is *antah-karana* that is the reflection of soul. When the *sadhaka* realises the *Vajrasattva,* he realises the universalised self as the perfectly—enlightened one. This realisation of the self is that of God and its directed that all *mudras, mantras* and *mandalas* are to be applied to the worship of the self. Thus, the self is God himself. God cannot be realised without realisation of self. It is obvious that Buddhism adopted the concept of self not directly but indirectly. The liberal and universal attitude of the Mahayanists with their ideal of all -–compassionate Buddha and Bodhisattva paved the way for the introduction of gods and goddess into the religion as it is mentioned in the Hindu philosophies.

Again, Buddhist *Tantra* system is also related to body. The *Tantra* considers body as a means or medium through which the truth can be realised. The Hindu philosophy considers the body as the epitome of the universe. Like that Buddhist philosophy considers body as the part of the universe in which entire universe may be realised. Many Buddhist *Tantras* like *Kalacakratantra* identifies the body and locate the seas, rivers, mountains and even planets in different parts of the body. They realise all truth in the nervous system and in the plexus and make the body, a perfect medium for realising the truth. This all happen when the *sadhaka* goes into deep meditation. The *Bhagvad Gita* and *Patanjali Yoga Sutra* of Indian philosophy talk a lot about *sadhana* and meditation. Through meditation entire truth may be realised. Not only that a *sadhaka* may achieve miracles through it.

The general term of *Tantric* Buddhism is given to the later aspects of Buddhism in India, i.e., *Mantrayana*, *Vajrayana* or *Sahjayana*. The importance given by the *Yogacara* School to *vijnana* and its cultivation gradually led to several esoteric developments in Buddhism. *Mantra, dhranis*, and diagrams in the forms of circles (*mandals*) and triangles began to assume increasing importance for a *yogi*. These *mantras* were supposed to possess great magical powers and had their counterparts in *parittas* in Pali literature, which were supposed to protect the reciters against the evils. Once the esoteric element was introduced into Buddhism, it was found necessary to restrict that element to a small inner group of 'initiates', and in order to maintain continuity it was also necessary to introduce the reinstitution of master and pupil (*Guru and Cela).*

In order to preserve the secret nature, they also had to use a language of symbolism which only the initiates could understand. To the common people the words carried together different meaning. Unfortunately, a language of double interpretation was used by the writers of this school, as a sort of *shocktherapy*. The apparent meaning of these words gave a shock to common people, but to the initiates carried an altogether different meaning.

Another feature of *Vajrayana/Mantrayana* of Buddhism is that it believed in a large number of gods and goddesses by whose favours the devotees were expected to attain *sidhi* or perfection. The Buddha has often been represented as sitting in the company of a large number of goddesses.

Allied to this branch of esoteric Buddhism, there is a still later phase of *Vajrayana* which, apart from the original principles on which the purer or brighter side was based, became mixed up with popular cults and assumed, among the lower classes of society a darker and objectionable form. It attracted a number of people hearing that one could get what he desired getting *sidhi* following the cult of *Vajrayana* and *Mantrayana*. So, the people, who lacked proper wisdom and understanding, joined the stream in great temptation. As a result, the path of *Vajrayana* and *Mantrayana* got corrupted. Wrong practices began. Corrupt practices like the use of five *makar, mamsa* (meat), *matsya* (fish), *mudra* (woman), and *Maithuna* (sexual intercourse), were encouraged and practices even by men who were supposed to be leading a religious life in *Vajrayana* works like the *Sri-samaja* (also called the *Guhya-samaja*), the *sadhana-mala,* the *Janana-sidhi* etc., began. It is found that violation of those very five rules which formed the basis of Buddhist discipline was recommended. Thus, the *Vajrayana* and *Mantrayana* got popularity, no doubt, but at the coast of big damage to the basic principles of original Buddhism. It is said that in the *Guhya-samaja* murder, falsehood, theft and intercourse with women were recommended.

This cult gained more popularity in the eastern part of India. Vikramasila was a centre of *Tantric* learning which gradually spread to Bengal, Assam and Orissa. No doubt, there was strong protest against such practices. The sane people totally disliked and abhorred it, but its popularity was so strong and followers were so great in number that it went on progressing expanding its hold inside and outside the country. Passing remark on such practices, one European scholar, namely, Sir John Woodruff who had the courage to rehabilitate the *Tantras*, especially the Hindu *Tantra* of the *Kundalini-yoga*, published his famous series of works of *Tantric* texts and philosophy under the pseudonyms of Arthur Avalon. In his foreword to the Sircakrasambhara *Tantra* he says:

The ignorant... envisage—spiritual truths so grossly that they come to be called superstition. All evil and ignorance is so much by its nature on the surface and affords so apt a subject for adverse judgement that it is readily seized upon, and the more so that it is convenient material for religious polemic. Nevertheless, I repeat that we must do credit both to our intelligence and sense of justice by trying to understand any religion in its highest and truest aspect."[10]

Even Avalon, however was under the impression that the Buddhist *Tantras* were merely an off-shoot of the Hindu *Tantra*, and that the texts, upon which his investigations were based, represented the original principles of the *Tantras*. This view was justified as long as Tibetan *Tantric* scriptures were comparatively unknown and unexplored, because even those few texts which were available in translation were far from being understood in their spiritual, historical and practical significance. The reason for this was the fact that these scriptures cannot be understood merely philosophically, but only from the point of view of *yogic* experience, which cannot be learnt from books. Moreover, those books, from which information was sought, were written in peculiar idiom, a language of symbols and secret conventions, which in Sanskrit was called *Sandhyabhasa* (literally twilight language), because of the double meaning which underlay in words).

Bapat is of the view that in the Chinese Ch'n and the Japanese Zen Buddhism, which in fact have much in common with the medieval Buddhist mystics, the so-called Sidhas, who flourished in India between the seventh and eleventh centuries AD, and were the main propagators of the *Tantric* teachings of *Vajrayana*. Their numerous mystic and poetical works were almost completely destroyed in the country of their origin when northern India was overrun by the Muslim invaders. Fortunately, a great many of their works as well as the bulk of *Tantric* literature that had developed up to that time, have been preserved in Tibet in faithful translations, together with thc living tradition of *yogic* and meditative practice, which was handed down through generations from *Guru* to *Cela*.

In India, however, the *Tantric* tradition went 'underground 'and lingered mainly in the lower strata of society, where it became mixed with various popular cults and finally deteriorated into superstitions, which discredited both the Buddhist and the genuine Hindu *Tantras*. These latter were built upon ancient *yoga* practices which apparently had been remolded under the influence of *Tantric* Buddhism.

Origin of the *Mantrayana* and *Sahajayana* in Buddhism

From among the many branches of Buddhism, *Mantrayana* and *Sahajayana* are the least known. Generally one is of the opinion that they are late development. *Mantras*, however, are already found in certain passages of the old Pali Canon. It may be assumed that because of the antiquity of the *mantras* the essentials of *Mantrayana* for a long time developed along lines parallel with the more intellectual schools of Buddhism, and were systematically codified and called a '*yana*' or a 'career' only later. *Mantrayana* and *Sahajayana* deal primarily with the psychologically effective aspects of spiritual development. Their instructions are of highly individual character and their contents must be grasped with the immediacy of experience. The *Mantrayana* is achieving what the other branches of Buddhism also claim to deal with, namely, the integration of human being, enlightenment or spiritual maturity. However, the methods are vastly different.

The *mantra* is by definition, 'a protection of mind', that is a formula which prevents the mind from going astray and therefore a positive help in meditative concentration. It is well-known fact that the human mind is not only influenced by the images within and without but also by words or even by syllable resists any attempt to be reduced to mere concepts of intellectual. Although the *mantras* have a definite relation to the energetic process they symbolise, the use of a particular *mantra* depends on the aspirant's personality and the spiritual discipline which suits him. It is this factor which has been mostly scientifically developed in *Mantrayana*. *Mantrayana* is strongly opposed to escapism and posits a positive aim and ideal against a negative one. All this is preparatory to the last phase, the *guru-yoga* as 'the means to have all sustaining power or reality settled on one's self.' The *guru-yoga* means the individual unity of one's self with the ultimate reality. The *guru-yoga* is a most exclusive discipline and its methods are intricate. In the ultimate sense, the *guru* is reality itself and reality is found in everything. The *guru* who himself has practiced this *yoga* is capable of guiding the aspirant on his difficult path. Thus, the message of *Mantrayana* remains a sealed book known to the *guru* and disciple only.

There is no much difference between *Mantrayana* and *Sahajayana*. According to the Tibetan scholar, it is the ultimate in Mind or *dharmakya* and ultimate in Appearance or the light of the *dharmakya* which are born together. In other words, reality and appearance are not separated from each other by an unbridgeable gulf, but are identical. This identity means that the reality is one and indivisible and is split up arbitrarily into a number of opposites only by the analytical methods and techniques of the intellect. Hence, the identity of Reality and appearance can be realised and experienced only by intuitive processes, and it is absolutely wrong and misleading to conceive of this identity as postulationally proposed hypothesis. In order to achieve this realisation, a course of meditation has been developed which is based on direct experience and takes cognizance of the fact that intellectual operations are inseparable from their emotional concomitants. The dichotomising activity of the mind (*vikalpa*) is accompanied and even supported by conflicting emotions (*klesa*). This turbulent state of mind can be remedied by meditative practices.

What *Sahajayana* teaches is no intellectual system but a strict discipline. Moreover, this school emphasises the intuitive approach to Reality, and it is a fact that the function of intuition is not the same as that of the intellect and that their modes of operations are completely different. This accounts for the fact that *Sahajayana* and *Mantrayana* successfully evaded the fate of turning into dead system. Both the *Mantrayana* and *Sahajayana* are concerned with the practical aspects of Buddhism which further developed in manifolds. Both had greatest influence on Tibetan Buddhism and there is sufficient evidence to show that. It is also the basis of Zen-Buddhism. They regard that man is not only a rational being but emotional being also. Emotions play greater role in shaping the practical life of the individual. Due to this opinion, the *Mantrayana* and *Sahajayana* have remained a living force of Buddhism till today. The living Buddhism of Tibet, China and Japan have been deeply influenced by the practices of *Mantrayana* and *Sahajayana*.

Mantrayana and Hindu's *Saivas*

Different opinions have been developed regarding the origin of the Buddhist *Tantra*. Some are of the view that it has been borrowed from Hindu society where the practice of *mantra* and magic was abundant. However, someone is of the view that it appeared in Buddhism from Tibet which was the centre of sorcery and witchcraft. The view that it originated from Hindu's cult of *Tantra* prevailed so long as Tibetan-*Tantra* scriptures were comparatively unknown and unexplored. The reason for this was the fact that these scriptures could not be understood merely philosophically, but only from the point of view of *yogic* experience which could not be learnt from books. Moreover, those books from which information was sought, were written in a peculiar idiom, a language of symbols and secret conventions; this symbolic language was not only a protection against intellectual curiosity and misuse of *yogic* practices by the ignorant or uninitiated, but had its origin mainly in the fact that the ordinary language is not able to express the highest experience of the mind. The indiscernible, which is experienced by the *Sadhaka*, the true devotee, can only be hinted at by smiles and paradoxes.

The western scholars spread that the *Tantric* cult prevailed among the Buddhist have the origin in the Hindu's philosophy of Saivas supported by Adi Sankaracharya in the ninth century AD. His works formed foundation of all Saivaite philosophy. However, the fact is that Sankaracharya was greatly influenced by the philosophy of Nagarjuna in this regard who had developed the theory of *sunyata* (dependent origination). Some of the Hindus scholars suspected *Sanskara* as the secret devotee of Buddhism while the Hindu *Tantras*, too took over the methods and principles and techniques of *yoga* to their own system of meditation. In the words of Bapat, "This view is held not only by Tibetan tradition and confirmed by a study of its literature, but has also been verified by Indian scholars after critical investigation of the earliest Sanskrit texts of *Tantric* Buddhism and their historical and ideological relationship with the Hindu *Tantra*."[11]

Another western scholar, namely, Austin Waddell, who is often quoted as an authority on Tibetan *Tantra* Buddhism, has written much about *Tantrism* in Tibet. In his estimation Buddhist *Tantrism* is nothing but *Saivaite* idolatry, *Shakti* worship and demonology. Its "so-called *dharanis*" are "meaningless gibberish ..." its mysticism a "silly mummery unmeaning jargon and 'magic circles'," and its *yoga* "a parasite whose monster outgrowth crust and cankered moist of the little life of purely Buddhist stock yet left in the *Mahayana*."[12] But the fact presented by Waddell is not correct. B. Bhattacharya, in his *Introduction to Buddhist Esoterism,* has come to the conclusion that "It is possible to declare, without fear of contradiction, that the Buddhist were the first to introduce the *Tantra* into their religion, and that the Hindus borrowed them from Buddhists in later times, and that is idle to say that later Buddhism was an outcome of *Saivaism*". Bapat is also of the view that to judge Buddhist *Tantric* teaching and symbols from the standpoint of Hindu *Tantras*, and specially from the principles of *Saktism* is not only inadequate but thoroughly misleading because both make use of the methods of *yoga* and of similar technical and philosophical terms, there is little justification for declaring Buddhism to be identical in the light of Hindu *Tantras*, or *vice-versa.*[13] One completely agrees with Bhattacharya when he says:

> The Buddhist *Tantra* in outward appearance resembles the Hindu *Tantra* to a marked degree but in reality there is very little similarity between them, either in subject matter or in philosophical doctrines inculcated in them, or in religious principles. This is not to be wondered at, since the aims and objects of the Buddhists are widely different from those of the Hindus.[14]

To declare Buddhist *Tantrism* as an off-shoot of *Saivaism* is only possible for those who have no first-hand knowledge of *Tantric* literature. According to Bapat, a comparison of the Hindu *Tantra* with those of Buddhism (which are mostly preserved in Tibetan and which therefore for long remained unnoticed by Ideologists) not only shows an astonishing divergence of methods of aims, in spite of external similarities, but proves the spiritual and historical priority and originality of the Buddhist *Tantras.*[15] Sankaracarya, the greatest Hindu philosopher of the ninth century AD, whose works form the foundation of all Saivaite philosophy, made use of the ideas of Nagarjuna and his followers to such an extent that orthodox Hindus suspected him of being secret devotee of Buddhism. On the other hand, the Hindus *Tantras*, too, took over the methods and principles of Buddhist *Tantra* and adapted them to their own purposes. This view is held not only by the Tibetan tradition and confirmed by a study of its literature, but has also been verified by Indian scholars after a critical investigation of the earliest Sanskrit texts of *Tantric* Buddhism and their historical and ideological relationship with the Hindu *Tantras*. B. Bhattacharya, in his *Introduction to Buddhist Esoterism*, has come to the conclusion:

> It is possible to declare, without fear of contradiction, that the Buddhists were the first to introduce the *Tantras* into their religion, and that the Hindus borrowed them from the Buddhists in later times, and that is idle to say that later Buddhism was an outcome of Saivaism."[16]

The cause of suspicion regarding whether the Hindus first used the Buddhist *Tantras* or the latter utilised the former's concept of *Tantras* is due to the mistaken idea, which was built upon the superficial similarities of Hindu and Buddhist *Tantras*. It was the Western scholar, Waddell who without having deep investigation into the related matters adopted that the Buddhist *Tantra* is nothing, but Saivaite idolatry. In this respect Bapat is very much near to the truth when he says:

> To judge Buddhist *Tantric* teachings and symbols from the standpoint of Hindu *Tantras* and especially from the principles of *Saktism* is not only inadequate but thoroughly misleading, because both systems start from entirely different premises. Although both make use of the methods of *yoga* and of similar technical and philosophical terms, there is little justification for declaring Buddhism to be identical with *Brahmanism* and therefore in interpreting the Buddhist *Tantras* in the light of Hindu *Tantras*, or *vice-versa*.[17]

Esoteric *Vajrayana*

In contrast to the common view, Tibetan reports that both the esoteric *Mahayana* and esoteric *Vajrayana* were taught by Shakyamuni in secret to certain disciples. The abundance of the evidence and common sense corroborates Tibetan reports that the raw materials of *Tantric* theory and practice were already available in Shakyamuni's days, but not systematically formulated, written or published until much later. From the

Indo-Tibetan perspective, the origin of the *Mahayana* and *Vajrayana* lay in the gradual unfolding of the Buddha's reform of Indian culture and society. Far from revisions or corruptions, these traditions extend the progressive role of the Theravada academy into the Indian mainstream, with rational and universal alternatives to the elite Sanskrit tradition of arts and science. As centrism emerged as definitive of Buddha's thought, it cleared the way for the *Vajrayana* to emerge as the definitive paradigm of the Buddhist contemplative science. The reason for this shift helped characterise the *Vajrayana* as a contemplative science. The *mantras* were formed in poetic form. According to *Tantras* life and the world are seen to emerge when the space of emptiness was planted with poetic seeds (*bija-mantra*). In *Tantras,* these seeds are planted not in the disembodied ground of a sub-conscious mind, but rather in the embodied soil of creative, bliss-void (*sukha-sunya*) states of mind, supported by the vital energy (*prana*) of a nervous system with channels (*nadi*) complexes (*chakra*) and drops (*bindu*). While this nervous system was mapped by contemplation rather than gross anatomy, *Tantric* psychology and medicine see it as made of subtle matter and ascribe to it all the normal mind/ body functions, modern science ascribes to the nervous in this the semiotic dimension of *Tantric* worldview, like the scientific phonetics of Sanskrit grammar, is not abstract or idealistic but embedded in the living context of mind/body interaction.

As for its therapeutic philosophy, the esoteric *Vajrayana* is often described as fruition or effectual vehicle in contrast to the causal vehicle of the exoteric *Mahayana*. It approaches the path of philosophy from the standpoint of its fruits or consequence, namely, the enlightened experience of a spiritual master. It does this by offering the disciple a master's eye-view of herself as a living Buddha within a Buddha perfected, natural social and cultural world as well as scripting his/her dialogue of enlightening speech (*mantra*) and repertoire of enlightening activities or gestures (*mudra*). Creative, imagery, poetic formulas and performative gestures provide a working linguistic construction and imaginative simulation of enlightened perception that serves as an alternative system of reference by which the disciple can critic his or her compulsive misperception of self and world.

Siva-Sakti* and Buddha's *Tantrayana

Bhattacharya is very much correct when he says that Buddhist *Tantra* in outward appearance resembles to *Siva-Sakti* symbol, but they differ in their approach and purpose both. Buddhist *Tantra* is not *Saktism*. The concept of *Sakti* or divine power of the creative female aspect of the highest God (*Siva*) does not play any role in Buddhism. *Siva-Sakti* symbol or concept of the Hindus represents Absolute God and (*Siva*) and His all pervasive creative energy *Sakti*. *Sakti* is also known as *Prakriti* that is upholding the entire creation. It is the first cause of creation. It creates, maintains and lastly destroys creation. It is the womb of creation. Everything in the universe comes out from the womb of the *Sakti* and lastly disappears in its fathomless dimension. Creation begins when *Siva*- and *Sakti* unites together. To the Buddhist *Sakti* is *Maya*, the very power that creates illusion, from which *prajna* can liberate mankind. It is therefore not the aim of the Buddhist to acquire power or join himself to the powers of the universe; either to become their instrument or to become their master. On the contrary, he tries to free himself from those powers, in order to liberate himself from their dominion. The Buddhist does not want the creation and enfoldment of the world, but the coming back to the uncreated, unformed world. The Buddhist concept of *nirvana* is related to the merger of the individual into the fathomless *sunyata* where there is neither birth nor death. The becoming conscious of this *sunyata* is *prajna* or highest knowledge. The realisation of this highest knowledge in life is enlightenment (Bodhi). *Sunyata* is the passive, all-embracing female principle, from which everything proceeds and into which everything recedes. The female concept of *sunyata* is united with dynamic male principle of active universal love and compassion which represent the means for the realisation of *prajna* and *sunyata*. The main difference is that Buddhist *Tantrism* is not *Saktism*. The concept of *Sakti*, of divine power, of the creative male aspect of the highest god (*Siva*) or his emanations does not play any role in Buddhism, while in the Hindu *Tantras*, the concept of power (*Sakti*) forms the focus of interest. The central idea of *Tantric* Buddhism, however, is *prajna* (Knowledge, wisdom).

To the Buddhists, *Sakti* is *maya*, the very power that creates illusion, from which only *prajna* can liberate mankind. So, there is not the aim of the Buddhists to acquire power, or to join himself to the powers of the universe, either to become their instruments or to become their master, but on the contrary, he tries to free himself from those powers, which for aenons kept him a prisoner of *sansara*. He strives to perceive those powers, which have kept him groping in the rounds of life and death, in order to liberate himself from their dominion. On the other hand, the attitude of the Hindu *Tantras* is quite different, if not contrary, "United with the *Sakti*, be full of power', says the *Kukacudamani Tantra*, "From the union of *Siva* and *Sakti* the world is created". The Buddhists, on the other hand, does not want the creation and unfoldment of the world, but the coming back to the 'uncreated, unformed' state of *sunayata* from which all creation proceeds, or which is prior to and beyond all creation.

The becoming conscious of this *sunayata* is *prajna* or highest knowledge. The realisation of this highest knowledge in life is enlightenment. If *sunayata*, the passive all embracing female principle, from which everything proceeds and into which everything recedes, is united with dynamic male principle of active universal love and compassion, which represents the means (*upaya*) for the realisation of *prajna* and *sunayata*, then perfect Buddhahood is attained. In the words of Bapat:

> Intellect without feeling, knowledge without love and rites without compassion lead to pure negation, to rigidity, to spiritual death, to mere vacuity, while feeling without reason, love without knowledge (blind love), compassion without understanding, lead to confusion and dissolution, but where both are united, where the great synthesis of heart and head, feeling and intellect highest love and deepest knowledge have taken place, completeness is re-established, and perfect enlightenment is attained."[18]

In Buddhism, the process of getting enlightenment thorough *Tantra* is different from that of Hinduism. In the Buddhist concept male symbol is active while the female symbol is passive, but in the Hindu *Tantra* the female aspect is represented as *Sakti* that is active principle, and the male aspect as *Siva*, the pure state of divine consciousness or 'being', *i.e.* the passive principle or the 'resting on its own nature. Again, in the Buddhist *Tantra*, the union of the male and female during sexual intercourse, knowing each other nature and quality, results into oneness giving *mahasukha*, but in the Hindu *Tantra* such union results in obtaining bliss (*ananda*). In the former the result of union is merger into *sunyata* where creation ceases while in the Hindu *Tantra* union of *Siva-Sakti* causes creation. In Buddhist symbolism, the Knower, (Buddha) becomes one with his knowledge (female symbol), just as man and wife become one in the embrace of love, and this becoming is the highest indiscernible happiness (*mahasukha)*. The Dhyani Buddhas (the ideal Buddhas visualised in meditation) and the Dhayani Bodhisattva of the active urge of enlightenment which finds its expression in *upaya,* the all embracing love and compassion, are therefore represented in the embrace of their *prajna*, symbolised by female deity, the embodiment of the highest knowledge.

Thus, by confusing Buddhist *Tantra* with the *Saktism* of the Hindu *Tantra*, a basic misconception has been created, which up to the present day has prevented a clear understanding of *Vajrayana* and its symbolism, in iconography as well as in literature, especially that of the *Siddhas*. The latter used a particular form of symbolism, in which the highest was clothed in the form of the lowest, the most sacred in the form of the most ordinary, the transcendent in the form of the most grotesque paradoxes. The language, symbolism and iconography of early Buddhist *Tantra* was so vague that it was difficult for common man to grasp the real meaning with the result that the *Tantra* falling in the hand of common unintelligent people, got perversion. Describing the same facts, Bapat says:

> Their (*Shidhas*) language was as unconventional as their lives, and those who took their words literally were either misled into striving after magic powers and worldly happiness or were repelled by what appeared to them to be blasphemy. It is therefore not surprising that after the disappearance of the Buddhist tradition in India, this literature fell into oblivion or degenerated into crude erotic cults of popular *Tantrism.*[19]

In early Buddhist *Tantra* the female figure presented *prajna,* the embodiment of knowledge and a sexless figure. The union of male and female represented union of active and passive, union of activity and knowledge, union of intellect and feeling, and union of knowledge and love. And not the union of male and female in physique as it happened later on. In the words of Galasenapp:

> The female Bodhisattvas figured in the *mandalas*, like *Prajanaparamita* and *Cudi,* are sexless beings from whom, quite in accordance with the ancient tradition, association of sexual nature are strictly excluded.[20]

Though the polarity of male and female principles is recognised in the *Tantras* of the *Vajrayana* and is an important feature of its symbolism, it is raised upon a plane which is as far away from the sphere of mere sexuality as the mathematical juxtaposition of positive and negative sign. In Tibet the male and female Ddhyani Buddha and Bodhisattvas are regarded as little as 'sexual beings' as in the schools of Japan. To the Tibetans even their aspect of union is indissoluble associated with the highest spiritual reality in the process of enlightenment, so that association with the realm of physical sexuality is completely ignored. In the earlier forms of Indian Buddhist *Tantrism* Mahamudra that represented divine figure, was represented as the 'eternal female' principle. About that eternal female it is said that "she shines fourth like the serene sky at noon during autumn, she is the support of all success; she is the identity of *sansara* and *nirvana*; her body is compassion (*karuna*) which is not restricted to single subject; she is the uniqueness of Great Bliss."[21]

Through the polarity of male and female principles is recognised in the *Tantra* of the *Vajrayana* is an important feature of its symbolism. It is installed upon plane which is as far away from the sphere of mere sexuality as the mathematical juxtaposition of positive and negative signs, which as valid in the realm of irrational values as in that of rational or concert concepts.

In Tibet the male and female Dhayni Buddhas and Bodhisattvas are regarded as little as 'sexual being' as in Japan. To the Tibetan even their aspect of union is indissolubly associated with the higher spiritual reality in the process of enlightenment, so that the associations with the realm of physical sexuality are completely ignored. Figural representation of these symbols is not looked upon portraying human beings, but as embodying the experiences and visions of meditation. In the worlds of Bapat, "In such a state, however, there is nothing more than could be called 'sexual'; there is only the super individual polarity of all life, which rules all mental and physical activities, and which is transcended only in the ultimate state of integration, in the realisation of *sunyata*. This is the state which is called *mahamudra*, the 'Great Attitude' or 'The Great Symbol, which I have given its name to one of the most important systems of meditations in Tibet."[22]

It is said that all women should be enjoyed by the *Saddhaka* in order to experience the *mahamudra*, but its hidden meaning is something else. It cannot be understood in physical sense, but that it can only be applied to that higher form of love which is not restricted to a single object and which is able to see all 'female' qualities, whether in ourselves or in others as those of the Divine Mother or transcendental wisdom. It does not grant permission to mingle with females. It is wrong to assume that the *sadhaka* "who has sexual intercourse with his mother, his sister, his daughter, his sister's daughter will easily succeed his striving for the ultimate goal."[23]

Thus, it is evident that to maintain that *Tantric* Buddhists actually encouraged 'incest and licentiousness' is as ridiculous as accusing the Theravadians of condoning matricide and patricide and similar heinous crimes. To quote Bapat once more:

> If we take the trouble to investigate the living tradition of the *Tantras* in their genuine unadulterated forms, as they exist up to the present days in thousands of none tries and hermitage of Tibet, where the ideal of sense-control and renunciation are held in the highest esteem, then only can be realised how ill-founded and worthless are the current theories which try to drag the *Tantras* into realm of sensuality.[24]

Thus, it is very much obvious that having union with women outside ourselves, we have to seek it within ourselves by the union of our male and female nature in the process of meditation. This is clearly stated in Tilopa's famous Six Doctrines upon which the most important *yoga* method of the Kargyutpa School is based. This method was applied by the mostly saintly people. There must be the relationship of the body and mind, of physical and spiritual interaction in a universal perspective. In this way, if the yogi comes out of the feeling of 'I' and 'mine' then only one may rise above reaching the stage of Buddhahood. In this sense, the Buddhist *Tantras* are not only the legitimate heirs of the Vijanavadians and *Yogacaras*, but the logical outcome and ultimate consequence of the central idea of Buddhism which consists in the Law of Dependent Origination.

Stages of Orgasm in *Sadhana*

Creation stage meditation on an ideal partner begins in earnest in the subtle creation stage, where it serves to arouse sexual bliss as a basis for contemplating the emptiness of touch in the co-called *Vajra* offering. The explicitly sexual nature of this practice is clear in its five stages mentioned below:

1. Envisioning a seminal drop at the tip of the male partner's *vajra* or *phallus*, dwelling within the lotus or vagina (*Bhaga*) of the female;
2. Imagining sexual intercourse and drawing the orgasmic release into the whole body to 'satisfy' all the archetypes of the body *mandala*;
3. Inscribing a microcosmic *mandala* complete with all 32 archetypes within the drop that has been released into the partner's womb;
4. Withdrawing those archetypes, one by one, up the *vajra* through the central channel to the heart, from where they emanate, one by one in all directions benefitting all living beings then returning to the heart; and
5. Converting those archetypes into seed *mantras* that circle the heart, then reciting them while envisioning that they radiates archetypes that travel out on exhalation, benefit beings and coalesce back into the *mantra* circle on the heart on inspiration.[25]

Use of Intoxication in Tantrism

Datura intoxication may have been wide spread in *siddha* culture. Many of *siddha* scriptures discuss ointments and drugs. The use of the various species of *datura* is particularly evident. Sometimes it is termed as 'crazy *datura*'. The use of *datura* in various rites is prescribed by a number of seminal *Tantras* that exerted a profound influence on Indian and Tibetan religious culture. Much *Tantric yoga* are intended to elicit extraordinary states of consciousness, including sexual *yoga* with real or visualised partners and energy *yoga* that manipulate body heat, respiration or dreaming. The concept of *Tantra* as a sex-positive religion devoted to embracing the material world is a modern construction that bears little resemblance to the historical *Tantric* practices and beliefs of Asia.[26] During 950-1200 CE, Tibet went under a period of upheaval followed by a renaissance in which the old Tibetan empire collapsed and reorganised into a society ruled by a complex network of powerful clans and religious institutions.[27] Thereafter, a new religious trend based on Buddhism appeared where many *Siddha* got their hold over the religion. They argued that the monks sitting within the four walls of monasteries and cutting their link from the rest of world cannot achieve the goal. So, the *Tantric Siddha*, began to express spiritual attainment in the world. They also began to commit outrageous acts of apparently reckless violence or sexual conduct.[28] In that course, they began to take intoxicative materials consuming enormous quantities of hemp, strychnos, nux-vomica and *datura*.[29]

In addition to accommodating the use of psychoactive, *tantric* texts sometimes include encyclopedic instructions for the use of medicinal plants. Ayurvedic medicines and *yogas* are two important antecedents to *tantric* and those disciplines provide a template for simultaneously developing mind and body both in the service of liberation. This holistic approach to spiritual practice is preserved in several important Buddhist *tantras* in which physical, mental and spiritual ailments form a single complex of related concerns that must be treated in tandem. This approach is an easy rhetorical fit with pre-*tantric* Buddhist scriptures, which sometimes describe Buddhas as a doctor and suffering as due to illness.[30] *Datura*, *bhang* and *ganja* are the intoxicating materials that intoxicate the mind and the individual in a different land where things are peculiar as well as the most highlighted. They provide the individual with special thinking and vision. It helps one to concentrate fully.

The psycho-active effects of *datura* have long been recognised in Tibet. Sachen Kunga Myingpo writes, "when *datura*.... eaten, appearance manifests as yellow." Dodrop Chen Rinpoche, a Tibetan scholar, writes "If one takes the nectar by itself the (subtle body) will receive blessings spontaneously and excellent accomplishments will be achieved, like being intoxicated by alcohol... and being deluded with vision by *datura* or thorn apple."[31] It is learnt that *datura* was used not only to intensify the brain and activate body, but also to harm enemies by giving them heavy dose of *datura*. Its effect is sometimes very much dangerous if big quantity is taken. It makes man mad also. The Tibetan commentator, Bodon Richen, explains that "five intoxicants, refers to the root, stem, leaves, flower and fruit of the *datura* plant all of which contain psycho-active alkaloids."[32] During the eighth century AD *Guhyasamaja Tantra* is generally considered one of the earliest extant Buddhist *Tantras*. This key scripture describes the basic architecture of *Tantric* practice and is venerated by several schools of Tibetan Buddhism. In the *Guhyasamaja Tantra*, Buddha *Vajradhara* gives instructions for undertaking the destructions of evil-doers.

Making an image of the enemy with excrement and urine of those who follow the great *Dharma*, wrathfully burn it in a fire of thorn-wood, and even the Buddha will certainly perish... So, he said black mustard seeds, salt, oil, poison and thorn-apple (*datru*'s fruit) these are taught as the supreme destroyer of all the Buddhas.[33]

Tantra scholar David Gardon White notes that cannabis use was a widespread part of the influential *Nath Siddha* Lineage. Additionally, he notes that in the Buddha Tara *Tantra*, cannabis is essential to 'ecstasy'. In that *Tantra*, Buddha says that drinking wine without having consumed cannabis "cannot produce real ecstasy."[34] Forty two of the *Mahakala Tantra's* fifty chapters include formulas for using medicinal plants, and many of these plants are psycho-active. The *Mahakala Tantra* says that a *yogi* who applies a *datura* ointment will "revolve like a bee."

Tantra as a Sex-positive Religion

The concept of *tantric* as a sex-relative religion devoted to embracing the material world is a modern thought that bears little resemblance to the historical *tantric* practices of Asia. *Tantra* began to take shape as a major religious movement in between the sixth and ninth century CE. Huge amount of *tantric* literature appeared during this period. The movement of *tantrism* remained in practice for several centuries. Most of the *tantrism* were composed in Sanskrit in India and central Asia and many were eventually exported to China and Tibet. During 950-1200 CE, major changes took place in the political arena of Tibet. It was the period of 'renaissance' where the old Tibet empire collapsed paving the way for arrival of a complex social system where powerful religious clans and religious institutions established their hold over power and society both.

There are several reasons to look to *tantric* for psycho-active substance use in pre-modern Buddhist Asia. The first and most important is that the non-monastic Buddhism is far less tolerant of violation of scriptural precepts than *tantric* Buddhism. The Buddha's injunction against consuming intoxicants precludes the open use of psycho-active substances by the members of the Buddhist Monastic establishments. In contrast, *tantric* Buddhism can allow for, and even applaud shocking transgression as a sign that the yogi has transcended ordinary patterns of valuation and behaviour. While non-*tantric* Buddhist practice was overwhelmingly the preview of ordained monks and nuns in medieval India, the *tantric*, or practitioner of *tantric* was often a lay person.

Geoffrey Samuel, author of several books and essays on Buddhist religious culture, suggests that the use of psychoactive plants in the Indian *siddha* cultural milieu may have been similar to current use observed among modern iterant ascetics in India.[35] Such use has been documented throughout the Himalayas, where the plants are consumed by *sadhus* for a variety of reasons, including healing, recreation and *yoga*.[36]

Notes and References

1. *Sankhya-karika*, Verse 2.
2. *Bhagvad Gita,* Chapter II, Verse 21.
3. *Vaisnavism*, p. 9.
4. Bapat, P. V., *2500 Years of Buddhism, op. cit.* p. 303.
5. Joseph Loizzo, *Vajrayana Buddhism in Tibetan Perspective*, Colombia University New York, p. 25.
6. R.A., 398cd, "*Gambhiram bhirubhijanam bodhisadhanam sunyatakaruna-garbham.*"
7. Quoted in Bapat, P.V., *2500 Years of Buddhism, op. cit.*, p. 45.
8. Quoted in *Ibid.*, p. 314.
9. *Ibid.*, p. 121
10. Bhattacharya, B. *Sadhanamala*, ii, xxxvi and iv, p. 147. Also see, Manindra Mohan Bose, *Post Citnya Sahajajiya Cult of Bengal*, Chapter III, pp. 134-42.
11. Quoted in Bapat, P.V., *2500 Years of Buddhism, op. cit.*, p. 317.
12. B. Bhattacharya, *Introduction to Buddhist Esoterism*, p. 47.
13. Bapat, P.V., *2500 Years of Buddhism, op. cit*, p. 316.
14. B. Bhattacharya, *Introduction of Buddhist Esoterism*, pp. 47-48.
15. Bapat, P.V., *2500 Years of Buddhism, op. cit.*, p. 316.
16. B. Bhattacharya, *Introduction to Buddhist Esoterism, op. cit.*, p. 147.
17. Bapat, P.V., *2500 Years of Buddhism, op. cit.*, p. 317.
18. *Ibid.*, p. 319.
19. *Ibid.*, p. 321.
20. Glasenappa, H.V., *Die Entstehung des Vajrayana*, Zeitsch *morgfenland, Gesellschaft*, Vol. 90, 560, 1936.
21. Edwin Obermiller, *Boston's History of Buddhism in India*, Tokyo, Sujuki, 1975, also see, Chattopadhyaya, A., and Chimpa. L., *Taranath's History of Buddhism,* Simla: Indian Institute of Advanced Studies, 1970.
22. Bapat, P.V., *2500 Years of Buddhism, op. cit.*, p. 323.
23. *Anangavajra Pranopaya-viniscaya Sidhi*, V. 25, quoted in *Yuganaddha*, p. 106.
24. Bapat, P.V., *2500 Years of Buddhism, op. cit.*, p. 324.

25. Buddhism of Tibet and Lamaism, pp. 11-12.
26. White, D.G., (1996), *The Alchemical Body: Siddha Traditions of Medieval India*, University of Chicago Press, pp. 19, 118-9, 412.
27. Davidson, R.M, *Tibetan Renaissance: Tantric Buddhism in the Rebirth of Tibetan culture,* Colombia University Press, 2006.
28. Abhayadattra, D., *Buddha's Lions: Life of the Eighty Four Buddhas*, trans. by James B., Robinson, Dharma Publishing, 1997.
29. Bhattacharya, B., *An Introduction to Buddhist Esoter*ism, Oxford University Press, 1931, p. 73.
30. Stablein W.G., *The Mahakalatantra: A Theory of Ritual Blessing and Tantric Medicine*, Colombia University, 1976, pp. 21-22, 80, 255-56, 286.
31. Thondup Rinpoche, T., *Hidden Teachings of Tibet,* Wisdom Publications, 1997, pp. 152-53.
32. Gray, D.B., *The Cakrasamvara Tantra (the discourse of Sri Heruka). A Study and Annotated Tanslation,* The American Institute of the Buddhist Studies, 207, pp. 371, 352, 373-74.
33. Fremantle, F.A., *Critical Study of the Guhyasamaja Tantra, Doctral Dissertation,* University of London, 1971, p. 103.
34. Maitra, A.K. ed, *Tara Tantra Varendra Res. Soc.* 1983.
35. Samuel G., *Personal Communication*, 2008.
36. Muller Ebeling, C., Ratsch C, Shahi, S.B., *Shamanism and Tantra in the Himalayas,* Inner Traditions, 2002.

25. Buddhism of Tibet and Lamaism, pp. 11-12.

26. White, D.G. (1996), *The Alchemical Body: Siddha Traditions of Medieval India*, University of Chicago Press pp. 19, 113-9, 412.

27. Davidson, R.M. *Tibetan Renaissance: Tantric Buddhism in the Rebirth of Tibetan Culture*. Columbia University Press, 2005.

28. Abhayadatta, D., *Buddha's Lions: Life of the Eighty Four Buddhas*, trans. by James B. Robinson, Dharma Publishing 1997.

29. Bhattacharya, B., *An Introduction to Buddhist Esoterism*, Oxford University Press, 1931, p. 73

30. Stablein W.G., *The Mahakalatantra: A Theory of Ritual Blessing and Tantric Medicine* Colombia University, 1976, pp. 21-22, 50, 253-76, 285

31. Thondup Rinpoche T., *Hidden Teachings of Tibet*, Wisdom Publications, 1997, pp. 152-53.

32. Gray, D.B., *The Cakrasamvara Tantra (The discourse of Sri Heruka): A Study and Annotated Translation*, The American Institute of the Buddhist Studies, 2007, pp. 371, 372, 373-4.

33. Freemantle, F.A., *Critical Study of the Guhyasamaja Tantra*, Doctoral Dissertation, University of London, 1971, p. 100.

34. Maitra, A.K. ed. *Tara Tantra*. Varendra Res. Soc. 1933

35. Samuel G., *Tantric Conversations*, 2008.

36. Muller-Ebeling, C., Ratsch C., Shahi, S.B., *Shamanism and Tantra in the Himalayas*, Inner Traditions, 2002.

8

Expansion of Buddhism Inside and Outside India

Buddhism that originated and developed on the soil of India more than 2500 years ago has achieved the status of a world religion spreading its influence in several foreign countries. Even today, Buddhism in other countries especially in South East Asia including Myanmar and Ceylon has deep-root and is the basic religion of their inhabitants. In ancient India, many *Brahmans* adopted Buddhism due to influence of Lord Buddha's attraction and of his teachings. King Bindusara was so much impressed with the Buddha's personality and his preaching that he invited him to his castle despite hard protest from his courtiers and his subjects. Ajatsatru, the famous king of Rajgriha and later Vaishali, was too much attracted to the personality of the Buddha. When the king gave the foundation of Patliputra after conquering Vaishali, he invited him with great honour. The main gate from which the Buddha came out was called *Gautam Dwar*. The place of the river Ganges from where the Buddha had crossed the river was called *Gautam Tirtha*. As the years rolled down, several followers of other S*anghas* giving up their original place joined Buddhist *Dhamma*. Even the wife of Bindusara adopted Buddhism and she indoctrinated Prasenjit to religion of Buddhism.

When Buddha reached Kapilavastu, people welcomed him whole-heartedly. Here, he indoctrinated his father, son Rahul, wife and a host of relatives to his *Dharma*. Among the Sakya dynasty those leading personalities who adopted Buddhism were king of Sakya Naresh Bhadrik, Anand, Anirudh Upali and Devdutta. Devdutta his cousin, later on, became rival to Buddha. He wanted to become the chief of Buddha *Sangha*, but he failed in his mission. Devdutta was so envious to the Buddha that he tried his level best to divide Buddha *Sangha*. He formed his own *Sangha* with hundreds of followers. He left nothing to criticise the Buddha and demolish his growing image. It is said that he applied the efforts thrice to kill the Buddha. In his first effort, he sent some persons to kill him with arrows. The Buddha was saved because those who came to kill him became Buddhists. In his second attempt, he threw a big piece of stone from the mountain when Buddha was passing below. This time also he got a little injury on his leg, but he survived. Third time, Devdutta sent an intoxicated elephant to the way on which the Buddha used to travel. It is said that Buddha was so charming that when the elephant came near to Buddha, it bowed down to him. Thus, Lord Buddha despite his opposition from his own blood and also from some vested *Brahmans*, went ahead successfully spreading the light of enlightenment and his message of peace, non-violence, universal brotherhood, *meti* (friendship), *karuna* (compassion), etc., which came to be known as Buddha *Dhamma*. Koshal always remained a lovely place for the Buddha. He passed at least 21 Varsavas at Shravasti, the capital of Koshal. The ruler of Koshal, namely Prasenjit was too much loyal to him. When he reached Lichhvi at the invitation of the people, he was highly welcomed. Many people of Lichhvi were suffering from natural epidemic. But they all got cure soon after arrival of Buddha there. Later on many people accepted Buddhism as their religion. The Buddha also went to Kaushambi and spread Buddhism.

Spread of Buddhism in India

Buddhism has a long history. Its ideas are various and multi-coloured, but all the Buddhist attitudes fall into either of the two notions. The first one holds the view that the man is utterly ignorant and has no wisdom. He cannot lead a right life. He is ugly and sinful. The other view holds that man is neither ugly nor sinful in his true colour. He is good and beautiful. He is pure and everyone is endowed with the light of wisdom (Buddha). The depth of the Buddhistic doctrine and the attitude of thought depend on the attitude which a particular school assumes. Generally speaking, *Hinayana* school stands on actuality and strives to attain Buddha's rank by removing evils while *Mahayana* school which emphasises immaculate human nature holds that evil is nowhere. Buddhism arose in India and was propagated in China and Japan. Doctrinally speaking, Indian and Chinese Buddhism may be characterised as intellectualistic. The intellectualism reached the peak in ancient China. Later it became practical with the rise of Zen, who interpreted Buddhism from new practical angle. In Japan, Buddhism bloomed as the religion of faith. Dogen, Shinren and Nichiren contributed much to its rapid development. Buddhism based on the idea of 'original enlightenment' seems to have reached its highest peak here.

No doubt, such anti-philosophy of *Vedanta* affected it, but it could fail to eradicate or abolish it. It remained in practice and faith both because its root was rooted in deep soil. However, such opinion and thinking paved the way for the growth of new philosophy related to metaphysics and existentialism. Among them two schools led by the Buddha and Mahavira in the six century BC became more popular and attracted followers from near and wide. This indicates that the tribal society of the time had reached a state of disintegration and new society came up which could meet the demands of the emerging new age. A new type of philosophy and religion, distinct from *Brahminical* ritual, had to emerge which could consolidate the various elements and components together for the benefit of a new society. These religious teachers preached self-restraint, detachment from worldly pleasures, penance and renunciation with a view to restoring the disintegrated tribal institutions.

Both Buddha and Mahavira who were born in Bihar did a lot to lead the people towards the light and goodness. After achieving enlightenment, the Buddha devoted his whole life to teach the people travelling from place to place. He spread the message of brotherhood, sincerity, honesty, simplicity and universality. They travelled place to place to enlighten the people. Buddhism appeared as a mid-way between the ways of Absolutism and nihilism. The middle-way of Buddha avoids both these end. [1] The theory of the middle-way has also been used in philosophical spheres. The Buddha neither approved the doctrine of perpetual eternity (*Sasvatavadins)* held by *Brahmavadins,* nor of those nihilist who believe consciousness to be a product of material elements, which is destroyed along with the destruction of the body. This doctrine can be well-compared with the doctrine of *anekantvada* propounded by Mahavira. This doctrine teaches that the truth is relative and reflected through various means in various ways. Therefore, there is nothing which can be called absolute affirmation and absolute negation.

Sangha or the monastic community played an important role in the organisation of Buddhist religion. The *Buddha*, *Dhamma* (religion) *and Sangha* (community) known as the 'three gems' in Buddhism are very important. The *vinayapitaka* gives the percept for the various details of the Order (*Sangha*) and regulates the entire conducts of the monks and nuns. There were a collective body of monks who lived together under the leadership of one teacher and who followed a code of rules and regulations laid down for them. It appears that the Buddha like Mahavira impressed by the unity and organisation of existing republican tribes introduced the idea of the S*angha.* Among the clan of the *Licchavis*, to which Mahavira belonged, there was provision how to live together and how to co-operate each other during the time of urgency and emergency. The Buddha after getting enlightenment formed the *Sangha* and directed his followers to move round with the message of Buddhism and spread it among the people who were yet in darkness. The Buddha advised his monks to spread out all over the world to spread *dhamma*. He declared, "Go unto all lands and preach the gospel. Tell them that the poor and the low, the rich and the high are all one, and that all castes unite in the religion as do the rivers in the sea."[2]

Buddhism and Upanishads

Like other great teachers and reformers of the age, Buddha, too, utilised the Hindu inheritance in order to bring about modification in it. The extremely rigid forms of religious sacrifices of the *Brahminical* period evoked a great spiritual unrest and revolt against the "formalism and exclusiveness of *Brahminical* system" in the *Upanishadic* period.[3] The expensive sacrifices and ritualism practiced by Hindus were denounced as 'irreligious and foolish' by intellectual stalwarts like Yajnavalkya, Janaka Videha, Ajatsatru of Kashi etc. The reaction and protest against this worn-out system proved so bitter that Janaka Videha refused to submit to the hierarchical pretensions of the *Brahmans* and asserted his right to perform sacrifices without intervention of priests. This conflict between the priest and the king may be compared with the conflict that had occurred in the ancient Roman Empire between the Monarch and the Pope. In Rome during the middle age when papal authorities had emerged the most dominant force, the Pope wanted to dominate the Monarch while the latter was not ready to surrender to the former. It was this conflict that paved the way for the growth of modernism in Europe. In India too, the conflict and aversion against the priestly system prepared the fertile ground for the growth of new religion and philosophy that appeared in the form of Buddhism and Jainism in ancient India.

The *Upanishads* talk of Supreme God that is too subtle to conceive. According to *Upanishads*, "all we can say about God is negative— it is not this, it is not that". The doctrine that Self yet essentially unknowable through the ordinary avenues of knowledge presents a puzzle, first propagated by Yajnavalkya, and has since then remained engrained in the *Vedanta* philosophy of later stage which found in *Sanskara* one of its most powerful exponents.[4]

It is generally agreed by scholars that Buddhism was but a natural reaction to this obscure and difficult philosophy of the Upanishads which was quite unintelligible to the ordinary mind. It was, as such, absolutely cut off from the ordinary mass and became an exclusive property of few scholars who had established mastery over them. It was natural to search out a new way that should have been simple to ordinary people and acceptable by reasonable persons. Thus, it was Orthodox Hinduism that paved the fertile land for the rise and growth of new philosophy where Buddhism appeared as the most dominant figure because it was simple to understand and reasonable to convince even by ordinary scholars. Buddhism originated in the same region as the *satpatha Brahman,* for instance, the country of the Videhas, the Koslas and the Sakyas. Moreover, the doctrine promulgated by Yajnavalkya in the *Brhadaranyaka Upanishad* is, in fact, less Buddhistic.[5] It is notable that by the advent of the Buddha, *Brahminism* had by now became 'an Iceland in a sea' in the following centuries till the rise of Sanskaraycarya.[6]

That is another fact that advent of Sankaracarya in the realm of Indian philosophy was such a notable period that by chasing Buddhism from the land of India successfully re-established *Brahminism* with new fervent and enlarged philosophy of Absolutism. Sanskar's commentary on the *Brahmasutras* gave birth to a host of commentaries and studies on Vedantism of great originality, vigour and philosophic insight, which was further championed by Mandana Misra (800 AD) of Mithila who strongly denounced the Buddhist. It is said that by his order the king Sudhanva downed thousands of Buddhists into the ocean and mercilessly massacred them.[7] Thereafter, the advent of the Muslims invaders and their subsequent conquests dealt a shattering blow to Buddhists.[8]

Buddhism and Vedanta: A Conflict and Adjustment

The teaching of the Buddha went against the grain of Hindu psychology and it failed to take an abiding root in India. Hinduism was based on *Sabdabramana* (the Vedas) where the Buddha repudiated all authority and traditions. The Hindus were prone to metaphysics while the Buddhists showed indifference towards it. The existence or non-existence of God did not at all interest the Buddha, as, according to him, man was the architect of his own future. There is no place for ritualism in Buddhism. On the other hand, ritualism was deep rooted in the Hindu's mind that is still prevailing in each and every Hindu's household. Buddha's conception of *Dharma* was not sufficiently concrete for practical purposes. The result was obvious. The Buddha gradually came to be defied and Buddhism was very much influenced by Hindu thought. On the other hand, Buddhism, too, exercised, almost great overwhelming influence on Hinduism. It gave birth to neo-

Hinduism which absorbed the best elements of Buddhism. It was the result of that influence that the *Shavas'* borrowed the monastic and contemplative elements of *Mahayana Sramanas* and the Buddha was given a place in Hindu pantheon as the tenth *avtara* (incarnation) of Lord Vishnu.[9] *Mahayana* was built on wholesale borrowing from Hinduism, and this process of intermingling went on until in the sixth century AD. In the words of Upendra Thakur, "Buddhism was borrowing even from *Saktism*, the most esoteric form of Hinduism. It ultimately gave rise to *Tantric*ism and *Vajrayana* with the result that the feminine divinities now found their way into the Buddhist patheon."[10] The Hindu society did not adopt Buddhism as a separate religion from Hinduism, but it borrowed a lot of things from the former to make Hinduism more effective. Adoption of the Buddha as an incarnation of the Lord Vishnu reveal the fact that the Hindus refused to practice Buddhism, but agreed to worship the Buddha.

Despite all these, Buddhism has not been totally uprooted from India. Till the death of Harsavardhana, the last Hindu king of the country, Buddhism prospered here, but after his death it began to decline specially in southern as well as plains of northern India. It did not completely disappear. It remained a visible force in the border areas of the country, especially in Jammu and Kashmir, Tibet, Meghalaya, Himachal Pradesh etc. The notable *Bhikhus* like Anagarika Dharmapala from Sri Lankas, Swami Bodhananda in Uttar Pradesh, Kripasarana Mahasthavira from Bengal, B.R. Ambedakar from Maharashtra, Rev. Negi Lama from Himachal Pradesh and others continued their sincere efforts to uphold the root and faith of Buddhism in India. The celebration of the 25000th *prinirvana* of Lord Buddha in 1956, heralded a new era in the history of Buddhism in India with the result that the Buddhist places of pilgrimage came to be renovated and Departments of Buddhist Studies set in some of the universities and institutions of India, particularly in Bihar (Deemed University of Nalanda Nav Bihar) to impart education in Buddhist region and philosophy. Today, the countries like Japan, Indonesia, and Ceylon Burma China etc., are taking deep interest to strengthen the position of Buddhism in India. They are generously contributing considerable funds to develop the palaces where Buddhism got root in the country and had left imprints.

The occupation of Tibet in 1959, by Red China created great problem for the Buddhist resided there. More than one lakh Tibet Buddhists, led by His Holiness, the Dalai Lama fled from Tibet to India as refugees and was mostly settled by the government of India at different settlements camps for Tibetan Buddhists in different states of the country. In India, Bodh Gaya, Nalanda and Rajgriha, Saranatha, Kusinara (where Buddha got *Mahaparinirvana)*, Sanchi, Lumbini etc., are the places where Buddhist activities may clearly be discerned. Thousands of Buddhists from foreign countries visit these places as pilgrimage. Nalanda Nav Bihar is the famous education centre for Buddhist education. Bodh Gaya where the Lord Buddha obtained enlightenment is the central visiting place for the Buddhists coming from inside and outside of the country. These places are well-protected and supported by the central as well as state governments of India. The South-East Asian Buddhist countries are also extending helping hand to maintain the sanctity and prosperity of these historical places where Buddhism arose and prospered.

Buddhism in New Shape and Garment

What we mean by Buddhism today is not the essence or fundamentals of this new Doctrine, but a religio-philosophical system which assimilated and adopted new ideas and beliefs from the environments in which it developed. In course of centuries, after the demise of its founder, Buddhism underwent so many changes and included within its fold so many thoughts that the original words of the Master changed beyond recognition. The history of the Buddhism is the history of developments, schism, corruptions and reforms, which the system underwent as it spread all over India and beyond. Advent of various schools in the main cult of Buddhism explicitly indicate that the mantle of Buddhism burnt by Lord Buddha has been handled by different scholars and propounders in such different ways and manners that originality of the Buddha *Dhamma* presented by the Buddha has lost its original colour and shape. It has travelled various mile-stones from its birth and met several thinkers who tried their best to make

Buddhism more expansive. In this course, Buddhism received various changes in its meaning and scope. As stated above, *Brahminism* that was at the climax when Buddhism appeared in India influenced the new religion (Buddhism) very much. Bishwanath Banerjee is also of the view that *Brahminical* ideals and principles have very much influenced and guided Buddhism, particularly (in its) later phases. The elaborate ritualistic system of the *Vajrayana* and its offshoots has given the religion a totally different form and flavour."[11] So, long as Buddha remained alive, there was no variation because there was no body to counter him. What he said or taught was treated as creed of Buddhism. Variation in the meaning of Buddhism began to take place after the demise of the great Lord. Emergence of as many as eighteen sects even before the time of Asoka disputes arose in the matter of interpretations of the words of the Buddha. Unfortunately the Buddha did not present any scripture except his words. The followers of this religion began to present different meanings of his words. In the Second Council of the *Sangha* held at Vaishali some dissenters refused to regard all *Arhats* as perfect. Thereafter, sects after sects appeared, eleven under the Theravada and seven under the *Mahasanghika*.

The *Lokotaravadins* and the sails of the *Mahasanghika* branch gave importance to the worship of *Caityas*, and defied Buddhas a super divine being. This action of the *Mahasanghika* led to the evolution of the Bodhisattva doctrine which attached much importance to the *paramitas*. The idea of the *Lokottaravadins* ultimately resulted in appearance of Mahayanism. *Mahayana* and *Hinayana* are two different Buddhist cult of thinking which developed after the demise of the Buddha. This all happened due to development of different schools of Buddhist thought. As it has already been stated, the Hinayanists are said to be upholders of the traditional and conventional interpretations of the words of the founder and branded as conservatives and *Hina* which means lower or lesser. The eighteen sections mentioned above are essentially Hinayanic. However, they never liked to be called themselves as Hinayanists. The orthodox and conservative Buddhists are always mentioned as Theravadians. The Buddhist of Myanmar,

Ceylon, Cambodia Thailand, etc., belong to the school of Theravada Buddhism, where as those of China, Japan, Mongolia, Tibet etc., follow the ideals of *Mahayana*.

Mahayana with its great emphasis on *maitri* (friendship) and *karuna* (sympathy), and also characterised by some more liberal progressive features and principles, may perhaps claim superiority over the so called Hinayanists. The Mahayanic idea is that the doctrine of *Hinayana* was preached by the Buddha as much as the *Mahayana* doctrines, but he used the former to descend to the weak intelligence of his early disciples. Since the early followers were not as much intelligent to grasp the progressive idea of Buddhism, the cult which was adopted by the Buddha at the time was traditional and conventional. There existed the conventions and traditions related to even other religions like Hinduism, Jainism etc. It was impossible to drop traditional ideas and develop totally progressive and radical idea. Banerjee has observed that "Whatever be the Mahayanic teachings, *Mahayana* is, in fact, a later phase of Buddhistic thought and religion—an advanced stage of Buddhism."[12] It is maintained that "The teachings of Sakyamuni are the seeds, those of *Hinayana* are the branches and leaves, those of *Mahayana* are the blossoms of fruits."[13] That is why the *Hinayana* is also considered as a stepping stone to *Mahayana*. The *Mahayana*, on the whole, emphasises the philosophical aspects of the religion and the Hinayanists are more ethical in their attitude. Both are so intimately related that any discussion on the one is incomplete without a look into the other.[14]

All these developments and changes in Buddhism convinced the leaders as well as followers of Hinduism that their religion is better than Buddhism. However, the kings like Ashoka and others took no much time to understand the significance of Buddhism in the interest of the people and the country as a whole. With the co-operation and sympathetic attitudes and behaviours of the kings, Buddhism availed prosperous circumstance and fertile land to develop in India.[15]

Buddhism during the Reign of Ashoka

During the first and second centuries after the *parinirvana* of the Buddha, Buddhism could hardly be distinguished from other ascetic movements. Evidently, in the Muarya period, Buddhism emerged as a distinct religion with great potentialities for expansion. In the beginning of the period, its activities were confined to Magadha and Kosla. It was the patronage of Ashoka the Great, the famous ruler of the Maurya dynasty that helped Buddhism enough to get propagation not only in the country but also out of India. He was known as Chanda Ashoka because of his cruelty and mercilessness. After the war of Kalinga where mass massacre was committed by him, his mind and heart both changed to such an extent that he took shelter in the Buddha *Dharma*, and as a sense of repentance of his act of cruelties committed during the war, Ashoka did all to expand the message of *Karuna, Metta*, *Sila* and Non-violence as well as universal brotherhood taught by the Buddha throughout the country and in the foreign countries also. He advocated tolerance for all religious sects and denominations, and respect for all pious men. It is said that he not only repented and considered the conquest of Kalinga war very painful and deplorable, but he also devoted himself to a zealous study of morality, to the love of morality and to the instructions (of people) in morality.[16] Since Buddhism carried all that Ashoka needed, he made no delay to adopt Buddhism and spread its message. Having saluted the Buddhist *Sangha* he professed his reverence and faith in the Buddha, *Dhamma* and *Sangha*.[17] In the words of Bapat, "The pillar edicts of Ashoka which were inscribed towards the end of his reign show that he was completely converted to the Buddhist ideas of kindness to all created beings. He drew up a list of different kinds of living beings which were to be exempted from slaughter."[18] He made a tour to the spots of Buddha's enlightenment and birth of the great teacher. He also visited Lumbini.

Buddhism that Ashoka embraced and propagated was characterised by *sadhamma* (true morality).[19] It did not include four Noble Truths of the Buddha, nor did it refer to Eight-fold Noble Paths. It did not discuss even salvation. He put emphasis on morality, compassion, liberality, purity, gentleness and goodness.[20] The root of Ashoka's new awareness emerged from the ashes of the massacre that he had committed during the war of Kalinga. It needed water of sympathy, benevolence, kindness, etc., that was abundantly available in the forceful current of the river of Buddhism. So, Ashoka's main concern was to heal up the people's wounds that needed sympathy and welfaristic attitude, not the doctrinal opinion. That is why he preferred moral principles of the Buddha, not his doctrinal opinions. What he received from the Buddha's teaching was not to hurt anyone even animals, birds and insects. One must be impartial and non-violent. It decried one not possessing self-control, purity of mind, gratitude and firm devotion.[21] In nutshell, he, while evicting or installing rocks, emphasised morality.[22] He wanted that all sects of religions should be united so far the case of morality and right conduct of behaviour was concerned. However, his moral and philosophical thinking moved round the 'periphery of the Buddha's teaching'.

Ashoka appointed religious officers of various grades to different provinces to help the people to lead a pious life. He had his edicts carved on rocks and stone pillars. The rocks pillars are mostly to be found at the places in the peripheries of his vast empire and the pillar edicts along with high roads or at places of pilgrimage where large crowds gathered. He wanted his subjects to follow the law of piety, and he and his family also practiced them. He visited various religious places like Bodh Gaya, Varanasi, and Saranath, etc. He performed pious jobs like planting trees alongside the roads, digging wells, opening hospitals for men and beasts both in his own land and in the lands of his neighbours like the Cholas and the Pandyas in Kerala and other countries as far south as Ceylon. Being the staunch follower of Buddhism, he offered large gifts upon the monastic establishments of the Buddhists. This attracted many non-Buddhists to the Buddhist *Sangha* for an easier life with the result that the purity of the *Sangha* suffered and consequently its periodical religious observances were interrupted. The sanctity of the *Sangha*s began to erode gradually.

Ashoka's Mission to Spread Buddhism in Foreign Countries

From the Buddhist literary sources it is evident that he sent various missions to various countries to spread Buddhism. Such missions were sent to the land of the Yavanas (Ionian

Greeks), Gandhara, Kashmir and the Himalayan regions in the north. To the western part of India, he sent missions to the places like *Aparntaka*. In the southern part the mission reached to Mysore, and further south to countries as far as Ceylon and Suvarnnabhumi (the land of the gold Malay and Sumatra. He tried to spread Buddha *Dhamma* not only in his territory or among the peoples of the border lands but also in kingdoms far off, such as those of king of Syria and the kingdoms of four other kings, still farther off, i.e., Ptolemy (Turameya of Egypt, Antigonos of Macedonia, Alexander of Epirus, (an ancient district of ancient Greece), and Magas of Cyrenia in North Africa. The evidences are still available in the rocks installed by Ashoka at different places.

Thus, it is clear that the efforts of Ashoka were largely responsible for the popularisation of the teaching of the Buddha in and outside India. It is he who paved the way for the Buddhist missionaries to Central Asia, China, Japan and Tibet in the north, and to Burma (Myanmar), Thailand, Cambodia and other countries in the south where Buddhism is still alive and active. Ashoka employed even his own son and daughter, Mahendra and Sumitra respectively, to spread Buddhism visiting foreign countries.

The rapid growth of Buddhism during the Ashoka's period to various parts of India resulted in the rise of Buddhist sects whose number is eighteen. With the spread of Buddhism, communities were founded in various parts of the country. These communities developed their respective traditions related to Buddhist teachings. However, these communities gradually merged with the major branch of Buddhism. The *Mahasanghika*, the splinter of Buddhism and which remained confined to the East and South India continued its activities. They developed a literature of their own and in fact it claimed to have preserved the most authentic tradition of early Buddhism in so far as it traced the lineage from Mahakasyapa who was responsible for convening the first Buddhist council. This school remained very much active till the fourth century AD.

Buddhism at the Time of Kanishka

Kanishka's reign is also a land mark in the history of Buddhism. He was a great religious man and his faith and devotion in Buddhism was great. There were a number of Buddhist masters during his time who played vital roles in spreading Buddhism by giving it a new meaning and direction. It was in this period that the Indo-Greek school of Buddhist art achieved its greatest development. Buddhist monks from India carried Buddhism to central Asia and China. A new form of Buddhism known as the *Mahayana*, also came to be evolved at the same time as a consequence. Kanishka contributed a lot to the development of Buddhism. It was the school of *Mahayana* that provided broader aspect of Buddhism separating its way from traditional school of *Mahasanghika*. The school of *Mahayana* developed its own authentic literature that is still available in India and also in foreign countries where Buddhism got string root. The things which are needed for a newly-emerged religion are authenticity of its creed and philosophy, the good number of followers, economic as well as royal support and faith of the people in it. Buddhism had the religious creed and philosophies of high quality and it had good number of supporters, too. What it needed further was economic assistance and administrative support. It began to receive it from the days of Ashoka. The Kanishka rulers developed their faith in sanctity and sagacity of Buddhism and spared nothing to enrich it. As a result, Buddhism became more and more prosperous in India and abroad both. The school of *Mahayana* that emerged forcefully during the region of the Kanishka's added new meaning, vigour and ethos to Buddhism. All these factors provided Buddhism the circumstance that prepared a fertile land for the growth and spread of Buddhism.

Gupta Dynasty and Buddhism

With the advent of the Gupta Dynasty, Buddhism achieved a new impetus. It is notable that the Guptas had faith in *Bhagvatas* and they honoured Hindu's religious scriptures, but their attitude toward Buddhism was not only liberal but sympathetic also. It is, perhaps, because of similarities of the Buddhist's philosophies to that of Hinduism at many points. From the beginning of the fifth century to the end of sixth century AD, evidences are available which indicate that the Kanishkas were liberal to give donation to the Buddhist monasteries. Bapat writes, "Buddhist arts with its relics at Mathura, Saranath Nalanda, Ajanta, Bagh and Dhanyakataka speak eloquently of the prosperity that Buddhism enjoyed in the Gupta period."[23] Again, Fa-Hien, A Chinese pilgrim who came to India during the reign of Chandragupta-II, testifies to the flourishing condition of Buddhism, especially in Uddiyana, Gandhara, Mathura, Kanauj, Kosala, Magadha, and Tamralipti. The foundations of the institutions at Nalanda were also due to the patronage of the Gupta rulers. The old Nalanda University was to play the biggest role in development of Buddhism not only in India but also in abroad. The high teaching of Nalanda University was so effective and meaningful that it attracted thousands of the teachers and students from the foreign countries to get acquainted with new knowledge and wisdom.

During the seventh century, though the mantle of Buddhism was not so bright, it yet brightened at Nalanda and Valabhi. King Harshavardhana in his later days became the follower of *Mahayana* Buddhism. In the west the rulers of the Maitraka dynasty at Valabhi had become patrons of the Buddhist faith from the middle of the sixth century AD. Numerous Buddhist relics discovered at Valabhi produce the evidence of Buddhism in that area in the 10th century AD.

Buddhism in India after Harshavardhana's Rule

So, long as Harshavardhana ruled India, there was peace, integrity and prosperity. He was a powerful ruler, and he was too much inclined towards religion. He had strong faith in existence of God and His power and prowess. Though his religious faith in Hinduism or in the Hindu's *Vedantic* philosophy was unshakable, he treated all religions alike. Hence, he honoured Buddhism. After his demise disputes and conflicts took place in his kingdom resulting in political anarchy. It badly affected the growth of monastic religion like Buddhism, which depended so much on the patronage of the rulers. From that time onwards, aversion among the orthodox Hindus towards Buddhism began to grow with the result that Buddhism began to fade away in India. However, in the place like Kashmir (Laddakh area), Swat Valley, Valbhi and other places in North India Buddhism remained active, no doubt, but its condition was not much prosperous. While Buddhism was slowly disappearing from other parts of the country, it experienced another great revival in eastern India under the patronage of the Pala dynasty. Most of the rulers of this dynasty were devout Buddhists. They were responsible for new endowments to the Nalanda monastery and also for the foundation of new monasteries, such as Vikramashila.

Bapat has recorded that "although some of the old centers of study had fallen into neglect before the rise of the Guptas, new and more vigorous centers came into existence under them. These new centers were numerous but, during the early Gupta period; Kashmir was the most predominant centre of Buddhist studies."[24] When the Buddhist study centre was set-up at Nalanda, the current of Buddhism shifted from Kashmir to eastern India. Nalanda became famous for Buddhist's studies not only in India but also in other countries. Thousands of foreign students were admitted in the old university of Nalanda and good management prevailed there for both the teachers and the students. Nalanda dominated the whole Buddhist world for nearly three centuries (from 6th to 9th century AD) or till it was badly ruined by the Muslim invader, Bakhtiyar Khiljee. The Pala rulers founded two other big universities for the study of Buddhism known as Vikramashila and Odantpuri. Eastern India with its new institutions Vikramashila, Odantpuri, Vikramapuri, etc., almost monopolised the commerce in Buddhist culture from 9th to the 12th centuries AD.

Buddhism in Central Asia and China

Bapat is of the view that it were the nomadic tribes like Sakas and Kushanas, as well as Indian merchants who carried elements of Indian culture with Buddhism to the different states of Eastern Turkestan at least a century before the birth of Jesus Christ. Positive evidence is now available to prove that small Indian colonies had been founded in the southern part of this region from Khotan up to the Labnor region before the Christian era. The Chinese annals of the 3rd century clearly state that there were nearly one thousand stupas and temples in Kucha in this period. Kuchean Buddhist monks had gone to China in this period and took an active part in the work of translation of Buddhist texts. Archaeological findings show that Buddhism was a flourishing religion in the north till about the 8th century AD. After the decline of these states Buddhism was patronised till the 11th century AD by the Uigur Turks who had their capital in the Turfan region.

It is said that China received Buddhism from the nomadic tribes of Eastern Turkestan towards the end of the first century of BC. Within a century Buddhism was officially recognised there as a religion worthy of toleration. Thereafter, Buddhist scholars began to come there and their activities were intensified more and more. A large number of texts were translated into the Chinese language. However, Buddhism in China had to struggle hard for its survival due to protest extended by the indigenous people. Confucianism, with its traditional prestige at the courts and its hold on the nobility, 'looked down upon Buddhism as a barbarian religion.' However, Buddhism succeeded in making its hold in China due to its richer religious tenets that lastly attracted the indigenous people who gradually developed interest in Buddhism and lastly accepted it. Moreover, the life of purity adopted by the Indian Buddhists who visited China also attracted Chinese people. Thus, Buddhism began to make deep hold in China. The foreign dynasties in China also helped Buddhism to prosper there.

Once Buddhism got strong hold in China and the Chinese scholar developed deep interest in Buddhist's philosophies, some of the Chinese scholar started to visit the places of India where centers of Buddhism was on work. Some of them were the pilgrims and scholars like Fa-hien and Huen-Tsang, who carried Buddhist literature from India to China and translated them into Chinese dialogues. Thus, a vast Buddhist literature, translated from Indian sources by Indian and Chinese scholars, helped the Chinese to read Buddhism in translation. Some of the translations also had great literary value and came to be looked upon as classics in Chinese literature. The influence of Buddhism on Chinese life and thought was tremendous. In the words of Bapat:

Besides certain forms of theistic religious beliefs, Buddhism introduced in China the doctrine of rebirth, the idea of causality, and belief in reward and retribution. Buddhist philosophy, especially its conception of reality, which permeates everything in nature and the notion of universal impermanence, had an abiding influence on the poets and artists and influenced China's atheistic outlook. Buddhism also brought to the Chinese a deep religious feeling and profound faith, which inspired the great works of art in China, such as we find in Yun-Kang, Hungmen, Tunhuang and other places.[25]

Buddhism in Korea and Japan

In Korea that is situated in the far East, Buddhism travelled during the 4th century AD. The Chinese monks were instrumental to introduce Buddhism in Korea. The chief significance of Buddhism in Korea lies in the role it played as an intermediary between China and Japan. Besides that, Buddhism in Korea also received royal patronage from the native rulers. Buddhism in Korea reached to the notable height during the 11th century during the rule of Wang dynasty of Korea. During this period several famous scholars visited China with a marked purpose to have deep knowledge about Buddhism. Due to the efforts of big scholars, Buddhism which made its hold among the aristocratic families of Korea became common faith attracting a number of indigenous people. There were several scholars who played vital role in spreading Buddhism in Korea, but the role played by Lamaism to strengthen Buddhism was greater. After the decline of Mongolian empire, the Rhee Dynasty of Korea accepted Confucianism as the leading principle of its culture and thus dislodged Buddhism from its place of honour. Nevertheless, even though it lost royal patronage in Korea, Buddhism continued to flourish as the religion of the masses.

Japan has been called as the land of *Mahayana* Buddhism where Buddhism got prominence. Buddhism in Japan travelled from China via Korea. Both the Chinese as well as Korean monks played great roles to introduce and spread Buddhism in Japan in the fourth century AD. In Japan there was practice of Shintoism, a native cult, where worship of ancestors prevailed. In the beginning, the Buddhists accepted their tradition of ancestor's worshipping and side by side with image of the Buddha, the gods of Shintoism, on the ground that these represented the various incarnations of the Buddha. In this manner Buddhism was gradually able to establish itself among the people without rejecting Shintoism outright. First, it was the aristocrats of Japan who accepted Buddhism. Once it was patronised by aristocracy, Buddhism rapidly spread throughout the country. Several emperors of ancient Japan adopted Buddhism and accepted its tenets as their guiding principles in life. They supported monasteries also. There were several sects of Buddhism that gradually found place in Japan. By the dint of the efforts of both the Tendai and the Shingon sects Buddhism became nationalised and gradually gained popularity. However, the philosophies that were introduced in Japan were yet to vague to be understood by common people of Japan who were much more inclined to superstitions. In due course of time, Buddhism in Japan got prominence by 13th century AD. Time came when common people like farmers, peasants and warriors accepted it.

During the Edo-period (1603-1867), Buddhism acquired the character of a national religion in Japan under the protection of the Tokugawa Shogunate. The chief reason for this development was that the government hoped thereby to undermine the influence of Christianity upon the life of the Japanese people. During this period various scholars appeared who helped Buddhism to be more popular. However, the opposition of this religion continued from Shintoism, but with the efforts of both monks and laymen the conflict was resolved and the government guaranteed freedom of religion under the constitutional provision. Many monks investigated the doctrine of Buddhism and tried scientifically to find a new meaning of the old doctrines. In this way, Zen-Buddhism appeared and prospered in Japan.

Japan is a Buddhist country and Buddhism has always got fertile land for its growth and expansion there. There have been many big Buddhist scholars who helped a lot to spread Buddhism and found strong centre of Buddhist study in Japan. With the adoption of European educational system several universities, colleges and research institutions came into being which have been contributing a lot to the growth of Buddhist studies there. A number of research intuitions are attached to particular Buddhist sects. There are also several institutes which specialise in Oriental studies in general, including Buddhism. Among them the most important are Toyobunka-Kenkyujo (The Oriental Cultural Research Institute) attached to the University of Tokyo, Jinbunkagaku Kenkyujo (The Research Institute of Science and Humanities) attached to the University of Kyoto.

The work of the society in London greatly influenced the outlook of Japanese scholars. Efforts have been applied to translate Pali cannons in Japanese language. The study of Pali Buddhism has now developed into that of the Agama, the *Abbhidhamma* and the *Vinya.* Each of these branches is under the supervision of competent scholar. The study of Sanskrit was introduced in Japan with research on *Mahayana* Buddhism. The comparative study of Sanskrit, Tibetan and Chinese versions of various texts has been made great progress in the recent years. Buddhist dictionaries of various kinds were compiled. The study of Chinese Buddhism has also been popular in Japan. Thus, Japan is a country where Buddhism flourished too much. The government of Japan is interested to provide monetary assistance to India for development and protection of Buddhist centers like Nalanda, Rajgriha, Bodh Gaya, Sarnath etc.

Buddhism in Tibet and Ladakh

It was not so easy to spread Buddhism in Tibet because most of the inhabitants were in the raw stage of philosophical understanding and their activities were yet confined to rustic traditional practices. However, Buddhism with some of its cultural advances and paraphernalia was brought to Tibet to replace the old animistic and Phon religious beliefs. The credit ushering in a new Buddhistic era in the history of Tibet goes to the first great monarch of Tibet, Stron-btsan-sgam-po who was a contemporary of Muhammad, the founder of Islam. Others who helped to establish Buddhism in Tibet were Emperor Harsha of Kanauj, and the famous pilgrim scholar, Yuan Chwang of China. Favour was done no doubt, but Buddhism had to cross over several oppositions extended by indigenous Phon beliefs. It had also to remove old superstitions, make compromises, adopt its own doctrines to the strange customs and traditions which had come down from time immemorial and suffer setbacks and banishment until the days of Atisa in the eleventh century, when at last Buddhism may be said to have truly became the national religion of Tibet.[26]

Tibet is a land where the practice of sorceries had taken deep root. Buddhism which believed in high tenets was beyond the reach of the common people. Hence, it was decided to send Padmasambhava, the powerful apostle of *Tantrism* with a purpose to spread it mingling with the process of sorceries. Thereafter, several other scholars of Buddhism were invited to spread Buddhism in Tibet, who tried their level best to implant the seed of Buddhist teaching there. The scholars like Santaraksita and Kamalasila, the able disciple of Santaraksita visited the place and applied the efforts to give foundation of Buddhism in Tibet. Chinese monks also entered into the land of Tibet with the same purpose. At the same time, the royal family was also disturbed due to constant conspiracy for power. It is only in the 11th century AD that Atisa may be said to have brought the last great spiritual impetus from India, with the result Buddhism struck deep roots in Tibetan soil and thereafter, flourished as an indigenous mode of religious and philosophical thought. The successors of Tibetan kings continued to rule in western Tibet through various political vicissitudes which that part of Tibet underwent, and the direct descendants of the mighty Sron-btsan-sgam-po, the first historical ruler of Tibet in Lhsa, still live in Ladakh.

From the time Atisa came to Tibet, Tibetan Buddhism developed into different indigenous schools. In relation to these the earlier heterogeneous and unreformed type of Buddhas came to be called Rani-ma-pa or the Old School with four main sub-sects. The followers of this school worshipped Padmasambhava as their founder and Guru, believe in fulfillment of both the divine and the demonical. They are generally recognised as such by their red caps. Atisa's reformed teachings, based upon the *Yogacara* traditions founded by *Maitera* and *Asanga*, led to the establishment of the Bkah-gdams-pa school by his Tibetan disciple, Hbron-ston. It took a systematic view of the teachings of both the *Hinayana* and

Mahayana. It was on the authoritative basis of this doctrine that the great Tibetan reformer, Tson-kha-pa, founded the 14th century AD the Dge-lugs-pa school, which purified the Bkah-gdams-pa of much of its elaborate ritualism. Today, it dominates Tibetan Buddhism both temporarily and spiritually through the religious succession of the Dalai Lamas. Besides that, in Tibet some other schools of Buddhism also appeared having their separate set of practices and beliefs.[27]

Nepal under the Influence of Buddhism

Like Tibet, Nepal is also a neighbouring country of India. It was Nepal near which (Lumbini) Gautam Buddha was born in the family of Shakya. In the third century BC Ashoka the great had already applied the effort to spread the message of Buddhism in Nepal. He himself had visited Lumbini twice and his daughter, Carumati, is said to have married a Nepalese noble man. Carumati built several stupas and monasteries in Nepal. The great Buddhist philosopher of the 4th century AD, Acarya Vasubandhu, is also said to have visited Nepal in order to propagate his own doctrine. However, Nepal assumed greater influence of Buddhism in 7th century AD during the days of the king Amsuvarman. His daughter was married to the powerful king of Tibet who helped enough to assist proliferation of Buddhism in Nepal. During the 9th and 10th centuries AD strong religious and cultural developments took place between these two countries. In the succeeding centuries, when the Muslims invaded Bihar and Bengal, Buddhist monks took shelter in Nepal. They took with them large number of valuable manuscripts some of which also found their way to the monasteries in Tibet. In Nepal, four sects mentioned below developed which still have its influence.

1. *Svabhavika*, which emphasises that all things in the world have their own ultimate characteristics which is expressed in two ways—*pravriti* (evolution) and *nivriti* (involution).
2. *Aisvarika*, which puts its faith in a self-existent god, who is perfect and infinite.
3. *Karmika*, which believes in a conscious moral effort through which the world phenomenon is developed on the fundamental basis of *avidya.*

4. *Yatrika*, which believes in the existence of conscious intellectual agency and free will.

This represents an almost complete fusion of various philosophical trends which originated in India and Tibet under the influence of both Hinduism and Buddhism.

Buddhism in Ceylon and Burma (Myanmar)

It was Ashoka the Great (273-236 BC) who applied the effort to bring Ceylon under the influence of Buddhist philosophy by sending various missions. He sent his son, Thera Mahendra, together with four others to Ceylon, and they preached the teaching of Gautam Buddha to the people and the king. It is said that the teaching was so impressive that it attracted thousands of people to adopt Buddha *Dharma* and became *Bhikhus*. Monasteries were erected all sides. There were several women who liked to become *Bhikhuni,* but it was not allowed because there was no one to admit them in *Sangha*. Thereafter, the sister of Mahendra, Sanghamitra was sent to Ceylon and ordination was given to the women of Ceylon. At the advice of Ashoka a branch of the Bodhi tree under which Gautam had attained Buddhahood was transplanted in Ceylon that created enchanting influence on the people. This served as an inspiration to the people who had recently embraced Buddhism. The second event was the bringing of the Buddha's tooth from India more than 500 years later. Thereafter, Buddhism got strong hold in Ceylon and most of the population adopted Buddhism as their religion.[28]

The great stupa was built during the reign of Dutthagamani (101-77 BC) and consecrated before a large assembly of Buddhist monks who had come from well-known monasteries in India. The Buddhist literature was transferred to Ceylon and Pali became the literary language of Ceylon. The Pali cannon was preserved there which became the ultimate sources of Buddhist knowledge in Myanmar, Cambodia, Shiam, Laos. Gradually, Thera Buddhism flourished. The archaeological remains at Hmawza, about five miles away from modern Prome, and the Chinese accounts leave no doubt that the Theravada form of Buddhism with Pali canonical texts was introduced in the region round from not later than the fifth century AD by

Indian missionaries who came from the eastern coast of Deccan and south India. At the same time the *Mula-sarvastivcada* and Mahayanism also entered there from eastern India.

According to the tradition preserved in the Ceylonese Chronicles, two Buddhist monks, namely, Sona and Uttra were sent by emperor Ashoka to preach Buddhism in Burma. However, such historical fact is the subject of controversy. Though Buddhism in Burma flourished from fifth century AD, but it appears that it had already influenced the Burmese people even before BC It was the Theravada school of Buddhism that spread its root there. There are good grounds for supporting that the Theravada form of Buddhism flourished among the Hinduised Monks or Talaings settled in Pegu, Thaton and other neighbouring regions collectively known as Rammnadesa, sometime before the 11th century AD. Thaton became a very important centre of this religion. Slowly, the Burmese of Pagan adopted the religion of Buddhism, language, literature and scripts of the monks. Aniruddha and his successors became the great champions of the Theravada form of Buddhism. Along with their political authority it spread all over Burma. The *Brahminical* religion that had prevailed there, gradually yielded to Buddhism. The ruler Aniruddha built numerous pagodas or temples and monasteries. His successors continued the work. Thereafter, the literature of Buddhism spread among the people.

Ceylon remained under the rule of Portuguese, Dutch and British in modern era. During their rule Buddhism in Ceylon fell to a low rank. Kittisiri Rajasing (1746-1779 AD.), the ruler of the Kandyan province, had to send emissaries to Siam to reestablish higher ordination in Ceylon. Other groups with similar purpose went to Burma at the beginning of the 19th century, and thus were established in Ceylon three fraternities Siamese, Burmese (Upper Burma) and Ramanna (lower Burma). When the British captured the land of Ceylon in 1815, the Christian missionaries applied the efforts to spread Christianity in the land. However, with the efforts of some committed Buddhist monks Buddhism remained in practice. The root of Buddhism in Ceylon was so deep that it was not possible for the Christian Missionaries to uproot it. The Theosophical Society of Colombo which controlled 350 Buddhist educational institutions played vital role to protect Buddhism. A number of steps including opening of new institutions and publishing Buddhist scriptures have been taken to popularise Buddhism in Ceylon. It may be observed that under the guidance of professor G.P. Malalsekera of the university of Ceylon, Ceylon has taken the lead in trying to bring all Buddhist countries together and to set-up the World Fellowship of Buddhism, which successfully met in Ceylon (1950), Japan (1952), Burma (1954), Nepal (1956) Thailand (1958).

Burma was ruled by its own kings right up to 1886, Buddhism continued to flourish without trouble. The country established its reputation for study of *Tripitaka*. A number of monasteries were built. Mandala has always been its educational and religious centers and its monasteries possess many rare manuscripts. Under the British occupation, practice of Buddhism remained undisturbed. After getting independence Burmese government has taken swift measures to bring about the revival of Buddhism and Buddhist teaching. A Buddhist Sasana Council was set-up and under its auspices several centers of Buddhist studies have been opened.

Malay and Buddhism

Mahayana Buddhism flourished in this region in the sixth century AD. This is proved by an inscribed clay tablet found near Keddah which may be assigned to the sixth century AD, on paleographical grounds. It contains the Sanskrit verse embodying some philosophical doctrines of the *Mahayana* school. *Mahayana* Buddhism continued to flourish in this region till the 8th century AD and possibly much later. An inscription found at Ligor refers to the construction of three brick temples for Buddhist gods and of five stupas by the king and priests. The stupas were built in Saka year of 697 which is equivalent to 775 AD.

Buddhism in Siam (Thailand)

Here Buddhism flourished from early period that is 1st and 2nd century AD. The archaeological remains available at Pong Tuk and Phra Pathom prove it. Phra Pathom is nearly 30 miles away from Bangkok, and Pong Tuk lies about 20 miles farther to the west. In these places, the image of the Buddha, inscribed terracotta and definite symbols of Buddhism like the *dharmacakra*, belonging probably to the first or second century AD have been found. About the 8th and 9th centuries AD both Siam and Laos formed part of Kambuja (Cambodia) politically and were influenced by the religious conditions of the country. So, both the *Brahminical* religion and Buddhism can be found flourishing side by side in all these regions. About the middle of the 13th century AD the Thais made themselves masters of Siam and Laos and put an end to the political supremacy of the Cambodians over them. Under the influence of the Thai rulers, Buddhism of the Theravad School and the Pali language flourished all over Siam and Laos. The Thai king Sri Suryavanasa Rama Maha-Dharmikarajadhiraja was not only a great patron of Buddhism, but he himself adopted the life of a Buddhist monk, preaching the doctrines of the Buddha all over his kingdom.

About 1361 AD, he sent some learned *Bhikkhus* and scholars to Ceylon and induced the great monk called Mahasami Sanghraja to come to Siam under his inspiration and the active efforts of the king, Buddhism and Paliu literature not only obtained a firm footing but also spread to a number of small Hinduised states in the territory now called Laos, such as Alavirastra, Khmerrastra, Suvarnagrama, Unmarga-Sila, Bonakarastra and Haripunzaya. Many of these still possesses their local chronicles written in Pali. From this time onwards Buddhism flourished in Siam and the neighbouring regions, and *Brahminism* declined until it almost disappeared, leaving only a few traces in public ceremonies and customs.

Today in Thailand, Buddhism is the state religion. Like Burma Buddhism here remained in practice without much disturbances. The state has a separate administration for religious affairs and the government spends large sums of money for the religious well-being of Buddhists, monks and laity alike. There are two great institutes of higher learning for the Buddhist monks—the Maha Makut Raja Vidyalaya Academy and the Maha Culankaran Raja Vidyalaya Academy. Sanskrit is now taught in Bangkok both at Culankaran University and the Academy for Buddhist monks. Thailand has always been in forefront of Buddhist studies and it is a matter of gratification that as many as forty five volumes of the Pali *Tripatika,* at least thirty volumes of *Attahkathas* and ten volumes of Pakaranas have been published in Siamese script. The country also preserves some rare books of Buddhism.

Kambuja (Cambodia) and Buddhism

Cambodia is a very small country, but it has always been the stronghold of Theravada Buddhism. The archaeological finds and the Chinese chronicles prove that from the end of the 5th century AD, Buddhism flourished in Cambodia though it did not occupy a dominant position, as it was less popular than some forms of *Brahminical* region like *Saivism*. The great emperor, Basovarman, who ruled at the end of the 9th century AD, established a Saugatasrama which was specially meant for the Buddhist monks, and elaborate regulations were laid down for the guidance of this *asrama* or hermitage.

King Jayavarman-VII (1181-circa 1220 AD) was a devout Buddhist and received the posthumous title *Mahaparamasaugata*. The records of his reign express beautifully the typical Buddhist view of life, particularly the feeling of charity and compassion towards the whole universe. His role in the founding of religious institutions was magnificent.

Buddhism continued to flourish in Combodia in 13th century AD. It must be remembered, however, that up to this, although Buddhism was in a flourishing condition it was neither the state religion nor even the dominant religious sect in the country. There is no definite information as to when Buddhism attained this position. But the change was undoubtedly due to the influence of the Thais of Siam, who, as already mentioned, were ardent Buddhists and had conquered large part of Cambodia. Whereas in the earlier period Siam was influenced by Cambodia, the role was now reserved, and Cambodia, under the influence of the Thais, was converted, almost wholesale, to Buddhism. Even the *Brahminical* gods in the great centuries like Angkor Vat were replaced by Buddhist images. It is not traceable exact stages of this conversion, but, gradually, Buddhism became the dominant creed in Combodia and today there is hardly any trace of the *Brahminical* religion in the country, except in some of the ceremonies and festivities of the people of Cambodia.

A school was set-up to diploma to the Pali students. This school has now developed into a college. In 1933, the authorities began to establish elementary Pali schools where the monks took a three year course. A royal library was also set-up in 1925. In the same year, a Buddhist institute appeared. Thus, Buddhism in Cambodia has been on rise constantly.

Laos and Buddhism

Laos is mostly mountainous and comparatively backward country. Although the country belongs to the Theravada school and the Pali *Tripitika* forms its sacred literature, it has few Pali scholars. It appears, however, that there exists in Laos many texts which are word-to-word commentaries of the Pali texts. In Luangbrabang, the capital, in a small temple on the hill, there is a library of manuscripts in which Laotian Nissaya are available. In this country, the *Jataka* enjoys great popularity and separate collections of ten to fifty Jatakas are available.

Vietnam

Vietnam was formerly known as Campa, a name evidently given to it by its Hindu colonist. Buddhism had obtained a footing in the country before the 3rd century AD. It may be inferred from the discovery of fine bronze Buddha image of Amravati School which may be dated about that period.

When the Chinese captured the capital city of Campa in 605 AD, they carried away 1,350 Buddhist works. From this important statement, it can be inferred that Buddhism must have flourished in the country for a considerable period before the 7th century AD. It is also found that the school of *Mahayana* was more dominant there. *Tantric* forms also prevailed there. Buddhism enjoyed the patronage of kings and high officials. Ruins of the great Buddhist establishment at a place called Dong Duong, including a temple and monastery built by King Jaya Indravarmana in 875 AD. are available. Buddhism of the *Mahayana* form continued as a living force in Campa right up to the 15th century AD, when the country was over-run by the enmities from the North. The enmities formerly liked in Tonkin, derived their culture from China. So, the Chinese form of Buddhism along with Islam replaced the old religion in Campa.

In the 20th century, there arose a new movement for the revival of Buddhism and Association of Buddhist Studies was started in Saigon (1931), Hue (1932), and Hanoi (1932). The new movement favoured the use of the Vietnamese language in Roman script for their religious books instead of Chinese. An awakening took place among the monks and the Laity and there was a movement to spread knowledge among the masses. However, the Second World War interrupted all these efforts. With the returns of peace, renewed efforts of reorganisation were made in 1948 in Hanoi in Northern Vietnam with the inspiring initiation and guidance of their eminences new schools were opened where Buddhist teaching continued. Hence, Vietnam is a place in the world where Buddhism is still alive with vigour and strength.

Indonesia under the Influence of Buddhism

Indonesia was under the influence of Hinduism from the beginning. It is evident from the statement of Fa-Hien who visited this island in 414 AD. According to him Buddhism was not much flourishing at that time. It was the missionary zeal of Gunavarman (an Indian monk) who introduced Buddhism there and obtained a strong hold on the island in less than a quarter of a century after Fa-Hien's visit. Buddhism was also introduced in the island of Sumatra, particularly in the kingdom of Sri-Vijaya, which is usually identified with Palembang. It appeared from some inscriptions found in this region that the king who ruled Sri-Vijaya in the year 683-684 AD, was a Buddhist. The famous Chinese traveller I-tsing who visited India in the last quarter of 7th century AD, said that the king of Sri-Vijaya as well as the rulers of neighbouring states favoured Buddhism and that Sri-Vijaya was very important centre of Buddhist learning in the island of Southern Asia. The Buddhist priests in Sri-Vijaya numbered more than a thousand and they studies all the subjects as in Madhyadesa (India) I-tsing spent some time in Sri-Vijaya in order to study Buddhist scriptures and he had left a very interesting account of the popularity of Buddhism in the island of the Southern sea consisting of more than ten countries. He gives a list of these ten countries and the states that "Buddhism is embraced in all these and other smaller islands and mostly the system of *Hinayana* is adopted except in Malayu (Sri-Vijaya) where there are few who belong to the *Mahayana*."[29]

A famous professor of old Nalanda University confirms the fact that Indonesia remained the centre of string of Buddhism from 7th to 11th centuries AD. A strong impetus to the *Mahayana* was given by the Sailendra Dynasty, who ruled over the Malay Peninsula and a part of Indonesia. The Sailendra kings were great patrons of this form of Buddhism and erected monumental structures. Under the influence of the Sailendra, Mahayanism flourished in Java and Sumatra for a long period but the influence of Bengal seems also to have been responsible for the introduction of the debased *Tantric* forms of Buddhism both in Java and Sumatra. We have a fairly detailed account of some later kings of both these countries, who were followers of these cults. We have also two important *Mahayana* tests viz., the Sang Hyang Kam, *Kamahayanan*, *Mantranaya* and the Sang hyang Kamahayanikan, which give us a fair insight into the leading conception of Mahayanism in Java. It is notable that Buddhism tried to spread its wings in the countries like Bali and Borneo, but it could not flourish their due to strong hold of Hinduism in these countries.

Concluding Remarks

Thus, it may be said that Buddhism having its root in India spread in several countries. Though it has declined in India, its influence in other countries where it reached is still very much alive. Buddhism is not a faith, but a culture, a way of life and a philosophy-based on scientific attitude. That is why it got strength in the countries where culture of the natives was either not matured or shaky. Ceylon, Burma, Siam, Cambodia Laos, Japan, Tibet, Magnolia, Nepal, Sikkim, Bhutan and Ladakh received not only their religion but practically the whole of their civilisation and culture. How much the introduction of Buddhism meant to the people of Japan, has been clearly stated by Dr D.T. Suzuki. Speaking of the eagerness with which they took up the study of the *Dhamma* in Nara period, he remarks, "Buddhism was to them a new philosophy, a new culture and an inexhaustible mine of artistic impulses."[30] Again speaking of the reason which led the government of that period to build temples and monasteries, maintain monks, and nuns and erect a gigantic bronze image of Buddha Vaiocana, he reminds one of the facts that in those days, the Buddhist temples worked as schools, hospitals, dispensaries, orphanages refuse for old age, and the monks were school masters, nurses, doctors, engineers, keepers of free lodges, cultivators of land explorers of wilderness etc. When the community was still in a primitive stage of evolution the Buddhists were leaders in every sense, and the government naturally encouraged their activities."[31] Buddhism in these countries, which were passing the phase of primitive cultured mostly-based on animism, appeared as a new bright light that broadened the spiritual as well as social aspects of life. It opened a new way which led people towards wisdom and enlightenment. As the years rolled down, the light of Buddhism spread throughout the central Asia to its East Bapat remarks:

Buddhism was in fact a spring wind blowing from one end of the garden of Asia to the other end causing to bloom not only the lotus of India, but the rose of Persia, the temple flower of Ceylon, the Zebina of Tibet, the chrysanthemum of China and the cherry of Japan Asian culture is, as a whole, Buddhist culture.[32]

To Quote Dr Suzuki Once More

> If the East is one, and there is something that differentiates it from the West, the differentiation must be sought in the thought that is embodied in Buddhism. For it is in Buddhism thought and in other that India, China and Japan, representing the East could be united as one each nationalist has its own characteristic modes of adapting the thoughts to its environmental needs, but when the East as a unity is made to confront the west, Buddhism supply the bond.[33]

As stated above most of these countries in the early period of their history were war like countries inhabited by the people who were ferocious by nature. Except China and India, they lacked ancient civilisation and culture. They were all disunited and quarreled among themselves. Buddhism having the slogan of peace and brotherhood appeared before them and taught them how to live and how to behave. It gave them the wisdom that made them civilised. Though Christianity had also appeared before them along with the Western rule, yet it failed to impress them more because of its selfish nature and intention to subjugate the people politically, culturally and religiously. Moreover, Christianity came to them from far-flung countries of European continent whereas Buddhism travelled to them from the Asian continent to which they belonged. In other words, Buddhism was the product of the soil to which they belonged. They, in fact, needed a religion, a culture, away and an outlook that could have led them towards peace, prosperity and well-being. Buddhism alone supplied all these qualities to them. So, it prospered in central as well as eastern Asia.[34]

References

1. *A History of Indian Philosophy*, III, p. 537 also see p. 528 ff.
2. Jagdish Chandra Jain, "Two Great Religion of Magadha", in P.N. Ojha, *Home to Bhikhu Jagdish Kashyap*, Nalanda Nav Bihar, 1986, p. 155.
3. *Samyutta Nikaya*, V. 421-23.
4. Jagdish Chandra Jain, "Two Great Religions of Magadha", in P.N. Ojha, *Home to Bhikhu Jagdish Kashyap*, *op. cit.* p. 160.
5. Rapson, *Ancient India*, p. 63. Also see, Upendra Thakur, *History of Mithila,* p. 97. and G.G. Pande, *The Origin of Buddhism*, p. 309.
6. *Ibid.,* pp. 98-104.
7. G.G. Pande, *op. cit.,* Chap. VIII.
8. Rapson, *Ancient India*, p. 148.
9. For detail study see Upendra Thakur, *Jainism and Buddhism in Mithila,* chap. II.
10. Cf, Madhva's Sanskara-digvijaya and also Buddhaachraya, Introduction II, fn, 1.
11. *Kryaratnakare Bible*, Indica Series, p. 105.
12. Upendra Thakur, "Buddhism in Bihar, Past and Present", in

P.N. Ojha, Ed. *Homage to Bhikhu Jagdish Kashyap, op. cit.,* p. 16.

13. Biswanath Banerjee, "A Peep into Modern Buddhism", in P.N. Ojha, *Home to Bhikhu Jagdish Kashyap, op. cit.,* p. 26.
14. *Ibid.,* p. 27.
15. Quoted in *Ibid.,* p. 27.
16. *Ibid.,* p. 28.
17. H. Hilutzsch, *Corpus Inscriptionum Indicarum* Vol. I, (Inscriptions of Ashoka), New Edition, Oxford, 1925, pp. 43-47.
18. Bhabru Rock Edict or Calcutta Bairat Rock Inscription.
19. Bapat, P.V., *2500 Years of Buddhism*, published by Director of Publications Division, Ministry of Information and Broadcasting, New Delhi, sixth reprint, 1997, p. 51.
20. Bhabru Rock Edicts.
21. Pillar Edicts II.
22. Rock Edicts VII.
23. Rock Edicts XIII.
24. Bapat, P.V., *2500 Years of Buddhism*, published by Director of Publications Division, Ministry of Information and Broadcasting, New Delhi, sixth reprint, 1997, 56.
25. Bapat, P.V., *2500 Years of Buddhism, op. cit.,* p. 57.
26. *Ibid.,* p. 60.
27. *Ibid.,* 66.
28. For detail study in this regard, see *Ibid.*, pp. 69-72.
29. For detail study in this regard see, *The History and Culture of Indian People*, Vol. II-IV (Bombay).
30. Quoted in Bapat, P.V., *2500 Years of Buddhism, op. cit,* p. 83.
31. Dr D.T. Suzuki, "Japanese Buddhism", *Essays in Zen-Buddhism*, Third series, Rider, London, 1953, p. 340.
32. *Ibid.,* p. 340.
33. Bapat, P.V., *2500 Years of Buddhism, op. cit.,* p. 397.
34. Dr D.T. Suzuki, "Japanese Buddhism", *Essays in Zen-Buddhism*, Third series, Rider, London, 1953, p. 348.

9

Revival of Hinduism and Declination of Buddhism in India

It is surprising to note that Buddhism that emerged on the soil of India and, spread its roots all over the world making strong hold in the countries like Tibet, Bhutan, Nepal, China, Myanmar, Japan, Ceylon, Cambodia, Laos, Java Sumatra, Indonesia, Vietnam, etc., gradually faded away in India. No doubt, the country still has some noted centers of Buddhism where thousands of foreign visitors or pilgrims visit them every year. Bodh Gaya where the Buddha attained enlightenment under the Bodhi tree is the place which is famous for Buddha's temple and *Dhammcakra*. Ruins of old Nalanda University which had remained the world fame educational centre for teaching of Buddhism and where thousands of students from different parts of the world landed for higher education, reminds the significance of the Buddhism and its teachings. Saranath (Kusinagar) where the Buddha remained for a number of years and took his *Mahaparinirvana* has become a pious place for Buddhist pilgrimages. Images of Buddha in different postures found in archaeological evictions from different places in India reveal the truth that there was a time when the Buddha was worshiped like God and Buddhism was the way of the life of millions of Indians. Various Pillars and Rocks having inscription of Buddhist teachings installed by several Indian kings from time to time remind one that Buddhism was very much popular in India having royal support and people's faith. Despite all that, Buddhism began to decline in the country with the revival of Hinduism with the advent of the great Indian scholar Sankaracarya from the 7th century AD. There are several factors responsible for declination of Buddhism in India, but the revival of *Brahminism* and its mounting attack upon Buddhism is the greatest factor. This chapter discusses and analyses about conflict of *Brahminical* cult of religion with the tenets of Buddhism along with other factors responsible for declination of Buddhism in the country. This chapter also discusses and examines the factors responsible for declination of Buddhism in India. It analyses the impact of *Vedanta* on Buddhist thought and its consequences.

Brahminism, a Corollary of Vedanta

In the Indian ancient religious scriptures the world '*Brahman*' has great significance because it is directly related to the Absolute Truth or Supreme God. Here *Brahman* does not mean a supreme caste/class of India that stood above all other castes or the system of *Varna-ashram*. Here *Brahman* means the creator of the universe, the sustainer of the universe and destroyer of the universe. According to the *Vedantic* philosophy, everything- living or non-living emanates from *Brahman* and ultimately merges into it. The *Brahman* is the ultimate source of creation and final abode of annihilation. The *Brahman* is Absolute Truth is permanent, eternal, endless, all pervasive, source of all energies, unlimited abode of everything, unmoveable, unseen, shapeless and formless, etc. The *Brahman* being the primary cause of everything is without any cause. Such notions of the *Brahman* are available in the Indian *Vedas*, *Upanishads* and other epics. The Hindus have the *Sanatan-Dharma* (a religion without beginning and end) that appeared and spread all over the country from time immemorial. It remains in existence even after final dissolution of the universe. The *Brahmans* having the knowledge of *Vedanta* emerged as a class, and, later on, they developed rituals for worshipping gods. They developed the practice of ritualism as a means to worship and please to God, and a number of gods and goddesses. The cult of worshipping God has Vedic resources based on *mantras* and *yjanas*. Since the *Brahmans* possessed the methods of *yjanas,* they developed a cult known as *Brahminism* which prevailed in the country inviting people to participate in it and get the Godly blessing and benefits. As the years rolled down, *Brahminism* became orthodox in its nature that paved the fertile ground for the growth of blind faiths and superstitions with the result that its basic tenets and utility were subdued by the practice of blind ritualism as well as formalism.

Protest against Orthodox Brahminism

The sixth century BC was an age of great spiritual upsurge. Ascetics and hermits roamed about, from place to place throughout the Gangetic valley of India advocating mental discipline and asceticism as means of salvation. As the ceremonial acts and sacrificial rites prescribed in the Vedic texts could not satisfy the urge of the philosophers, it became necessary to go to deeper to the depth of the ultimate truth. Here comes the period of the Upanishads (700 BC to 600 BC) that started to make inquire and investigation to know the divinity and the reality. Here is an ardent desire to know, to go beyond the Vedas. The question that perplexed the mind of the contemporary philosophers was: what is *Brahman* (ultimate truth)? Wherefrom do we come? How should we live? What is this universe like? How did it start? When will it end and so on?

The neo-philosophers who appeared in the sixth century BC denied the authority of the Vedas as having superhuman origin and rejected the usefulness of sacrificial rites enunciated by the priestly class. They denied the existence of an intelligent first cause of this universe. They did not believe in efficacy of caste, but enunciated the thesis that it is not through birth but through one's own deeds, a person either an untouchable or a Brahmin should be counted. At the same time, the philosophy of *Carvakas* that taught non-existence of God or soul, prevailed. He denied the existence of any supernatural power. Rather he advocated the philosophy of materialism. They held that consciousness was not the quality of any unperceived non-material or spiritual entity, but a by- product of material elements such as the earth, fire, water, air and ether. *Carvaka's* philosophy also denied the concepts like next transcendental world, rebirth of soul and salvation. Thus, numerous philosophical schools outside the spell of *Brahminism*, of the days of the Buddha and Mahavira prevailed that created more confusion and caused more conflicts among the people. Need was felt to develop a religious as well as spiritual knowledge without complicacy. It has already been thoroughly discussed that how Gautam Buddha, the prince of Sakya dynasty, renouncing the royal life and family, appeared as the Buddha claiming that he had obtained full enlightenment visualising truth.

Upendra Thakur is of the view that "Like other great teachers and reformers of the age, the Buddha, too, utilised the Hindu inheritance in order to bring about some improvement in it."[1] Though, the Buddha went against the teaching of *Brahmans*, the *Vedantic* philosophy served as the fundamental base for the development of his doctrines. The extremely rigid forms of religious sacrifices of the *Brahminical* period evoked a great spiritual unrest and revolt against the 'formalism and *Brahminical* system' in the *Upanishadic* age.[2] It has already been discussed that the expensive sacrifices and ritualism were denounced as 'irreligious and foolish by intellectual stalwarts like Vijnavalkya, Janka Videha, Ajatasatru of Kasi, etc. The reaction and protest against this worn-out system invoked Gautam to protest it. This *Brahminical* cult overlooked the philosophy of Upanishads that emphasised on significance of Brahma and *Atman*. But a close analysis of the Buddha's teachings and ways of the life prescribed by him has some direct or indirect association with the philosophies of the Hindu.

The Buddha's Attack upon *Brahminism*

The Buddha who appeared in the sixth century BC confronted with such conflicting philosophies. He had fully realised the futility of orthodox *Brahminism* in the life of mankind. He took no time to understand that it was on shaky foundation of blind faith. He also realised that the superstitions developed under the shadow of *Brahminism* were not only useless but harmful also to the general mass. So, his first attack was on excessiveness of *Brahminism* and secondly, he too, denied the existence of any supreme power like God as a creator of the universe, and soul as an integral particle of God. However, the path which he developed was not on the line of *Carvakas* nor it accepted the view of nihilism. Rather he preferred a middle way. He neither approved the doctrine of perpetual eternality (*Sasvatavada*) nor of those nihilists who believe consciousness to be a product of material elements, which is destroyed along with the destruction of the body. Though he condemned ritualism of *Brahminism*, he did not reject the doctrines of *karma* and rebirth as well as *nirvana* which existed in the Hindu religion prior to the advent of Buddhism. Main concern of the Buddha was not the metaphysics, but the mundane world and the people. He emphasised on pragmatic aspect of philosophy preferring psychology and morality. He thought that the mankind had been caught in the whirlpool of ignorance resulting in pains and suffering. So, he devoted his efforts to get the man realise the reality of life and adopt the ways searched by him to get rid of pains and suffering. He was either unknown to the idealist and speculative theory of Ultimate Reality or knowingly avoided its usefulness in the practical life of mankind.

Upanishads, too, were not clear about the concept of Absolute Truth. Its Dogma related to God, *'Na iti, Na iti...'* created more confusion. The Buddha had to find out the reality not for him but for all common people. The scholars are of the view that Buddhism was but a natural reaction to this obscure and difficult philosophy of the Upanishads which was quite unintelligible to the ordinary mind. So, the knowledge related to absolute truth reflected in the Upanishads had become the property of a few who could understand it. Popular discontent began to grow and seek some outlet elsewhere. According to G.C. Pande, thus, the leaders of Hinduism had themselves prepared the ground which proved very fertile for the new religion—Buddhism- - to thrive on. The Buddhism originated in the same region as the *Satapatha Brahman*, for instance, the country of Videhas, the Koslas and the Sakyas. Moreover, the doctrine promulgated by Yajnavalkya in the *Brhadaranyaka Upanishad* is in fact more or less Buddhistic.[3]

The Buddha vehemently denounced the heretical views of the time 'fruitless'. The Buddha was not alone to criticise *Brahminism*, but attack was made from other scholars also. *Brahminism* had by now become "an island in a sea."[4] The majority of the people followed the new order till the rise of Sankaracarya.[5]

Buddhism at the Cross-road of Schism

In the words of Lokesh Chandra, "It (Buddhism) sought a dispassionate analysis of the causes of suffering and scientific search for their remedy. Away from ritual the human personality and its will for virtue were elevated to a supreme height. The gods became epic figures, possessing the majestic and crystalline impersonality of principles that governs the universe."[6] It searches the point that governs all and that point is inner-development, to know oneself.

No doubt, Buddhism became popular not only in India but even beyond India attracting millions of people all over the world. But like other religions, it, too, met the fate of division and schism that has already been discussed in the succeeding chapter of the book. As it generally happens, when a religion or religious philosophies take birth, in course of time various sects related to the original theme appear in pursuit of more clear explanation and interpretations. So, Buddhism, too, in due course of time or rather to say after the demise of its profounder the Buddha, met the fate of division and schism.

In the words of Lokesh Chandra:

> Sakyamuni was transformed from Master into Lord. Solar myths, fire cults, and immemorial fantasies transmuted him into an idealised figure. The Enlightened One became the Enlightening One, the radiator of Light. From Buddha the interest shifted to the abstraction of Buddhahood. From an individual he became a symbol. *Nirvana* was transformed into paradise, and *karma* became modifiable by prayer. Elaborate patterns emerged. Buddhism was face to face with Absolute, the Ultimate, the First, the Eternal, the everlasting and the All-pervading which now had the adamantine purity of the Adi-Buddha. With metaphysical daring this Eternal *par excellence*, definable

> by negatives alone, became the bejeweled *sambhoga kaya,* passionately embracing his transcendent consort or *prajana.* Extreme serenity was identified with extreme passion, the crystal light with the fire of love, the intangible with all the intoxication of the senses. Sensuality and symbolism metaphysical filigree of jewel, caresses and cerebrality, earth and sky were celebrated in proportion, and harmony in portraiture and cryptograms. Hymns crystallised into miniature and scrolls, and into statues to carry eternal depth to the eyes of the faithful of the earth.[7]

The statement of Lokesh Chandra gives immense indication how Buddhism falling in the hands of those who lacked real wisdom and who preferred material enjoyment, went from the best to the worst. Morality which was foundational base of Buddhism began to decline paving the way for growth of indiscipline and immorality.

Buddha's Doctrine of *Anatmavada* (Soullessness)

One of the greatest causes of declination of Buddhism is the 'Doctrine of *Anatmavada.*' In the Hindu philosophy God, Soul (*atman*) and World is the base of spiritualism as well as religion. The entire edifice of Hindu philosophy as well as the spiritualistic views is related to these three words—God, Soul and World. If soul is removed from the trinities, there is no philosophy of spiritualism. On the other hand, the Buddha denied the concept of soul and developed the doctrine of *Sarvam Anatman* that means "All is without soul." Buddhist philosophy denies soul as "an eternal substance exempt from the vicissitudes of change and incapable of entering into combination with anything else."[8] According to Dharmapala, *Atman* means supreme authority which is identical with freedom, eternality and absolute unity. Such an *Atman* is an organism associated with five aggregates, an absolute existence separate from the aggregates while living together. But the Buddhist philosophers did not approve such views. The denial of the Buddhist philosophy of *Atman* is fully-based on the universal principle of impermanence. When the doctrine of impermanence is accepted, in that case, the acceptance of eternality, absolute unity or supreme authority in any case becomes meaningless.

As a result of it, an existence like the above cannot have *Atman* or Ego. However, at the same time, they do not discard non-existence of *Atman* or Ego at all. Once they agree to the view of *nirvana,* existence of soul or ego is a must. Thus, the Buddhist theory of soul is conflicting and controversial. The quotation mentioned below clearly substantiates the fact.

> The *Tathagata*, sometimes, taught that the *Atman* exists and at other times he taught the *Atman* does not exist. When he preached that the *Atman* exists and said to be the receiver of misery or happiness in the successive lives as the reward of its *karma*, his object was to save man from falling into the heresy of Nihilism. When he taught that there is no *Atman* in the sense of a creator or perceiver or an absolutely free agent, apart from conventional name given to the aggregate of five *skandhas,* his object was to save man from falling into the opposite heresy of externalism or *sasvatavada.*[9]

It means Buddha developed two doctrines related to existence of *Atman*. In the broader sense there is no *Atman* because there is nothing except complete *sunyata*. In another sense, the *Atman* (ego) exists so long as it realises the reality. Here he seems to stand very near to the *Sankhya* philosophy of the Hindu. According to the Buddha, the soul which he called consciousness loses its identity while merging into *Sunyata*. The two doctrines were preached by the Buddha for two very different objects. He taught the doctrine of *Atman* when he wanted to impart to his hearers the conventional doctrine; he taught the doctrine of *Anatman* when he wanted to impart to them the transcendental doctrine. According to Buddha, if there is any concept of soul, it is not immortal. It has existence in the mundane world in the form of ego or consciousness. But when one crosses the boundary of mundane world and land in the transcendental world where there is nothing except complete tranquility, and realisation of consciousness ends forever with the result that there is neither birth nor death because there is no *karma* at all. The same fact has been said in the following words:

> The existence of the *atman* and the *dharma* of the Ego and the phenomenal world is affirmed in the sacred canon

provisionally and hypothetically and never in the sense of possessing a real and permanent nature.[10]

Buddhism like any other system of Indian philosophy, is not merely a theoretic consideration of things to satisfy intellectually curiosity or an speculative luxury, but is primarily concerned with the awareness of human suffering in all its intensity, inexorability and extent. It is at once an attempt, a very convincing and glorious attempt, to eradicate all sufferings and attain a state of final peace and cessation. The Vedangs, on the other hand, holds that though literally we cannot speak of *Brahman* as meant by the word, it can still indicate the presence of *Brahman* in a metaphysical or symbolic way. In fact, it is through the scriptural word that we initially derive our knowledge of *Brahman*. *Brahman* is known only through the Upanishads. Madhayamika school of Buddhism is opposed to the *Vedantic* conception of the function and use of language. However, its theory of *sunyata* has deep spiritual purpose. It is through *sunyata* one can get rid of all sufferings. *Sunyata* is *nirvana* where nothing exists. The philosophies either realistic or idealistic declare the individual soul or *atman* to be underused, immortal principle, whose fulfillments consist in the manifestation or attainment of its own essential nature.

Buddha's middle path is the non-acceptance of two extremes—the affirmative and the negative (the *sat* and *asat)* view of all views. In the *Yogacara-Vijnanavada, sunayata* is accepted, but with modifications. The formula is—that which appears (the substratum) is real; the form of its appearance (the duality of subject and object) is unreal. The middle path, thus, is the avoidance of both the dogmatic of realism and the skepticism of nihilism. The acceptance of two truths is vital for any correct understanding of the Madhayamika. These two truths are – Conventional Truth and Ultimate Truth. Those who do not know the distinction between these two truths, they singularly fail to appreciate the deeper significance of Buddha's teaching. Ultimate reality (*Pramartha Satya*) is the knowledge of the real as it is without any distortion. Categories of thoughts and points of views distort the real. They unconsciously "coerce their mind to view things in a cramped, biased way, and are thus inherently incapable of giving us the truth." The *Pramartha* is the utter absence of the function of reason which is therefore equated with *samvriti.* The Absolute Truth is therefore beyond the scope of discursive thought, language and empirical activity; and conversely, the object of these is *samvritisatya*. So, it is said, "The *Pramartha Satya* is in fact the unutterable, the unthinkable, etc. Devoid of empirical determination; it is the object of inner most experience of the wise; it is so intimate and integral that we cannot be self-conscious of it.

Buddha declined certain questions of a distinctly metaphysical character. The questions are:

(i) Whether the world is eternal, or not, or both, or neither;

(ii) Whether the world is finite (in space), or infinite, or both, or neither;

(iii) Whether the *Tathagata* exists after death, or does not, or both, or neither; and

(iv) Is the soul identical with the body or different from it?

Silence of the Buddha on the questions mentioned above is of metaphysical nature, and it indicates that he either had no answer to the questions or he avoided answers because the answers are vague, conflicting and non-convincing. The Buddha, in fact, refused to accept certain things like, permanent, the *atman,* the abiding and identical nature of things. He considered things in a sequential manner, as dynamic as becoming (refuting being), probably because it took its stand on the efficacy of the moral law. It does not mean that he was quite blind to the existence of *atman*. The question is if there is no soul being an agent of action, how could a Buddhist accept change without accepting an observer of change, one who takes note of change and is therefore unaffected by the process of change. The Buddha could not be blind to the fact that there is a Self for which everything else is meant and which is not meant for other things. That is why he developed two theories of truths—conventional and transcendental. Conventional is meant for ordinary people while transcendental is for wise or perfect one who has the intelligence to know 'Ultimate Reality'. He kept silence on transcendental questions because he did not want to be involved in controversy. His purpose was different, to emancipate mankind from worldly sufferings, not to involve them in the vague and conflicting matters of metaphysics. On the other hand, among the Hindus the belief deeply prevailed that soul is the integral particle of God, and it is as immortal and pure as God Himself. These two conflicting views of Buddhism and Hinduism remained as a barrier between them so long as later Buddhists accepted the doctrine of soul.

Two realities of the Buddha have to be related or connected and they obviously cannot be brought under any conceivable relation, and yet could not also be left unrelated either. The inseparable difficulties could be resolved by either denying the reality of the objects (which the Adaivta *Vedanta* did adopt and declared the phenomenal world as *maya*) or deny the reality of the elusive Self or *atman* and declare only the observable phenomena as real. It is this attitude that was adopted by *Abhidharmika* philosophy. Nagarjuna was thus led to point out that the Real or Ultimate Truth is Transcendental to thought—categories, it is *sunya.* Since the Buddhists have basic concern with moral law, they repudiated the existence of any being not subject to the law of *karma,* such as *Isvara* and even the Permanent Identical Human Self or the substance in things. They were also led to deny the stand of the materialists who denied Free Will and its result. No school of Buddhism ever accepted God as the creator or the sustainer of the universe. The *karma* of beings was the necessary and sufficient cause of the variety and difference in the universe. In the words of TRV Murti, "The Buddhists considered them (God, *atman,* substance, etc.), as unreliable, as words without reality behind them. They were aware of the *atman* as something unreal, as something to be sunned and abandoned, as the root cause of all suffering."[11] Such views of Buddhism kept many Hindus out of the cult of Buddhism. Soul or *atman* in the Hindu philosophy has been dominant from the beginning, and to deviate from such thinking was to commit philosophical as well as religious suicide by the Hindus of the time.

Declination of *Brahminism* and Advent of Sankaracarya

With the rise and growth of new philosophies developed by

different scholars and also the mounting attack upon it by the philosophies of Buddhism, the *Brahminism* came to its lowest ebb. Its philosophy, based on Upanishads was too tough to be understood by common people. Its ritualism-based on blind faith and conventions, its exclusion of the lower castes from participation of ritual performances proved too much harmful as well as destructive to itself. Buddhism and even Jainism opened the flood gate for all people in participation of religious performances denying the philosophy of *Varna-ashram*. Though *Brahminism* still existed as a force but it lost the capacity to reckon with the rivals. It began to shrink. People's faith in ritualism started to recede. At that very moment the need was felt to revive *Brahminism*. It was not an easy task. Buddhism as well as Jainism had spread their hold everywhere in the country. Buddhism had appeared in the neighbouring countries of India and also in the countries of Central Asia which extended support to it. To defeat Buddhism or to subdue its philosophies required a more powerful convincing philosophy having scientific base and common understanding. This task was fulfilled by Sankaracarya who was born in South India in a Brahmin family in the eighth century AD. He possessed, in fact, gigantic philosophical knowledge of Indian religious scriptures. He knew Vedas, Vedangs, *Brahmans*, and Upanishads, etc., fully, and had the spiritual capacity to reinterpret them in new light. Various *Commentaries* presented by *Sanskara* put new life in Hinduism that was on the verge of declination.

According to Upendra Thakur, "the age of Kumarila and Sankaracarya (788 A.D) was the age of great religious ferment and Brahminic revival, for they are supposed to have been avowed opponents of Buddhism."[12] Samkara's *commentaries* on the *Brahmasutra* gave birth to a host of commentaries and studies on Vedantism of great originality, vigour and philosophic insight.[13] This philosophy was further championed by Mandana Misra (800 BC) of Mithila who strongly denounced the Buddhists.[14] According to a popular legend, in Mithila and elsewhere Samkara-chased the Buddhists out of India. He not only defeated and discomfited them in logical debates, but it was also by his order that king Sudhanva drowned thousands of Buddhists into the ocean and mercilessly massacred them.[15]

Such inhuman acts committed by *Samkara* and his followers have no historical base. It is true that *Samkara* who was busy with revival of the *Vedantic* views was dead against Buddhism and its preachers as well as followers, but he could not commit those heinous acts. It is evident from the fact that at the time of *Sanskara* under the patronage of Pala kings of Bengal, Buddhist universities like Vikramasila (in Champa or Bhagalpur) and Odantpuri (in Magadha) came into being. The numerous archaeological remains, grants, endowments, monasteries Buddhist images and brilliant pieces of art and sculpture also tell another stories related to Buddhism.[16] This is another fact that Sankaracarya who had fully visualised the Buddhist doctrines and that stood against the long established philosophical truth of the country, disliked Buddhists and their religion.

Samkara, being the champion of the cause of Hinduism, travelled entire country spreading the significance of Indian *Vedanta* and other religious scriptures. He wrote several commentaries wherein he tried to interpret transcendental philosophy with a view to regaining the faith of people in Indian ancient scriptures. He established four famous sits (*dhamas*) of worshipping at different places in the country. These are Vadrikashram in northern India, Rameshwaram temple in Southern India, Jagnathpuri in Odisha and Dwarikanath in Dwarkiapuri (Gujarat). These places became famous for Hindu pilgrimages. He set-up the school of *Kevaladvaitavada* (Absolute Monism) which put emphasis on one reality. The doctrine of Monism stood for not only of one God or absolute, but *Brahman* and *Brahman* alone or absolute and absolute only is the sole reality. *Jiva-jagta* or this universe of souls and mater is false (*mithya*). So, there is only one *Brahman* and one Reality. To Sankaracarya *Brahman* is *Ekamedvaitam.* (*Chandogya Upanishads*, 3, 14, 1) which means one only without second and all other characteristics of *Brahman* follow from the same. The *Brahman*, according to Sanskara, is *nirvisesa* or without *visesa or bheda* or difference of any kind whatsoever. *Brahman* is all pervasive so there is no question of *sajatiya* or *vijatiya* or *bhedas* (differences). There is no other god outside him from whom he can have *sajatiya bhedha*, and there is no Satan outside him from whom he can have *vijatiya bheda*. He has not even *savagata Bheda* for he is not a whole of parts, but he is absolutely *niramsa* one and one only, with no internal parts (*amsa)*.

Thus, *Brahman* is *nirvikara* or absolutely changeless. Change is in *vikara*. Since *Brahman* is *nirvikara*, there is no question of change in Him. So, *Brahman* is *nirguna, nistriya, nirvikara, nirnjana*. *Brahman* is *suddham* (absolute pure) sinless, free from all blemishes, sins and stigma and always pure. In his several commentaries, he interpreted the meaning and significance of Advaitism (Non-dualism). He taught people that the *Brahman* is absolute, alone, being the primary cause of everything.

Monotheism being the corollary of Monism followed by Ramanujacharya recognised the monistic doctrine so far the existence of one Absolute God is concerned, but it propounded the doctrine of three realities—God or Absolute *Brahman*, *Jiva* and *Jagta* (soul and matter). He also propounded the doctrine of *Saguna Brahman* that, out of mercy, incarnates on the earth with special purpose to help devotees and finish up devil souls. He pleaded that God listens to prayers of devotees and showers mercy and blessing upon his true devotees. Hence, *Bhakti* cult began among Hindus and gained popularity being the easiest path to approach God and obtain His blessing. According to Sanskara, *Brahman* and *Jiva-jagta* are absolutely identical with one another, and due to our *avidya*, only we take them to be different. For instance, *ghatakasa* seems to be different from *mathakasa*, but after breaking the pot the either side becomes absolutely merged in the universal ether all around. Because of *upadhis* (bodies with sense organs*) java* or the individual soul appears to be different from *Brahman* and when the *upadhis* are no longer taken to be real, *jiva* and *Brahman* are realised to be one. This is the doctrine of Absolute Monism.

Thus, it is very much evident that the philosophy of Hinduism is quite different from that of Buddhism. According to the former soul is integral part of absolute *Brahman* that is in captivity of ignorance (*Maya*). Liberation of soul or its *moksha* means its complete identification with Absolute *Brahman* that is possible with full realisation of the individual soul and understanding of *Brahmans*. Moreover, soul can be liberated obtaining God's blessing. But in the Buddhist's view there is neither soul nor *Brahman* and *nirvana* means realisation of consciousness of the individual that finally nothing exists, and cause of birth is unfulfillment of desires. The Buddha used to keep quiet about the discussion of any numeral existents and carefully avoided such questions rising out from discussions. Nevertheless, the questions would arise about the metaphysical targets like *atman* or God, rebirth and after life and similar other points. The Buddha maintained that there is conglomeration of *Rupa* and *Nama* or an assemblage of *Rupa, Vedana, Sarijana, Sanskara* and *Vijnana,* and that is all about a *Jiva*. This assemblage is wrongly viewed as *atman* if *Samyak-Dristi* is adopted the *Atmagraha Dristi* goes away and nothing remains after the disintegration of the five enmeshes or *skandhas*. This position is clear enough to be differentiated from that of the *Carvakas* who maintained that there is no soul. The Buddha, too, ultimately came to the conclusion that there is no anything like soul. If soul is accepted logically, its existence is not permanent because with the achievement of *nirvana*, it disappears. Such views related to soul could hardly convince the Hindus.

In the Hindu philosophy *moksha* is of four types *Salokya-moksha, Saristi-moksha, Samipya-moksha and Sarupya-moksha.* The first type of *moksha* (*Salokya-moksha*) means to reside in the land of God which further means to rise spiritually as high as God himself. The second type (*Saristi-moksha*) is a higher stage than the first one. Here one spiritually rises to the height where there is no feeling of pain and pleasure because all of his desires and longing disappear forever. The third type of *moksha* that is (*Samipya-moksha*) is nearer to God. While reaching to this stage all godly opulence is available to one who rises up to this stage of *moksha*. The last one that is *Sarupya-moksha,* is the final stage where there is complete merger of soul into the *Brahman*. Here there is no duality. The Buddhist concept of *nirvana* is not elaborative like that of the Hindus. In Buddhism *nirvana* simply means dispersion of five *skandhas* into *sunyata* that is Absolute Brahmin. This dispersion is possible only when the *sadhaka* succeeds to rise above *trisna,* desires, lusts, etc., and constantly maintain the ascetic life. Ramanuja and others further expounded that soul being the integral part of God never distinguishes. The liberated souls always remain in the *Dhama* (location) of God which never perishes.

The Buddha's idea of *anatmavada* created misconception and brought about new question related to soul and rebirth. Most of the Buddhist schools agree to the idea that after life *swarga* (heaven) and *narak* (hell) are the results of our mind's working or reflection as if in dream. The rebirth is a more difficult question to be answered but is, logical understandable. This idea of rebirth is connected ordinarily with the idea of *Atman* which is a non-existence in Buddhism. So, it is interesting to note that the path of rational thinking with which Buddhism carefully removes the possibility of soul's existence, puts the questions such as if there is no soul, who gets salvation, and who takes new birth. But to those who have grasped the meaning of Hindu's religious philosophy related to *Atman and Paramatman* may never agree to the Buddhist's view regarding the futility of soul's doctrine. If there is no soul, there is no rebirth, if there is no soul, there is no bondage and liberation. In later Buddhism, this concept gradually began to change. Even the cult of worshipping and notion about different gods appeared. Mahayanists developed faith in Buddha's supernatural character and later on began to allow worshipping the Buddha and the Bodhisattvas in the Church. Such changes brought Buddhism near to Hinduism on the one hand, and philosophical differences of both the religions began to disappear on the other.

The Buddha taken as a God

Whether the Buddha was worshipped in life of physical existence or not is not traceable. However, it is said that he was fully committed to his mission and remained always strict to disciplines that annoyed some of his followers. After his demise, his image was erected, and process of worshipping his image came into being. According to D.S. Trivedi, "The necessity for such worshipping was felt within the human hearts which could remain satisfied with reason alone. Thus, naturally, later

Buddhism had to provide for worshipping Buddha's image; at first the symbol of Lotus or Lotus feet should be worshipped; once introduced the spirit became, further and further popular..."[17] He further writes, "Later the images began to bear palpable proofs of the local colouring and regional character. And, in the later years, *Mantrayayana*, *Vajrayana*, *Sahajayana* and *Kalacakrayana* or *Tantric* Schools came into existence and later Buddhism became a new development altogether having almost nothing in common with its earlier phase. Buddha's images varied from place to place and Buddha's teaching began to assume symbolic charcter."[18]

Decline of Buddhism in India

The varying characters of the Buddha and different interpretations of Buddha's teaching by different schools though expanded the scope of Buddhism, no doubt, but it damaged the spirit of Buddhism creating confusion about thought and thinking of the Buddha. The emergence of the school of *Vajrayana* and *Mantrayana* which allowed wine, women and meat in practice of Buddhist *sadhana* totally damaged the earlier significance of Buddhism at least in India where the *Vedantic* philosophy and revival of Hinduism was on rise during the time of Sanskara. Outside and inside the peripheries of Buddhism there were many who not only disliked the practice of *Mantrayana* but they abhorred it. Even all types of intoxication were allowed in the practice of *Mantrayana Yogacara*. It attracted a number of those people who belonged to the lower sections. They joined the stream with the marked objective to enjoy the life and establish their reputation in the society. The confusing situation related to sanctity as well as sagacity of Buddhism provided favourable circumstance to *Brahminism* to overpower Buddhism and strengthen its hold all over the country.

One of the vital causes of declination of Buddhism in India is the vehement attack of Muslims upon India and their destructive activities against both Hinduism and Buddhism. The Muslims invader like Bakhtiyar Khilji ruined the University of Nalanda by putting its rich library on fire. It is said that the fire was so strong and powerful that it continued burning the library for a week. Most of the literature preserved in the library burnt into ashes led to an unbearable loss to the University of Nalanda. The Muslim invaders destroyed a number of central Buddhist places. Most of the Buddhists being afraid of invaders escaped away from India and took shelter in other neighbouring countries of India. Besides that, even among the fundamentalist Hindus there were some who disliked Buddhists and applied all the efforts to eradicate Buddhism from the soil of India by harming the Buddhist monks. It is all because the Buddha and his follower had disregarded *Brahminism* and claimed Buddhism as a superior *dharma*. In the 14th century AD, they treated the Buddhists, and not the Muslims, as their worst enemies, even two hundred years after the destruction of the Nalanda University and other Buddhist centers of learning. They denounced the Buddhists as 'degraded and dangerous.' The story of the massacre of the Buddhists and their patron, King Arjuna of Saptri (Nepal), by Dronavara Maithila , king Puraditya of Raj Banaili after *Siva* simha's death, is yet another pointer to it. These stray references manifest the bitterness that a small section of the *Brahmans* against the Buddhism.[19]

With the advent of Sankaracharya and revival of Hindu's Philosophy by him presenting several commentaries of Indian philosophy of monism, the Hinduism was gaining new vigour and strength. Buddhism that stood like a rock on the way of *Brahminical* cult of Hinduism was to be suppressed if the latter had to prosper. So, it was natural to subdue Buddhism in India. Secondly, the Buddhist philosophy from the beginning taught the religion that denying the existential Hindu's concept of God and soul presented the theory related to God and soul that was too vague to understand or grasp the real meaning. In India, the insistence was on the devotion and prayer from the beginning, and Buddhism prohibited both. The *Bhakti*-movment enunciated by Ramanuja, Sufis, Chaitnya Mahaprbhu, Kabir, Surdas, Tulsi Das, etc., during the 16th and 17th centuries had revolutionised the faith of Hindus in the cult of devotion to God. It was not possible for the Hindus to discard God and give up prayer as well as worshipping to Him. So, reaction against Buddhism was natural. Thirdly, the various schools of Buddhism developed religious doctrines expanding Buddhism in such a manner that they differed not only among themselves but also confronted to each other. This move of the Buddhist scholars created confusion and confrontation among the common mass. As a result, aversion arose against Buddhism in India. Fourthly, Hinduism had been the mightiest religion of the country having the *Vedantic* support. Doctrines of devotion and prayer propounded and developed by various saints, poets and authors and also the movement of *Bhakti,* provided very strong base to Hinduism. Consequently, Buddhism began to disappear from the country slowly. Lastly, but not the least, various adoptions related to the Buddha's supernatural nature and divine strength created a feeling among the Hindus that the Buddha was another creation of Lord Vishnu on the soil of India. Most of the Hindus began to worship him as Lord Vishnu. Thus, Buddhism that emerged and prospered in India and remained in practice for centuries lost its strength and fervour leaving some signs and symbols here and there.

The, revaluation of the testimony of the foreign scholars, inscriptions and contemporary digests make it clear that, with the advent of the 13th century A.D., Buddhism was at its last gasp. The Buddhism tried to cope with the changing times and successfully brought in a reformation. *Mahayana* Buddhism was replaced by *Tantric* Buddhism which led to further decline and fall of the religion in India. And the process of this disintegration could not be checked in spite of strenuous steps of Acarya Atisa of the Vikramasila University, who expelled the *tantric* teachers from the monastery of Vikaramasila in order to maintain purity of *Mahayana* Buddhism.[20] Again, the introduction of the school of Sahajiya Buddhism that opened the flood gate for entry of people belonging to lower society was another severe blow to the decline of Buddhism.

The teaching of the Buddha went against the grain of Hindu psychology, and, as such, could not take an abiding root in India. Hinduism was based on *subdapramana* (the Vedas) whereas the Buddha repudiated all authority and traditions. The Hindus were prone to metaphysics while the Buddhists showed indifference towards it. The existence or non-existence of God did not interest the Buddhas at all. According to him, man was the architect of his own future. Naturally, therefore, there is no place for ritualism in Buddhism. Moreover, the Master did not succeed in compelling his followers to adopt an attitude of suspended judgement on the ultimate question. His conception of *Dharma* was not sufficiently concrete for practical purposes. The result was obvious. The Buddha gradually came to be defied and Buddhism was very much influenced by Hindu philosophy. On the other hand, Buddhism, too, exercised a great, almost overwhelming, influence on Hinduism. It gave birth to neo-Hinduism which absorbed the best elements of Buddhism. It as a result of this influence that *Saivas* borrowed the monastic and contemplative elements of *Mahayana* Buddhism and the *Vaisnavas*, borrowed the devotional and humanitarian elements. This view is expressed by Upendra Thakur. But in my understanding the fact is that the Saivas and *Vaisnavas* did not borrow something substantial from Buddhism because the literature of the Hindu philosophy in this regard is richer than that of Buddhism. This is another fact that both the *Dharmas* which developed in the same country on the same soil could not remain ineffective to each other.

With the emergence of *Vaisnavism* in a new form in the 12th and 13th centuries, the Buddha was taken as an *avtara*, entirely different from the *Bhagvata* by Jayadeva in Bengal and others in Mithila. The Sahajiya, though flourished in Bengal and other places, it also inclined to *Vaisnavism*. The image of the Buddha is worshipped here and there in West Bengal, Mithila and other places as a form of Viṡnu and sometimes as *Siva*. *Vaisnavism* finally incorporated the faith of the Buddha into the 'parent stock'. In the latter part of the 16th century, Buddhism became fully incorporated into the body of Hinduism through the medium of 'neo-*Vaisnavism*. Once the Buddha was accepted as incarnation of God by the Hindus, it was difficult to bring him out from the heart of the later.

The Buddha in the Form of God (Tathagata)

So, long as the Buddha lived physically, he never claimed that he was God or was incarnation of God. After his demise his followers regarded him like God. He was called *Tathagata* which means Absolutism or Absolute. *Tathagata* is the essential being of all elements of existence. *Tathagata* is the revealer of truth. He is the personalised reality. If the *Tathagata* assumes a personality, his freedom does not limit his personality. Buddha was called *Tathagata* because he came on the earth to lead people to adopt real path, to liberate them from bondage, and to reveal them the truth. He possessed all absolute power. It was believed that he was capable of doing anything. Ordinary persons cannot know real truth. It is *Tathagata* who knows, and he is capable of knowing the Absolute. So, the Buddha is identical with the Absolute, the universal and the impersonal reality of the world and so is the *Tathagata*. Being endowed with power and perfection Buddha is God. In Him all power, spelndour, fame, wealth, knowledge and act dwelled. (*Madhyamikakarik*a XXXIV, 12). He possessed variety of wisdom.

It were these attributes related to the Buddha which made him God and his followers, taking him the centre of final refuse, began to worship him. However, such view has been discarded by Kumaril who pleaded that only the impersonal or eternal world (Veda) can be omniscient. No person can be omniscient because he is subject to passion and the peculiarity of his mental constitution.[21] The logic was also advanced that it is very difficult for man to have knowledge of many things including the minutest. So, Kumarila remark, "There is no existence of super sensuous seer, those who know something, know the means of the eternal word (Veda)."[22] However, there were many who accepted him as God. According to Nagarjuna even when he did not utter a single word, all his devotes were content.[23] Candrakriti says that the Buddha spoke only once at the time of attainment of Bodhi. This dispelled the ignorance of sundry.[24] In the *Bodhicaryavatvara Panjika,* the Buddha has been compared to the Cintamani, i.e., the wish fulfilling stone and the *Kalpataru,* the immortal heavenly tree that is capable of giving anything to devotees. These satisfy different desires of the devotees.[25]

In the *Vedanta*, the Absolute reality is *Brahman* whereas in Buddhism Absolute reality is *Sunyata*. In both the cases, the absolute transcendence of the empirical or phenomenal reality is necessary in order to teach the Absolute. A medium is needed to reach Absolutism. In *Vedanta Isvara* is the medium while in the Buddhism medium is *Tathagata*. Both *Isvara* and *Tathagata* is the subject of worshipping. It has been established that as *Isvara* of the *Vedanta* is related to *Brahman*, therefore the *Tathagata* of Buddhism is related with the absolute or sunyata. Thus, it appears that the Buddhist's concept of *sunyata* is not much different with that the Hindu's concept of *Brahman*. So, in due course of time, both the philosophical terms *Sunyata* and *Brahman* came very much near to each other convincing the Hindus that Buddhism is not a different thing, but a new branch of Hinduism.

Lord Vishnu in Hindu *Dharma*

In the Hindu *Dharma*, Lord Vishnu is regarded as the symbol of Absolute *Brahman* who is the first cause of creation. He is not only the creator and upholder but destroyer of creation. He exists in Trinity Brahma, Vishnu, Mahesh. Brahma creates, Vishnu sustains and Mahesh destroys creation. According to the doctrine of incarnation, it is Vishnu who incarnates on the earth with the purpose to re-establish *Dharma* and protect devotees. *The Bhagvad Gits* states:

Although I (*Isvara*) am unborn and my transcendental body never deteriorates, and although I am the Lord of all living entities, I still appear in every millennium in my original transcendental form. (*Bhagvad Gita,* Chapter 4, Verse-6)

It further states:

> Whenever and wherever there is a decline in religious practice ... and a predominant rise of religion at that time I descend Myself." (*Bhagvad Gita* chapter 4, Verse-7)

Regarding protection of *Dharma,* the *Bhagvad Gita* says:

> To deliver the pious and to annihilate the miscreants, as well as to establish the principles of religion, I Myself appear, millennium after millennium." (*Bhagvad Gita*, chapter 4, Verse 8.

Thus, it is very much evident that in the Hindu *dharma* the concept of God and soul is very much prominent. The universe is God's creation and it is the responsibility of God to protect universe by protecting *dharma* that is the base of the survival of the creation. To serve the purpose God incarnates in different forms. So far the case of human being is concerned, man the highly developed creature of the earth, represents God's will on the earth. Since the mundane world is showed in *vikaras*, it maligns the individual soul causing sufferings and pains to him. His liberation is possible, provided he gets God's mercy and kindness, and for that faith and devotion are needed unconditionally. On the other hand, according to the philosophy of Buddhism, the theory of God and soul is unscientific and vague. To believe in an unseen power and rely upon its mercy is not wise. In other words, it is like to live in fool's paradise. Let man try himself to get rid of world's problems. Buddhist logic and philosophy are characterised by a deep-seated disrupt of conceptual knowledge. Buddhist logic does not accord validity to inferential cognition. In Hinduism emphasis is on prayer and devotion while in Buddhism stress is on one's self efforts to realise reality.

Description of the Buddha as Lord Vishnu amongst Hindus

A perusal of the history of the period (13th century) reveals the fact that Buddhism by this time was not disparaged by the Brahmin community and the followers of the *Brahminism*, barring a few exceptions. Shriharsa and Laksimidhara assign an honourable place to the Buddha in the *Brahminical* pantheon. In the *Naisadhacaritam* the Buddha is regarded as an incarnation of Vishnu. Laksmidhara in his *Krtyakalpatru* prescribes that the Buddha is to be worshiped on two occasions: (1) on the first of *Caitra* and the seventh of *Vaisakha*—both times along with other deities. [26] Besides that, the Buddha had long been recognised as an *avtara* (incarnation) of Vishnu in the *Matsya, Bhagvata, Garuda, Linga Prunanas,* etc.[27]

According to Upendra Thakur, "The incorporation of the Buddha into the cosmopolitan and ever-expanding Brahminic pantheon as one of the ten incarnations in which Lord Vishnu comes down on earth at different times, by orthodox *Brahmans*, who were at one time the severest critics of the Buddha and his new order finally put a finish to the long-long story of the bitter, wordy duel and violent wrangling between the adherents of the two opposite schools of thought."[28] The reference is in the *Varahpurana* which states that as a result of the observance of the vow of *Buddhdvadsi*, king Suddhodhana had as his son, Lord Vishnu in the form of the Buddha.[29] Similar festivals in honour of other incarnations of Vishnu to be performed in different months of the year are also described. In reality, Buddhism, in its essence, was not hostile to *Brahminism*. Therefore, it is not surprising to find the Buddha later came to be worshipped as an incarnation by the followers of the Brahminic faith. In fact, there are a number of things in Buddhism that have similar description in the religious scriptures of Hinduism. For instance, the Buddhist concept of *Sunyata* is similar to that of Hindu's view of *Brahman*; the doctrine of *karma* and rebirth has relevance in both the *Dharmas*; both talks of pains and suffering in the mundane life and both teach to attain *nirvana* (salvation).

In the later Buddhism, the worshipping of cult of *Sakti* has been regarded as the source of power that has been borrowed from Hindu *dharma* where *Sakti* is worshipped in the form of goddess Durga. There are various forms to perform *Sakti-puja* and please her. The *Mantrayana* and the *Vajrayana* of Buddhism have very close relevance with that of the Hindu's adoptions. Both the religions have the mentioning of *Mahakalcakra*. In Hinduism, it is said that it is *Mahakal* that governs the universe and lastly annihilates it completely. All creatures of the universe including gods, semi-gods and others are in the grip of *Kalcakra*. Both put equal emphasis on good moral conducts, universal brotherhood, non-violence, etc. Both agree to the points that desires, lusts, greed, hatred, violence, non-tolerance, etc., are the root cause of sufferings and bondage. The way to get rid of suffering and pains forever is to be pious in both thought and action and prefer renunciation. Both, Buddhism and Hinduism, prescribe *sadhana* or meditation as the suitable method to visualise reality and acquire wisdom. Thus, it is obvious that apparently or even inwardly Hinduism and Buddhism are not different. The Buddha denounced not Hinduism, but wrong views and practice of *Brahminism*. So, it is not surprising to note that the Buddha was adopted by the Hindus as the tenth incarnation of Lord Visnu.

Relevance of Buddhism in India Today

From the above discussions it is very much obvious that Buddhism in India having its deep root began to fade away due to different reasons. However, to say that Buddhism has been uprooted from the country is not correct. Buddhism though in changed form and at limited places, still prevails having the support of the Hindus. In the border areas of India like Kashmir, Himachal Pradesh, Arunachal Pradesh, Buddhism is still alive and there are a number of followers of Buddhism. Buddhism did not completely disappear from India. The celebration of 2500 years of *Parinirvana* of Lord Buddha in 1956, heralded a new era in the history of Buddhism in India. Thousands of Buddhist pilgrims come to visit the historical places of the country every year. There are several Universities in the country where departments of Buddhist studies and teaching of Pali language have been running.

The establishment of the Bihar Buddhist Association under the guidance of Krtipasarana Mahathera during the early part of the 20th century was a big step in reviving Buddhism in the country. The Bengal Buddhist have played greater role in reviving Buddhism and strengthening its root. In course of time, many Buddhist monasteries, shrines and temples have been erected at several places, especially in Bihar. The role played by Baba Ambedkar to expand Buddhism is highly appreciable and notable. The partition of the country in the year of 1947, uprooted thousands of Buddhists living in East Pakistan (Bangladesh), but most of them crossed the country and settled in India in West Bengal.

The subjugation and occupation of Tibet by the Chinese government in 1959, badly affected Buddhism in Tibet. But with the best efforts of Dalai Lama, the expelled Buddhist leader of Tibet who took shelter in India along with a number of Buddhists, has kept the banner of Buddhism up till today. The refugees who came from Tibet to India and who are mostly the Buddhists have been given honourable settlement by the government of India at different settlement camps. Thus, with the coming of Tibetan Buddhist, Buddhism has received new energy and vigour in India. The Council for Religion and Cultural Affairs was established soon after His Holiness the

Dalai Lama came to India in 1959. It is this Council that is responsible for preservation of Buddhist culture and tradition living in exile. During the last 23 years, about 150 monastic universities and religious centers accommodating 6022 monks and nuns have been built with assistance from the government of India, Buddhist organisations and the Tibetan people themselves. In some of the Indian universities Buddhism is taught at the post-graduate level. For instance, The Department of Ancient Indian and Asian Studies and Buddhist Studies in Magadh University and the Nav Nalanda Mahavihara set up at Nalanda by the government of Bihar and India are doing marvelous service to the cause of Buddhist studies. Here large number of Buddhist students even from foreign countries is getting benefits of Buddhist teaching. Several new centers at Bodh Gaya and other places have also been set-up for meditation and training of Buddhist monks. The international Buddhist Meditation Center in Bodh Gaya has become the place of attraction for the students of foreign roots.

Besides all these, there are a number of the places of pilgrimage where Buddhists from all over the world come to worship. These notable places are Bodh Gaya, Saranath, Kusinara, Nalanda, Rajgriha, Sanchi, Lumbni etc. These places are well-protected and maintained by the central and state governments with the active support of various South-East Asian Buddhist countries. The department of the Archaeological and Survey of the government of India keep constant eyes over these places to protect the monuments, ruins, maintenance and conservation. The Buddha Purnima is celebrated with great pomp and show every year at Bodh Gaya and other Buddhist places in India. Many Buddhist periodicals and journals are published from India that carries more authentic knowledge about Buddhism. The celebration of the Buddhist *Jayanti* in Vaishali to commemorate the birth-anniversary of the Lord Buddha has its own attraction for the local people there. It is interesting to note that Buddhism in India amongst all sects of people is gaining wider support and honourable place. The people of India are proud of the Lord Buddha, who was born in India and who left nothing to highlight India's religious as well as philosophical tradition. Among the common mass the

Buddha is the Lord, the Hero, the incarnated God, and the great Muni who taught people how to live, what to do and what not, how to get rid of worldly suffering and pains, how to liberate one from the shackle of bondage and attain *nirvana*. The Buddha, thus, is immortal in India.

References

1. Upendra Thakur, "Buddhism in Bihar: Past and Present", in P.N. Ojha, (ed.*), Homage to Bhikhu Jagdish Kasyap*, published by Nav Nalanda Bihar, 1986, p. 2.
2. Rapson, *Ancient India,* p. 63. Also see, Upendra Thakur, *History of Mithila,* p. 97. G.C. Pande, *The Origin of Buddhism*, p. 309.
3. G.C. Pande, *The Origin of Buddhism*, Chapter II.
4. Buddhist India, pp. 155-56.
5. *Ibid.*
6. Lokesh Chandra "Buddhist Oikoumene", in Bapat, *op. cit.,* p. 95.
7. *Ibid.,* pp. 96-97.
8. Yamakami Sogen, *System of Buddhistic Thought*, p. 17.
9. Nagarjuna in his Commentary on the *Prajnaparamita Sutra.*
10. Dharmapalacarya in his commentary on *Vijnanamatra Sastra.*
11. T.R.V., Nurti, "*Buddhism and Sunyata*", in C.S. Upasak and C.S. Prasad (eds.), *Nav Nalanda Mahavihara Research Publication*, Vol. IV, *op. cit.,* p. 102.
12. Upendra Thakur "Buddhism in Bihar: Past and Present", in Bapat, *op. cit.,* p. 3.
13. Dasgupta, S.N., *History of Indian Philosophy*, Vol. I pp. 429-94, pp. 36-58.
14. *Ibid.,* Vol. I, pp. 429-94, pp. 36-58.
15. *Ibid.,* p. 118ff, Vol. II, pp. 82-102. For other details see Upendra Thakur, *Jainism and Buddhism in Mithila*, chapter II.
16. Cf, Madhva's *Sanskara-Digvijaya* and also Buddhacharyya, Introduction, II, fn. I.
17. D.S. Trivedi, "Date of Lord Buddha", in C.S. Upasak and C.S. Prasad (eds.), *Nav Nalanda Mahavihara Research Publication*, Vol. IV, published by Nav Nalanda Mahavihar, 1979, p. 59.

18. *Ibid.,* in P.N. Ojha, (ed.*), Homage to Bhikhu Jagdish Kasyap*, p. 5.
19. Upendra Thakur, "Buddhism in Bihar", in P.N. Ojha, (ed.).
20. *Journal of Asiatic Society of Bengal* (JASB), 1864.
21. Obermiller, *The Doctrine of Pranjanaparamita*, p. 45.
22. *Tatvasangraha of Santarakssita*, p. 895.
23. Nagarjuna's *Catuhstva.*
24. *Bodhicaryavatra Panjika* IX, 36.
25. *Ibid.,* p. 419.
26. Radhakrishanan, *Indian Philosophy*, Vol. I, p. 608ff. Also see *Journal of Asiatic Society of Bengal,* (*Buddhajainti* Special Issue Vol. I) 1956, pp. 33-34.
27. For detail study see, B.P. Majumdar's paper in the *Journal of Bengal Royal Society (JBRS),* (*Buddhajayanti* Special Issue), Vol. I, pp. 180-82.
28. Upendra Thakur, "Buddhism in Bihar", *op. cit.,* p. 13.
29. *Journal of Asiatic Society of Bengal* (JASB), 1864, p. 360.

10

Conclusion

Buddhism, as a religion and philosophy, emerged in India more than 2500 years spreading its dynamic impact and influence over a number of countries in the continent of Asia. Buddhism among other religions, cults and religious belief systems is one of the world religions possessing a history that states how did it came into being and when it spread its influence in other countries. The history of Buddhism also presents emergence of different sects of Buddhism that played vital role in expanding Buddhist philosophy and enlarging its scope. The two dominant schools of Buddhism, namely, *Hinayana* and *Mahayana* provided Buddhism stable strength by defining and explaining the teachings of the Buddha. The former laid emphasis on traditional Buddhist views while the latter provided Buddhism a broader concept and new meaning. Buddhism started in a specific period in a particular territory in the Indian sub-continent by a unique human personality popularly known as the Buddha. He was born to human parents and lived an exemplary earthly life, inspiring awareness in others to be one and 'strive for one's own betterment by oneself. In consideration of his extraordinary conduct and wisdom with which he addressed to human reason, he was, and still he is, honoured as an incomparable teacher of human kind, the world has ever produced. Since the doctrine that he invented and preached for forty-five years of his earthly life is based on complete metaphysical wisdom as well as psycho-analytical interpretation. Today, in the world of ours where morality and honesty of mankind has fallen down due to growth of material prosperity and emergence of greed and temptation, Buddhism has become more relevant to provide the right path to the world of humanity and emancipate man from bondage of lust and frustration.

Buddhism abounds in ethical as well as aesthetic exhortations particular to itself together with a cogent presentation of epistemological data on a sound footing. Regarding logic, Buddhism adheres to induction while finding fault with deduction as a valid means of knowledge. However, on an empirical level, logical coherence and consistency of propositions are encouraged for better understanding, but speculative reasoning and abstractions on such reasoning are discouraged. Besides, in some instances, dialectics, too, has been employed as a logical apparatus for the purpose of highlighting the pragmatic aspect of his doctrine. Buddhism has interest in neither ontology nor cosmology, however the descriptions of planes of existence found in the canonical texts, are referred to as Buddhist cosmology by some writers. In philosophical studies cosmology is a study of the origin and structure of the universe. Since the Buddhist description of planes of existence does not deal with the origin or structure of the universe, Buddhism has no cosmology in the sense that it has been used in philosophy.

Scientific Base of Buddhism

His outlook was broader, balanced, analytical and observational. His vision was based on his inner-insight. He did not accept any truth until it was reasonably verified. The truth that he discovered was not new but the ways which he prescribed to obtain the truth through personal effort is unique in itself. His views are not based on speculation, but on experience. The philosophical truth that he established related to existence or denial of God, salvation, the way of attainment of truth etc., are all scientific. His various doctrines like *sunyata, anatmavada,* theory of *karma,* death and rebirth, etc., are scientific. His every attitude and angle is scientific. The vagueness of Veda's teaching and complicacies of *Brahminical* ritualism could not attract many people, but the Buddha's teaching became popular because it was simple and understandable even to common mass. Moreover, his teaching helped number of people to come out from the captivity of *karmkandas* and ritualism. His teachings were based on the principle of humanism where man is preferred, not his birth or caste. That is why the orthodox *Brahmans* became bitter critics of the Buddha and Buddhism both.

The Buddha, who was a progressive thinker in the guise of a super monk, wanted a new society-based on new scientific thinking, a new way of life-based purely on right understanding and a new religious philosophy related to pragmatism, not to abstractionism and dogmatism. He discarded dogmatism and authoritarianism in thinking. He did not favour miracles and superstitions. Rather he applied the power of reasoning-based on scientific spiritualism. Lord Buddha believed in moral and social values not in metaphysical and dogmatic discussions. He postulated that there is no absolute truth, it is only relatives. If there is any absolute theory of ultimate truth, that stands above human sense and reasoning. He denied neither the existence of God nor absence of God. Rather he preferred to remain silent about the question related to existence of Super God only because nothing definitely could be said about such unseen power. Whenever the issue related to existence or non-existence of God appeared before him, he remained silent knowing that the concept is too vague to say anything definitely. He avoided both agnosticism and nihilism. He preferred the middle way that is neither absolute nor skeptical. He maintained that no scientific doctrine related to existence or denial of god may be produced due to vastness and vagueness of the divine concept. Therefore, we should try to understand the point of view of others. In this regard, he confirmed the Vedic version about God that *"Na iti, Na iti"*, which means whatsoever is presented about existence and meaning of God is not final. There is something more to be said about endless reality.

Teaching of Buddhism

Entire thinking of Buddhism is based on the principles of

non-violence, *karuna* (compassion) and *meta* (friendship). Buddhism preached non-violence brotherhood and love. It taught people that hatred cannot remove hatred. Rather it is love and compassion that may govern and correct others. It put emphasis on self-controlled life and discipline. Buddhism condemned superiority and inferiority of caste and held that everyone can attain the highest status through perseverance. The Buddha believed that each amoeba has the quality to become Buddha. His emphasis was on *meta* (friendship) and *karuna* (compassion). He asked people to be kind enough to all creatures of the world and let them live. All beings are the same in their inner-quality. Weaker beings need sympathy from the higher one. Since man is the highest being, he must be friendly and sympathetic not only to other people but to all living beings including animals, birds and even insects. This is the right path of living. Ill-will and hatred bring about more problems and harm the society.

The Buddha had no faith in a sectarian religion. He used the word *Dhamma* in Pali which means truth and law. *Dhamma*, according to him is the way to liberation and to the end of suffering. His teachings are universal and applicable to all religions and people from all backgrounds. He put emphasis on *vipassana* which means insight. It is *vipassana* that leads to the inner-calm of relaxation and also to the insight or wisdom of reality. He emphasised that the truth would be realised through the practice and not by the sermon or preaching of some individuals. The answer to life and the end to suffering are found by oneself as one becomes his own teacher and discoverer. Truth is achieved through the practice of insight meditation, not by hearing sermons and performing Y*janas*. The Buddha's enlightenment is related to light which means absence of darkness. Once the ignorance is removed, darkness disappears itself providing one inner-light that helps one to follow the right path. This light cannot be transferred to anyone, but one has to achieve it through practice of *sadhana* following controlled life.

Thus, Buddhism is a religion of kindness, humanity and equality. The Buddha aimed at a new spiritual existence attained through *jnana or Bodhi* or absolute illumination. The

Buddha deemed "the highest goal of a man to the stage in which there is neither old age nor fear, nor disease, nor birth nor death, nor anxieties, and in which there is no continuous renewal of activity."

The Buddha's Search for Truth

Siddhartha, the son of Suddodhana born in the Shakya dynasty at Lumbini, was in search of reality or wisdom from his early childhood. It was his wish that made him a *sanyasin* in pursuit of truth. The truth which he wanted to realise was not the ultimate truth related to supreme Brahmin as stated in the ancient Indian religious scriptures like Veda and others, but the truth related to our life and the world where we live. He totally disliked the truth based on traditions blind faith and superstition that existed in Indian society during his time. His concern was to search the nature of the world and destiny of the man. He wanted to know the cause of sufferings (*Dukha*s) in this world and find out the ways to get rid of sufferings. After obtaining enlightenment under the Bodhi Tree at Gaya which came to be known as Bodh Gaya later on, Buddha realised fully the causes of sufferings and also the ways to get rid of sufferings. He realised that there are two aspects of truth— one aspect is relative while another one is absolute. The former reflects through various elements of the mundane world while the latter exists in wholesome that is beyond human understanding. Truth is covered by ignorance. Without wasting his much time to explain the origin and nature of the universe as well as Supreme God, the Buddha explained his followers the causes of effects related to constant circle of birth and death, sufferings of mankind and meaning of *nirvana* and ways to obtain it. The Buddha said that greed, hatred and delusion (ignorance caused by illusion) are 'Three Poisons'. Of the Ten Evil Deeds, three of them are evils done by the mind. Greed poisons the mind, and once the mind is poisoned, there is illusion and diversion. In the absence of right vision man falls prey to greed.

Buddha was not an Atheist

Traditionally in most *Dhamma* books Buddhism in generally has often been described as atheistic. But this does not state the whole picture on the issue for many reasons. The Buddha was not so much atheistic as he was opposed to discussing metaphysical questions in general. He described his teachings using the analogy of a physician who treats the patient without keeping in mind who he is or what caste and community does he belong to. The doctor's only mission is to cure the ailment of the patient. The Buddha without going into depth of the metaphysics simply adopted that it is the human mind that creates the world. The mind is the creator in the sense that it develops a world on its own. So, there is no creator, except for what man mentally wishes to create. The Buddha adopted the middle way whereby his emphasis was on the reality, not the abstract idealism. He had no faith in abstraction. Some Buddhists tend to be atheistic because of the measurable silence of the Buddha on such issue. The Buddha was, in fact, opposed to a concept of an all powerful God who exists somewhere. He rejected the idea of a first beginning or creation or that there is a creator sitting somewhere. It is his adoption that makes some people to take him as atheist. In other religion existence of God, His mercifulness and benevolence are described in such a manner that He is listening to the prayers of mankind and He grants blessings, being pleased. The Buddha discarded such faith. God has been taken as a personal entity in other religions, but in Buddhism there is no place for personal god. The Buddha talks of *nirvana* that is liberation of the bonded soul. Though his theory of soul is not clear, he believed that there is something inside man that is to be liberated.

Buddhism and Vedanta

Buddhism as stated above arose on the land of India that is the abode of metaphysical philosophy and a place of incarnations of God in different forms. Hence Buddhism, has directly or indirectly been influenced by philosophy of *Vedanta*. *Vedanta* is the base of Indian Hindu society and Hindu *Dharma*. It talks of Absolute *Brahman* that is alone, indivisible, all powerful, omnipotent, omnipresent and what not. The concept of *Brahman* is such that it cannot be understood in words and it cannot be defined. It is the subject of experience and belief. The Mundane world is nothing, but manifestation of the absolute *Brahman*. The world where we live is not real, but temporary because of its transient nature. Everything in the world is at constant move that causes its appearance and disappearance. The life is also the subject of advent and disappearance. Here no one is happy because of lust, *trisna*, desire, greed, envy, jealousy etc. These all are the products of great *Maya* created by Lord Vishnu. Each soul that is the integral particle of Absolute God becomes a bondage to *maya*. Involvement of man into the worldly affairs in search of pleasure makes man's life more troublesome. To get rid of such state one has to obtain salvation that is possible either through meditation or through constant devotion and absolute surrender to God. Until blessing of God is obtained sufferings of man has no end.

When one closely investigates into the tenets of Buddhism and analytically examines Buddhist philosophy, one finds corollary between Buddhism and *Vedanta*. Though Buddhism differs from *Vedanta* at several places, but it draws a lot from *Vedantic* philosophy. For instance, the transient nature of the world and sufferings of the world are available in the *Vedantic* philosophy. The *Bhagvat Gita* talks of the form and nature of soul and prescribes the ways to liberate soul and obtain salvation.

In the Hindu philosophy God, Soul (*atman*) and World is the base of spiritualism as well as religion. The entire edifice of Hindu philosophy as well as the spiritualistic views is related to these three words— God, Soul and World. If Soul is removed from the trinities, there is no philosophy of spiritualism. On the other hand, the Buddha denied the concept of Soul and developed the doctrine of *Sarvam Anatman* that means "All is without soul." Buddhist philosophy denies Soul as "an eternal substance exempt from the vicissitudes of change and incapable of entering into combination with anything else." According to Dharmapala, *Atman* means supreme authority which is identical with freedom, eternality and absolute unity. Such an *Atman* is an organism associated with five aggregates, an absolute existence separate from the aggregates while living together. But the Buddhist philosophers did not approve such views. The denial of the Buddhist philosophy of *Atman* is fully-based on the universal principle of impermanence. When the doctrine of impermanence is accepted, in that case, the acceptance of eternality, absolute unity or supreme authority in any case becomes meaningless. As a result of it an existence like the above cannot have *Atman* or Ego. However, at the same time, they do not discard non-existence of *Atman* or Ego at all. Once they agree to the view of *nirvana,* existence of soul or ego is a must. Thus, the Buddhist theory of Soul is conflicting and controversial.

The Buddha had been a bitter critic of *Brahminism* because of latter's involvement into false traditions and superstitions. With the revival of Hinduism by Sankaracarya it regained its lost position, no doubt, but it could hardly eradicate the practice and influence of Buddhism in India. It was not possible to finish up the root of Buddhism because the root germinated and prospered in India relying directly or indirectly upon the metaphysical principles of *Vedanta*. After the demise of the Buddha his followers who divided themselves into several groups following converse opinions and ways, Buddhism began to lose its strength and influence in India. On the other hand, there were many Hindu religious leaders and scholars who realising the Buddha as the tenth incarnation of Lord Vishnu, honoured the Buddha like God with the result that no much difference was left between Buddhism and Hinduism. Thereafter, Buddhism, in India, became an integral part of Hinduism. Today both the religions are corollary to each other at least in India.

Bibliography

Adhikaram, E.W., 1946, *Early History of Buddhism in Ceylon*, Ceylon.

Annual Report, Archaeological Survey of India, 1906-07 and 1912-13, Calcutta 1910 and 1913.

Anacker , Stefan, 1984, *Seven Works of Vasubandhu,* Motilal Banarsidas, Delhi.

Arthur Wale, 1931-32, *New Light on Buddhism in Medieval India,* Vol. I.

Bapat, P.V., 1919, (sixth reprint), *2500 Years of Buddhism,* Sixth Reprint, Ministry of Information and Broadcasting, Publications Division, Government of India, New Delhi.

Bhartiya Vidyabhavan, *The History and Culture of the Indian People,* Vol. II, Bharatiya Vidyabhavan, 2nd edition, 1953.

Bharatiya Vidyabhavan, *History and Culture of Indian People,* Vol. III, 1954.

Barua Dipak, 1971, *An Analytical Study of Four Nikaya,* Rabindra Bharti University, Calcutta.

Bhattacharya, B., (ed.), 1929, *Two Vajrayana Works*, Gaekwada's Oriental Series, No. XLIV.

Bocking Brian, 1995, *Nagarjuna in China,* the Edwin Millen Press, Lewiston.

Bose, P.N., 1927, *Indian Colony of* Siam, Punjab.

Brown Thomas, 1994, *The Dhammapada: the Sayings of the Buddha,* Bell Tower.

Burges, A., 1921, *Buddhist Art in India* (translation).

Charles Elliot Sir, 1954, *Hinduism and Buddhism*, Vol. III, London.

Chatterji, B.R., 1926, *Indian Cultural Influence on Combodia*, Calcutta University.

Chimpa, L., 1970, *Tranath's History of Buddhism,* Indian Institutes of Advanced Studies, Shimla.

Conze Edward, (Translator), 1979, *The Large Sutra on Perfect Wisdom,* Banarsidas Publishers, New Delhi.

Conze Edward, 1957, *Buddhism: Its Essence and Development,* Cassirer, Oxford.

Conze Edward, 1962, *Buddhist Thought in India*, George Allen & Unwin, London.

Conze Edward, 1964, *Buddhist Texts Through the Ages*, Harper & Raw, New York.

Conze Edward, 1967, *Thirty Years of Buddhist Studies*, Cassirer, Cxford.

Conze Edward, 1960, *The Prajnaparamita Literature*, Mouton, The Hague.

Conze Edward, 1973, *The Short Prajnaparamita Texts*, Luzac, London.

Coomaraswamy, A.K., 1927, *History of Indian and Indonesian Art,* London.

Cowell, E.B., *et al.*, 1969, *Buddhist Mahayana Texts*, Dover Publication, New York.

Das Gupta, S.N., 1932, *A History of Indian Philosophy,* Cambridge University Press.

Danial Cozort, 1979-80, *Highest Yogha Tantra*, Ithac: *Snow Lion.*

David Grey, 2007, The *Chakrasamvara Tantra,* (AIBS) Colombia University Press.

Debidas Chatterji, 1986 (ed.), *Homage to Bhikhu Jagdish Kashyap* Nav Nalanda Mahavihara, Nalanda.

Edwin Obermiller, 1975, *Buston's History of Buddhism in India*, Suzuki, Tokyo.

Evams-Wentz, 1935, *Tibetan Yoga and Secret Doctrines*, London.

Edward Said, 2003, *Orientalism*, Vintage Books, New York.

Erricker Clive, 1995, *World Faiths Buddhism*, Hodder Headline Pub.

Fitzgerald, C.P., 1942, *China—A Short Cultural History*, London.

Frankey E. H., 1914 and 1926, *Archaeological Survey of India, Antiquities of Indian Tibet*, New Imperial Series, Vol. XXXVIII,

Geiger, W., 1912, *Mahavamsa* (translation), Calcutta.

Geshe Kelsang Gyatso, 1994, *Clear Light of Bliss*, Tharopa Publications, London.

Giles, H.A., 1923, *The Travels of Fa-Hien*, Cambridge.

Grouset Rene, 1931, *In the foot-step of the Buddha.*

Guenther H.V., 1952, *Yuganddha the Tantric View of Life*, Banaras.

H.H. 14th Dalai Lama, 1997, *The Buddha Nature*, Bluster Communications.

H.H. 14th Dalai Lama, *The Art of Living*, Thorsons Publications.

Joshi, 1980, *Studies of the Buddhist Culture of India*, Motilal Banarsidas, New Delhi.

Joseph Loizzo, 1977, "Renewing the Nalanda Legacy," Amherst Independent College Studies, Thesis.

Josheph Loizzo, 2006, *Wittgenstein and the Madhayamika*, Amherst Independent College Studies, Thesis.

Joseph Loizzo, 2001.*Candrakriti and the Moon-Flower of Nalanda: Objectivity and Self Correction in India's Central Therapeutic Philosophy of Language*, University of Michigan, University of Microfilm, Services.

Joseph Loizzo, 2008, "Kalcakra and the Nalanda Tradition: Science Religion and Objectivity in Buddhism and in West", In R. Tharman, *et al. The Kalcakra Tantra: Essays in Honour of the H.H. the Dalai Lama*, Ithaca, Snow Line.

Kimura, R., *History of Early Buddhist School*, Vol. III, Part-I, Oriental.

Legge, J., 1886, *Fa-Hien's Records of Buddhistic Kingdom*, Oxford.

Law, B.C., 1994, *Life of Buddha*, London.

Majumdar, R.C., 1953, *Inscriptions of Kambuja*, Asiatic Society, Calcutta.

Majumdar, R.C., 1944, *Kambujadesa*, Madras University.

Majumdar, R.C., 1927, *Suvernadvipa*, Calcutta.

Majumdar, R.C., 1944, *Hindu Colonies in the Far East*, Calcutta.

Malalasekra, G.P., 1928, *Pali Literature in Ceylon*, London.

Miranda Shaw, 1994, *Passionate Enlightenment: Women in Tantric Buddhism,* Princeton, Princeton University Press.

Mukherji, R.K., 1947, *Ancient Indian Education*, 2nd edition, London.

Nihar Ranjan Ray, 1946, *Theravada Buddhism in Burma,* Calcutta University.

Matheu Ricard, 2003, "The Relevance of Competitive Science", in Allan Wallace (ed.), *Buddhism and Science*, Colombia University Press, New York.

Matheu Ricard and Trinh Xuhan Thuna, 2001, *The Quantum and the Lotus,* Corwun Publishing, New York.

Matheu Ricard and Trinh Xuhan Thuna, 2001, *Nalanda – Buddhism and the World, Research,* Vol. VII, Nav Nalanda Mahavihara, Nalanda.

Matheu Ricard and Trinh Xuhan Thuna ed, 2004, *Buddhiasm and Culture of North-East India*, Nav Nalanda Mahavihara, Nalanda.

Nilkanta Sastri, K.A., 1950, *History of India: Ancient India,* Part-I, Madras.

Narda Mahathera, 1873, *The Buddha and his Teachings*, Vajrarama, Colombia.

Patra C.R., 1991, *Present Buddhist Tribals in West Bengal*, Calcutta.

Ray Chaudhury, H., 1853, *Political History of Ancient India*, 6th edition, Calcutta.

Rabindra Pant, (ed.) 2001, *Buddhism in Universal Perspective*, Nav Nalanda Mahavihar, Nalanda.

Richard King, 1999, *Orientalism and Religion and Science*, Routeledge Press, New York.

Robert Thurman Richard, 1992, "Vajra Hermeneutics", in D. Lopez (ed.), *Buddhist Hermeneutics*, Honolulu, University of Hawaii Press,

Rowland, B., 1953, *The Art and Architecture of India*, Penguin Series.

Rockhill, W.W., 1884, *Life of Buddha*.

Samuel Beal, *Life of Hiuen Tsing by the Kawui Li*, 1914.

Samuel Geoffrey, 2005, *Tantric Revisionings: New Understanding of Tibetan Buddhism and Indian Religion*, Burlington, VT, England.

Salmony, A., 1924, *Sculpture in Siam*. London.

Sanayana Souvenir, *Buddha Sasna Council*, Rangoon.

Sangitivamsa, *Bhadanta Vanaratana Somdej* Phravanar.

Sarat Chandra Das, 1993, *Indian Pandits in Land of Snow*, Calcutta.

Sarkar, S.C., 1928, *Some Aspects of Earliest Social History of India*, London.

Sen A.C., 1956, *Buddhist Remains in India*, Delhi.

Sprung, Mervyn, 1979, *Lucid Exposition of the Middle Way*, Rutledge, London.

Aurel Stein, 1907, *Sand-buried Ruins of Khotan*, Oxford.

Charles Eliot, 1954, *Hinduism and Buddhism*.

Sirkar, D.C., 1975, *Inscriptions of Asoka*, published by Ministry of Information and Broadcasting, Government of India, New Delhi.

Sogyal Rinpoche, 1993, *The Tibetan Book on Living and Dying*, Harpan Collins Publishers.

Stcherbatsky, F. Th., 1965, *The Conception of Buddhist Nirvana*, Mouton, The Hague.

Subadhano Bhikhu, 1961, *A Guide to Awareness*, Buddha *Dharma* Meditation Centre.

Suzuki, D.T., 1963, *Outline of Mahayana Buddhism*, Schoken Books, New York.

Takakusu, J., 1996, *A Record of the Buddhist Religion as Practiced in India and Maly Archepilago* Trans. (671-95 AD), Oxford.

The Dalai Lama, 2006, *The Universe in a Single Atom*, Broadway Press, New York.

Thick Nath Hanh, *The Five Mindfulness Training*, www plumvillage org.

Thomas, E. J., 1963, *History of Buddhist Thought*. Rutledge, London.

Thomas Yamell, 2008, *Tsong Khapa on the Creation Stage*, Colombia University Press, (AIBS).

Thomas L. and Thomas L. W., 1917, *The Beginning of Buddhist Art and other Essays on Indian and Central Asian Archaeology*, (translation), Paris.

Thurman, Robert, 1995, *Essential Tibetan Buddhism*, Harper, San Francisco.

Upasak C.S., and Prasad, C.S., 1978, *The Nav Nalanda Mahavihara Research Publications*, Nav Nalanda Mahavihara, Nalanda.

Upasak C.S., and Prasad, C.S. 2001, *Dictionary of Early, Buddhistic Monastic Terms,* (Based on Pali Literature), Nav Nalanda Mahavihara, Nalanda.

Vesna Wallace, 2002, *The Inner Calachakratantra*, Oxford, Oxford University Press.

Vesna Wallace, *Calachakratantra: The chapter on the Individual,* American Institute of Buddhist Studies, New York.

Vidya Bhushan, S.C., 1907, *Indian Logic: Medieval School,* Calcutta.

Vogel, J. Ph. 1936, *Buddhist Art in India, Ceylon and Java,* Oxford.

Waddell, L.A., 1895, *Buddhism of Tibet or Lamaism*, Allen & Company, London.

Warder, A.K., 1970, *Indian Buddhism*, Motilal Banarsidas, Delhi.

Waters, T., 1804-05, *On Yuan Chwang's Travels in India,* Calcutta.

Watson, Burton, 1993, *The Lotus Sutra*, Columbia University Press, Columbia.

Williams Paul, 2009, *Mahayana Buddhism: The doctrinal foundations*, Rutledge, New York.

Winternitz, M., 1933, *History of Indian Literature,* Calcutta University.

Wells David, *The Penguin Dictionary of Curious and Interesting Number*s, Penguin Books.

Yangchen Gawai Lodoe, 1995, *Paths and Grounds of Gyhyasamaja According to Arya Nagarjuna,* Library of Tibetan Works and Archieves, Dharmsala.

Young, Shinzen, 1998, *Algoritham and Emptiness*, www. shinzen org.

Zimmer, H., 1955, *The Art of Indian Asia,* Bolligen Series XXXIV. Vols. 2, USA.

Index